Contractor's Year-Round Tax Guide

Revised Edition

Michael C. Thomsett

Plan Your Business to Minimize Your Taxes

Craftsman Book Company
6058 Corte del Cedro / P.O. Box 6500
Carlsbad, CA 92018

The Library of Congress has cataloged the first edition of this book as follows:

Library of Congress Cataloging-in-Publication Data

Thomsett, Michael C.
    Contractor's year-round tax guide.

    Includes index.
    1. Construction industry--Taxation--United States.
I. title.
HD9715.U52T48 1983   343.7305'585624   83-15160
ISBN 0-910460-34-5 347.3035585624

© 1983 Craftsman Book Company

Second edition ISBN 1-57218-006-4
© 1995 Craftsman Book Company

Edited by Claudia Stebelski
Design and Page Composition: VersaTech Associates
Cover Design: John Wincek, Emil Ihrig

Contents

Taxes and Forms of Organization

This is a tax guide for construction contractors. If you're running a construction company, this manual will help you to:

1. steer clear of tax problems, and

2. reduce your tax burden, so you can

3. make a better living at your chosen profession.

I'm going to offer dozens of tax-planning ideas that can reduce both your taxes and the risk of loss when (and if) your return is audited. No one has to pay more tax than the law requires. And, in spite of what you may have heard, the tax code doesn't have to be an impediment to building a successful construction company. There are perfectly legitimate ways to both minimize your tax liability and limit the time you spend complying with the Internal Revenue Code. I hope that's what you want from this book, because that's exactly why I wrote it.

But please understand: This manual won't take the place of professional tax counsel. It doesn't have the technical details and references to the Internal Revenue Code an accountant or tax lawyer needs. And I'm not going to explain line by line how to fill out a 1040. (Dozens of good tax preparation manuals are published for that purpose every year.) But this manual will help you reduce legal and accounting expense by:

- making you more aware of what can (and can't) be done under the tax code,

- helping you recognize when expert tax advice is needed, and

- equipping you to evaluate the quality of the tax advice you're getting.

Very few construction contractors can afford to keep accountants and lawyers standing by, ready to give tax advice. Most of the builders I know wouldn't even try do business under those conditions. Better that you, the decision-maker in your company, have the knowledge and background needed to make sound tax decisions when and where decisions have to be made. Let the lawyers and accountants review the paperwork and clean up the details later. For most day-to-day work, rely on your own knowledge of what the tax law requires. If that's the way you like to conduct business, this book will suit you to a T.

You don't have to be a tax whiz to make it in the building business. Tax law is just one more area where construction contractors need a working knowledge of the basic principles, like estimating, accounting, labor relations, debt collection, and finance.

There's a basic body of tax law that most contractors can and should understand, even if they have an accountant and never fill out their own tax return. Most successful contractors take care of many minor tax problems themselves. When a tougher problem comes up, they usually have the decision pretty well thought through before they get counsel from a tax professional. That saves time and reduces accounting fees. Your knowledge of the tax law will help your accountant give you better service at a lower cost.

Finally, this book should help you avoid expensive tax mistakes. No one should have to learn tax law by trial and error. That's the most expensive, most painful way to learn what the code requires. Because you've read this far into Chapter 1, I suspect that you agree.

A New Tax-Planning Strategy

During my lifetime the tax code has changed dramatically. There was a time when the code was far less fluid than it is today. Twenty or thirty years ago, we knew that changes would occur in the tax law. We also knew that most of the changes would be little more than tinkering with the details.

The Economic Recovery Act of 1981 introduced new and significantly different ways to compute depreciation, take investment tax credits, and contribute to retirement plans.

Change accelerated in the late 1980s and early 1990s as Congress redefined the way most business is taxed. In the process, entire industries were decimated. What had been good investment strategy in 1988 became foolish a few years later. Look at what happened to commercial construction between 1988 and 1992.

We can expect more of the same in the future. But don't be concerned. Change isn't necessarily bad. It just means that the rules are different. Some will be helped and others will be hurt. Those with the foresight and flexibility to adapt will continue to thrive.

❏ Major Changes Coming?

Contractors and their tax advisors face special questions and problems in tax planning. For example, are you allowed to use the completed contract method of accounting for major jobs? Under completed contract accounting rules, you delay recording income for a job until the year when work is actually completed. The tax advantages should be obvious. Under completed contract accounting, the tax collector makes an interest-free loan of the tax money that will be due in later years.

As this book is being written, Congress is considering liberalized capital gains treatment and possibly even a new investment tax credit. There's no way to know what compromises Congress will make between the conflicting goals of maximizing tax revenue and stimulating the economy. No tax law on the books today or being written tomorrow can be permanent. Everything is up for negotiation every year. And that brings me to an important point.

While the information in this book is up-to-date with the latest tax rules at the time of publication, there are no guarantees about the future. So what's a construction contractor supposed to do? My advice is to rely on the IRS. The Internal Revenue Service is an excellent source of general information on the rules and rule changes. You're paying them to take your money. It's only fair that they provide assistance on figuring out how much you owe. They offer many free publications and have a telephone hotline where you can get answers to specific questions. That number is 800-829-1040.

❏ Professionals and Tax Planning

As I said, this book isn't a substitute for professional advice. Instead, you'll find it a good supplement to the professional help you're getting now. Master the information between the covers of this book and you'll save many hours of your accountant's time and prevent at least some of the more common mistakes builders make when paying taxes.

Most construction contractors doing between several hundred thousand and several million dollars in business annually retain an accountant or CPA who prepares an annual tax return and provides counsel from time to time. That may be all the tax assistance some contractors need. But as your business grows, so does the need for tax planning. In fact, your need for tax planning will probably grow considerably faster than your business grows.

Proper tax planning can save you a lot of money. It's legal and it's smart. Most construction contractors can both reduce their liability and defer payments to later tax periods — while operating strictly within the law.

Experienced accountants who counsel and prepare tax returns for contractors and builders will tell you that some of the most successful contractors know the most about taxes, even though they have little or no formal training in accounting. They've learned enough of the basics over the years to recognize the important tax considerations in most of the decisions they make.

And the most basic decision of all is how a company is organized, as the tax liability and the way it is calculated are different for each type of organization. So we'll begin with that important subject. There are three choices: proprietorship, partnership or corporation.

Proprietorship, Partnership or Corporation?

A construction company operated as a corporation has to file a tax return and pay tax at corporate rates.

A construction company operated as a proprietorship (someone doing business under their own name) doesn't file a tax return and doesn't pay any tax. Instead, business income and expenses are listed on Schedule C of the proprietor's tax return. The proprietor pays tax on net income from the business.

Partnerships file an informational tax return but don't pay any tax. Instead, net income to the partnership is divided among the partners. Each pays tax on a share of that income. If three partners are taxed on a third of the year's profits, it's likely that each will pay a different rate of tax. For example, if one is single and has income from other sources, he or she will pay a relatively high rate. If the second partner is married, has several children and sizable deductions, his or her taxable income will be considerably less. The third partner may be able to offset part of his or her income with losses from other ventures.

Let's take a closer look at these three forms of organization and the tax obligations of each.

The Corporation

Corporations pay taxes on net income (profit) on a graduated scale. As income increases, more of each dollar earned goes to tax. Corporations have more rate classifications than individual tax payers. If you're running a contracting company that's a corporation, you may want to consider each of these graduations or plateaus. Here's an example.

Suppose at mid-year you forecast that income for the year will reach the top tax bracket. Every extra dollar of profit earned during the year will be taxed at the highest rate. So every job you bid for the remainder of the year will offer about 10 percent *less* after-tax profit. Now ask yourself this: How does that affect your competitive position against contractors who will be paying tax at lower rates?

Tax planning is in some ways easier for partnerships or small contracting businesses run by individuals. Even though individual tax rates are also graduated, the rate changes aren't as abrupt as they are for corporate profits.

For example, let's look at a father-and-son business run as a corporation. The two owners set their own compensation each year in the form of salary. Within limits, they can adjust their wages to control the amount of tax the corporation has to pay. What are those limits? The owners should get some tax advice *before* adjusting compensation, especially if they've adjusted compensation to match net income in previous years. The IRS considers this form of "planning" to be abusive and has authority to assess additional taxes.

A corporation has to file at least a four-page tax return every year. It includes not only a summary of income, like individuals have to file, but also a beginning and ending balance sheet for the year, and a record of all changes in retained earnings. Supplementary schedules are appended to explain or substantiate key items on the tax return.

Larger corporations file detailed returns because of the complexity of their business organization. A corporation is treated as a separate entity for tax purposes. A corporation is a taxpayer, just like you and me. But the IRS wants more information about corporations than about individuals. The corporate tax form, Form 1120, requires a listing of assets and liabilities, retained earnings, and dividends paid to stockholders. Even if one person owns all stock in a corporation, the corporation is a separate entity.

Stock traded on stock exchanges is stock issued by publicly-held corporations. Anyone can buy stock in one of these companies. Most construction companies organized as corporations aren't publicly held. They're closely-held companies owned by a few individuals, often members of the same family.

Most publicly-held corporations pay dividends to stockholders. A section of the corporate tax return, Form 1120, is dedicated entirely to dividends. Many closely-held corporations don't pay dividends, preferring to invest after-tax earnings in the company.

❏ The Advantages

The corporate form of ownership allows you to deduct some expenses that unincorporated businesses can't deduct. And in the past, a lower tax rate made the corporation an attractive alternative to partnerships or sole proprietorships. But today, tax rates are very nearly the same for individuals and corporations.

The real advantage of the corporate form has nothing to do with taxes: It is that a corporation doesn't stop operating just because ownership changes. In a proprietorship or partnership, if one of the owners wants to sell out, or dies, the business terminates and a new business entity has to be formed. This usually requires closing the books in the middle of the year and starting a new set of books.

A corporation can continue in business forever. If a stockholder dies, the stock can be sold to someone else. The company, however, can continue without interruption. That's a major advantage when your company has major jobs under contract. Imagine how hard it might be to dissolve a partnership, form a new company, and then have the company write new contracts on all the existing jobs.

Financing business growth may also be easier for the corporation. A new corporation probably won't be able to borrow from the bank without the personal pledge of an officer or stockholder. But a corporation can raise capital by selling stock or trading stock for equipment. Of course, there's a disadvantage to selling stock rather than borrowing money. Each new stockholder becomes a part owner of the business. Lenders expect to get repaid, but they don't own a part of the company.

If a corporation goes into bankruptcy, stockholders aren't liable for the corporation's debts. Federal liens attach to corporate property only.

Individual owners aren't liable unless corporate assets were distributed to them when insolvency was declared. A tax assessment against the corporation doesn't affect individual stockholders — except that the value of their stock might fall or even become worthless. The owners of proprietorships and partnerships are usually liable for company debts.

❏ The Disadvantages

The corporation also has disadvantages. Its dividends are taxed twice under federal law. The corporation must pay taxes on the profits from which dividends are paid. When the dividend is paid, recipients must declare the money received as income on their individual returns.

In some cases, corporations are taxed more heavily than individual taxpayers. If the corporation is used to avoid taxes, an accumulations tax is levied. The IRS proves this by citing an unreasonable level of retained earnings, more than the company needs for day-to-day operations. Also, in the past, an "excess profits tax" has been temporarily imposed only on corporations.

Finally, the constitutional guarantee against self-incrimination (the Fifth Amendment) doesn't apply to corporations in tax matters.

The S Corporation

For tax purposes there are two types of corporations. Up to this point we have been talking about "C" type corporations that are taxed at corporate rates. The S corporation, or "Small Business Corporation" is taxed more like a partnership. That is, the stockholders pay tax on net income of the corporation (even if none of that income is actually distributed to the stockholders).

A corporation can elect to be treated as an S corporation. In effect, this hybrid form of organization enjoys the advantages of a corporation (like perpetual existence) but is taxed more like a partnership. Here's a point worth remembering: S corporations are created under federal law. How that corporation is taxed under state law varies from state to state. If your state assesses an income tax, you'll probably have to file a state corporate tax return for an S corporation. The S corporation also files a federal tax return, but on a different form than the one used by C corporations.

Type of Corporation	Year	Profit (Losses)	Carry-over Losses	Losses Taken by Shareholders
S corporation	1996	(43,000)	—	(43,000)
S corporation	1997	(4,500)	—	(4,500)
Regular	1998	(2,100)	—	—
Regular	1999	5,900	3,800	—
Regular	2000	(1,400)*	—	—
Regular	2001	2,100	700	—

Figure 1–1

Example of S corporation

*Losses can be carried back to previous years, but if you expect future profits, the wisdom of carry-backs is questionable.

In an S corporation, all income is "passed through" to the owners, just as in a partnership. The owners pay tax on the income, whether or not they withdraw it. For example, your S corporation might have been very profitable last year, but the profits were used to pay down debt, buy new equipment and pay subcontractors. Since the profits were earned by the company, they'll be taxed to the stockholders even though no money was actually received. See Figure 1–1.

You can elect to have your corporation treated as an S corporation if you meet the following rules:

- First, you have to be a domestic corporation. No foreign corporations can elect to be treated as an S corporation. And none of the stockholders can be nonresident aliens.

- Second, you can't have more than 35 shareholders. And, among those 35 shareholders, no partnerships or other corporations are allowed. (A corporation's stockholders can include not only individuals, but other companies as well. But you can only become an S corporation when all of the stock is owned by individuals.)

- Third, you can have only one class of stock. In some corporations, different types of stock are issued in different circumstances. For example, there might be common stock and preferred stock. That won't be possible for a corporation wanting to switch to S corporation status.

Plan to get professional assistance before forming either a C or S corporation. All states and the federal government have laws that regulate how stock can be sold and to whom you can offer stock. If you plan to sell stock to raise capital, you'll need legal assistance.

Partnerships

A partnership is two or more individual taxpayers working as a team. But for tax purposes, they're considered individuals.

Partnerships are not taxed. The partners are taxed whether profits are distributed to them or not. In a good year the partners could be pushed into higher brackets, even if all profits remain in the company and none are distributed.

The partnership must file a tax return which includes both an income statement and a balance sheet. In addition, there is a reconciliation of the partners' equity accounts. An additional schedule (Schedule K-1), must be filed for each stockholder, showing his share of income and credits.

So a partnership lacks some of the corporation's major advantages and must file a more complicated return. And many accountants agree that partnerships are more likely to be audited.

The partnership offers a key advantage: Losses are passed directly to its members. In low-income years or years when the organization loses money, losses can be used to offset other sources of income, lowering an individual's tax bracket.

Proprietorships

Most builders go into business as proprietors. There's nothing about a proprietorship that promotes poor record keeping, lack of tax planning, or failure to coordinate business strategies with personal tax considerations. But many accountants would say that these characteristics are more common in proprietorships than in other forms of organization.

A proprietorship is usually a one-person show with the owner too busy handling construction problems to do much planning or to spend much time on business records. The result is that most proprietorships never mature into other forms of business. But nearly all successful corporations have their roots in a proprietorship that *did* succeed!

One of the most serious accounting errors made by business owners is mingling business and personal funds. Business transactions must be kept separate from personal accounts. Don't try to run a business from the family checking account. IRS regulations require that all businesses keep separate records.

Even if your business is a proprietorship, estimate your income tax liability from time to time so you can plan your business affairs to minimize taxes. The tax code requires that you estimate liability for the year and make quarterly estimated tax payments. Our system of taxation is a pay-as-you-go system. All taxpayers — individuals, corporations and associations — are required to pay estimated income taxes in installments during each year. For employees, this is done by withholding from each paycheck. The self-employed individual must pay estimated taxes. Estimates are due on the 15th of April, June, September and January, on Form 1040-ES.

Like a partnership, the sole proprietor is taxed on all profits, whether taken out of the business or not. Without good tax planning, this can lead to some problems. For example, suppose Jack Smith, Builder showed a profit of $78,000 in a calendar year. Jack will pay substantial taxes on these profits. But even though profits were good, there may be little ready cash available to pay taxes. Assume the total tax bite (including self-employment tax, covered later in this chapter) was $24,000. Jack's $78,000 in profits may actually have been used as follows:

In increased outstanding accounts receivable	$12,000
Used to reduce long-term liabilities (notes, etc.)	16,000
Used to purchase new equipment	18,000
Withdrawn for living expenses	32,000
Total	$78,000

It may be very tough to raise the cash needed by April 15. Tax planning wouldn't create any more cash, but it would make meeting the payment deadline easier. Accurate quarterly estimated tax payments split the burden over several months. This would have disclosed the problem much earlier. The builder might have decided to pay off liabilities over a longer period, promote additional financing, purchase his new backhoe at a different time (or lease it), and pressure his clients to accelerate payments.

With a minimum of tax planning, the dilemma could have been avoided. In addition, the liability itself could have been reduced substantially through proper timing. If you don't anticipate tax liabilities and adjust business transactions accordingly, you can't expect a tax savings. If Jack Smith expects another year with profits of $78,000, it's probably time for him to incorporate his business.

Figure 1–2 compares the forms of organization. Tax reporting requirements are summarized in Figure 1–3.

Self-Employment Tax

Employees have Social Security tax (FICA and Medicare) withheld from their pay checks each pay period. Employee contributions are matched by the employer. Those who are self-employed don't have these taxes withheld. Instead, they make an estimate of the taxes owed and remit that amount with their tax return. The tax rate for the self-employed is higher than the rate for employees because the self-employed have no employer to match their contributions. The self-employed have to pay at a rate that is approximately one and one-half times the employee's rate. The contribution rate for the self-employed is, at the time of this printing, around 15 percent. The contribution required for a year's income is a significant amount of money. Don't overlook it when estimating taxes due.

Self-employment taxes are computed on Schedule SE and filed with the individual tax return. The amount to be reported on this form is the net profit from Schedule C (business income). If you have more than one business, the reportable amount is the combined profit.

There's no legal way to avoid the self-employment tax. Paying yourself as an employee would actually increase your tax burden. Although the withheld amount is less, as an employer you would have to match the amount withheld. In addition, there are the added expenses of disability insurance, workers' compensation and filing payroll tax returns.

	C Corporation	S Corporation	Partnership	Sole Proprietorship
Taxes	Paid by company. Rates set by law.	Paid by shareholders. Rates vary with individual	Paid by partners. Rates vary with individual	Paid by individual. Rates vary with individual
Losses	Are carried back or forward	Applied against other earnings	Applied against other earnings	Applied against other earnings
Tax Return	Four pages, including balance sheet	Four pages, including balance sheet. Schedules for shareholders	Four pages, including balance sheet. Schedules for partners	Individual return; Schedule C, Schedule SE
Life of Organization	Outlives shareholders	Outlives shareholders	Must dissolve and re-establish with ownership changes	Dissolves when business stops
Owner Limits	None	35 or less	None	One
Liability	Stockholders usually liable only to the value of stock	Stockholders usually liable only to the value of stock	General partners jointly liable for partnership liability	Full liability
Tax Years	Can choose any fiscal year	Usually has to use the calendar year	Usually has to use the calendar year	Usually has to use the calendar year

Figure 1–2
Comparison of types of organization

Self-employed business owners are allowed to claim a deduction for one-half of the self-employment tax they pay. That means that, while you have to pay an additional tax for being self-employed, you are also given some tax relief.

The total self-employment tax is called SECA (Self-Employment Contributions Act). It includes two parts: Old Age, Survivors and Disability Insurance (OASDI), which is generally referred to as Social Security; and HI (Hospital Insurance), also called Medicare. The distinction is important even though they represent the sum of self-employment tax, because the tax rate is different for each part of the tax.

When to Incorporate

Doing business as a proprietorship or partnership limits your ability to accumulate earnings or avoid heavy taxes in unusually good years. The corporate form can be beneficial in both good and bad periods. Use the S corporation to take losses and small profits as an individual. When larger profits are expected, change to the regular corporation form. If you expect an extended period of growth for your construction company and need to accumulate earnings in the business, the corporation is the best form of organization.

Before incorporating, talk to an accountant. You need a full understanding of how the changes will affect your particular business and how to keep your records. Once the corporation is formed, dissolving it isn't as simple as terminating a partnership or sole proprietorship.

A successful, growing business will usually convert to a corporation. See Figure 1–4 for an example.

Subsidiary Corporations

A corporation may acquire other corporations or create other corporations (called *subsidiaries*) to handle related business. There are many reasons to do this.

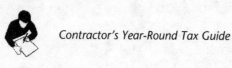

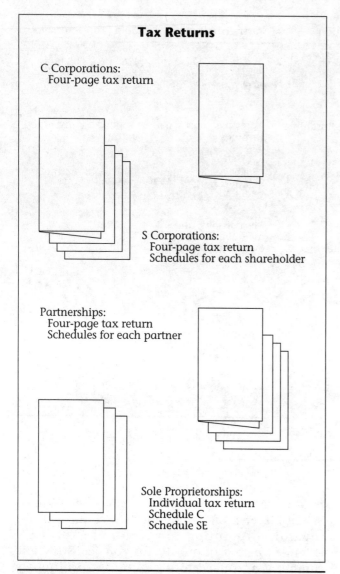

Tax Returns

C Corporations:
  Four-page tax return

S Corporations:
  Four-page tax return
  Schedules for each shareholder

Partnerships:
  Four-page tax return
  Schedules for each partner

Sole Proprietorships:
  Individual tax return
  Schedule C
  Schedule SE

Figure 1–3
Comparison of tax reporting requirements

Specialization: Many builders specialize in one type of work. But a company that specializes in new construction may decide to form a subsidiary to handle remodeling work. Some of your customers may prefer to do business with a company that caters exclusively to their needs.

Financing: Many banks have limits as to how much they will loan any one corporation. To get around this, subsidiary corporations may be formed. Usually loan officers will require financial statements from all corporations in an affiliated group.

Accounting reasons: If you have one corporation that does service work, you might want to have it keep books on a cash or accrual accounting basis. A related corporation that handles larger, long-term contracts might use completed-contract accounting. A third related corporation that maintains a large supply of material might use a cost basis (or market value basis) for valuing inventory. Creating subsidiary corporations will increase the administrative overhead, but will also offer more options when filing tax returns.

Liability protection: If you anticipate the possibility of large lawsuits, creating separate corporations may insulate each part of the company from any liability of the other parts.

Benefit plans: Consider creating subsidiary corporations so compensation or benefits can vary widely for employees in different lines of work. That may help avoid a claim that the company pension plan discriminates against a class of employees.

Unemployment insurance: To avoid overall unfavorable experience ratings for an entire company, you can concentrate high turnover positions in a separate corporation.

Union considerations: Specialized subsidiaries in different areas of activity or geographical locations can avoid union jurisdictional debates. This also prevents union auditors from seeing the accounting records of the entire organization.

Segregation of products or services: To keep the quality of one operation from affecting the reputation of another, create a subsidiary corporation for the less desirable business.

Personalities: Some key employees may have personal conflicts. A subsidiary corporation can separate them.

Geography: It may be impractical to manage business over a wide area. Subsidiary corporations can be used to deal with the problems of distance.

Local directors: There may be advantages in appointing Board of Directors members from the communities served. Use subsidiary corporations to have representatives from several areas.

There are three categories of controlled groups:

Parent-subsidiary: The parent corporation owns 80 percent or more of the subsidiary's stock or voting powers.

Brother-sister: Two or more corporations, in which 80 percent or more of the stock is owned by five or fewer stockholders.

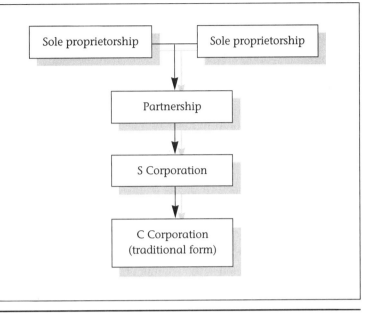

1. Builders individually form their own companies

2. A partnership is formed to reduce competition and pool resources

3. Limited liability protection and permanence are provided by forming a corporation and making an S corporation election

4. Increased income and larger number of shareholders necessitate reversing S corporation election

Figure 1–4
Evolution of a business

Combined group: Three or more corporations meeting the specifications of parent-subsidiary or brother-sister groups.

Figure 1–5 shows a typical set of subsidiary corporations.

❑ Consolidated Returns

Consolidated returns (several corporations combining their operating results on a single tax return) are allowed for affiliated groups. Your tax consultant will have specifics on this. Consolidated returns offer several advantages:

- Operating losses in one corporation may be absorbed by gains in another.

- Capital losses (not deductible by individual corporations) can be used on a consolidated return to offset capital gains.

- Inter-company transactions (for example, the paying of rent from one company to another, creating income on one side and an expense on the other) are eliminated on consolidated returns.

- A group of controlled corporations is allowed only one surtax exemption (the $25,000 level of taxation), but it can be used in many ways and can be varied from year to year.

Two major disadvantages of consolidated returns are:

- The election to file a consolidated return is considered permanent; it can be reversed only with IRS permission.

- When losses of one corporation are absorbed by gains in the other, the right to carry losses into future years is lost.

Even with the proper inter-company connections through stock ownership, consolidated tax returns could be disallowed by the IRS. If a corporation is established only for tax benefits, without a true business purpose, a consolidation may be denied. However, there are many legitimate reasons to operate subsidiary corporations. Only blatant abuse will cause problems. Many of the provisions related to subsidiary corporations and consolidated returns are designed to discourage the formation of scores of corporations for the purpose of burying income.

When considering the formation of a subsidiary corporation, remember that additional accounting documentation, payroll accounting and administration will be required. The extra paperwork burden may outweigh even a sound business reason for splitting operations.

Some builders just aren't able to manage multiple corporations. I've seen many subsidiary corporations

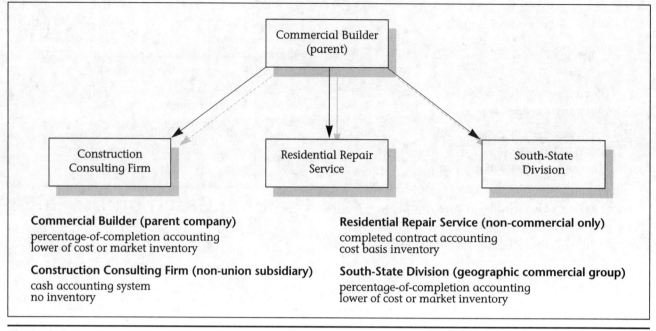

Commercial Builder (parent company)
percentage-of-completion accounting
lower of cost or market inventory

Construction Consulting Firm (non-union subsidiary)
cash accounting system
no inventory

Residential Repair Service (non-commercial only)
completed contract accounting
cost basis inventory

South-State Division (geographic commercial group)
percentage-of-completion accounting
lower of cost or market inventory

Figure 1–5
Typical subsidiary corporations

abandoned, merged, or sold to decrease the burden placed on management. Be sure you have the good management you need to help run a subsidiary corporation before forming one. The tax problems you solve may be less important that the management problems you create by forming a subsidiary.

First-Year Tax Strategy for Corporations

Most larger construction contracting companies are corporations because of the flexibility that this form offers. From the time a corporation is organized, it has more options, especially tax return filing options.

❑ Choosing the Fiscal Year

During the first year, the corporation has the choice of ending its first fiscal year in any month it chooses. For example, a corporation which begins operations in July may close its books and file a tax return as early as July 31 — a one-month first year — or as late as July 30 the following year, a full twelve months.

Here's how to use this flexibility to your advantage: Try to include less profitable periods in the same tax year with more profitable periods. That way the tax due on the year as a whole will be smaller. A new business might absorb its early months of flat or money-losing operations into later profitable periods. Or, if you have an early profit, let the first year stretch through a slower period.

Here's an example: A contractor incorporated in July. He had an initial contract which was to last through the summer months. During this period profits were good. But he had no commitments for future jobs once the initial contract was completed.

When the first job was finished, the contractor had a net profit of $50,000. He laid off most of his crew and cut back on overhead during the slow winter months. By early spring the $50,000 profit had dropped to less than $20,000. In March he got another large contract that was expected to be reasonably profitable. It was scheduled to begin in mid-May.

The contractor reviewed the estimate and work schedule for the new job. May and June looked like very profitable months since he was using percentage-of-completion accounting. The expected profit was recognized for accounting purposes as the job was completed. During these months he expected to show a profit of $20,000 a month. It was obvious that the first corporate fiscal year should end on April 30.

Here are the advantages of cutting off the first year at April 30:

1. The year ended at the close of a natural cycle of business.

2. In the first fiscal year profits were controlled so that taxes were low.

3. In the second fiscal year profits will be partially absorbed by the slower winter period.

4. Profits in May, June and July are pushed into the next fiscal year, so that the tax liability is put off for one year.

If the situation changes in future years, he can file an election to change the fiscal year to another closing date. (You can't do this too often, however. The tax code restricts arbitrary changes in the fiscal year.)

❏ S Corporation Election

Here's another option you have in the first year of incorporation. You may file as an S corporation. It's especially useful if your business loses money the first year. The C corporation can't pass losses to individual stockholders, although it could carry forward those losses and apply them against future profits. But the S corporation can pass losses through directly to stockholders who can claim those losses to offset other income.

S corporation status gives you the protection from liabilities that all corporations enjoy. But at the same time, you have the tax advantages of a partnership. You can eliminate or reduce personal income taxes. For example, if you had capital gains, or your spouse had substantial income from a job, a loss from your business reduces your tax liability. Be careful, though. You can only claim losses up to the limit of your investment in capital stock. That is, if you invested $40,000 in the corporation, you can't deduct accumulated losses over $40,000.

You have to make the election to be taxed as an S corporation within 30 days of the end of the fiscal year. (In most cases, the fiscal year is also the calendar year.) Remember, too, that to make this election, all stockholders have to agree to the idea. Being taxed as an S corporation must be a unanimous decision by all stockholders.

If you're a stockholder in an S corporation with a substantial operating loss, you might be able to eliminate your tax liability altogether. This assumes that you don't have income from other sources in excess of your losses and that your losses don't exceed money you've invested in the S corporation. If you don't take the S corporation election during the first year, losses can be only be carried forward to future corporate years.

Planning Based on the Rules

The decision to incorporate or not, and then which type of corporation to use, all depends on your personal tax situation and what is most advantageous. Remember, you can't switch your election every year as circumstances change. Make a good decision and then be prepared to live with it.

Let's say that you want to incorporate because you have associates who want to be partners. As a partnership, each of you would be jointly liable for business liabilities. That means your exposure to risk is virtually boundless. So you and your partners need and want the corporate protection. But at the same time, you expect losses during the first two or three years. So you elect to be taxed as an S corporation. That makes sense.

Here's another possible situation. Let's say your corporation is very profitable, but your spouse also has a business which loses money every year. It might make sense to take an S corporation election and have profits passed through to you. Your profits could be offset against your spouse's losses, saving taxes. Why pay corporate tax when you, individually, have losses to report? One problem with this idea: If you have other partners, they have to agree to the election as well. This plan would work only when all the stockholders are in your immediate family, or when your business partners would also like their profits passed through to them each year.

A number of business deductions are legitimate for a corporation but not allowed to proprietorships or partnerships. For example, corporations get favorable tax treatment for organizational expenditures, dividend income, and charitable contributions. Corporations have some additional leeway in deducting employee benefits such as health insurance premiums. Sole proprietorships and partnerships are either limited or excluded from deducting expenses like these.

Owners As Consultants

An owner-employee of a corporation has taxes withheld on regular income. In addition, the corporation must pick up the employer's share of withholding taxes. This increases the cost of each employee by from 10 to 12 percent over the wage cost. Compare the advantage of hiring a consultant instead of an employee. There's no "employer burden" because the consultant is either employed by another company or is self-employed. In either case, you're not responsible for employer taxes and insurance on that employee. Thus, there's a temptation to hire more consultants and less employees.

In some cases, it's perfectly legitimate to receive substantial consulting fees from a corporation, even if you are part or substantial owner. But be cautious. The IRS may view this arrangement solely as a means to minimize taxes. The result could be a major tax liability.

For example, suppose Joe Contractor pays himself as a consultant but takes personal deductions for home office, entertainment, travel, and business use of his car. On audit, the IRS decides that the relationship was one of employer-employee. Joe will be liable for the taxes that should have been withheld. He will probably also lose the deductions for office, entertainment, travel and auto, even if they would have been legitimate deductions for other employees. The best rule is to pay yourself as a consultant only after getting very specific accounting and legal advice.

CHAPTER

2

Capital Assets

C apital assets get special treatment under the tax law. Most of the money a business spends can be taken as an expense immediately. That's not true of capital assets, such as equipment used in your work and the office where you do business. Today's tax rules consider any property with a useful life beyond one year as a capital asset. That's appropriate, because capital assets can be expected to last more than a year. Business properties that fall under this rule generally include machinery and equipment, furniture and fixtures, autos and trucks used in business, and buildings (but not land). Items like stationery and supplies are not capital assets. The process for "recognizing" (writing off) a portion of the cost of capital assets each month or year is called *depreciation.*

Under former tax law, you claimed depreciation by subtracting an estimated salvage value from each asset, and then writing off part of the balance each year. That system was changed early in the 1980s. Now, depreciation is claimed under a system called *cost recovery.* There is no allowance for salvage value under the new rules. The entire cost of qualified assets is subject to depreciation. The IRS publishes extensive tables showing the amount of depreciation you can claim each year, depending on the type of asset, its "recovery period" (or, useful life expressed in years), and the depreciation method allowed.

In some cases, you can claim depreciation on an accelerated basis. That means you get greater tax benefits earlier in the recovery period and have to accept less tax benefits in later years. Higher depreciation encourages investment in capital assets. That's good tax policy if we assume that investing in capital assets increases productivity. That translates to a more prosperous economy and, ultimately, to higher tax revenues for the government.

In past years, businesses were also allowed to claim an investment tax credit. A tax credit is more valuable than a deduction because it reduces tax dollar for dollar. Up to 10 percent of what you spent on qualified assets could be deducted from the tax owed. That credit was repealed in 1986. But through the modern history of taxation, the investment tax credit has been reinstated and repealed a number of times. Expect another comeback in the future.

Modified Accelerated Cost Recovery

The older, Asset Depreciation Range (ADR) rules provided guidelines that set up minimum and maximum periods for depreciation under a number of asset classifications. Then the Accelerated Cost Recovery System (ACRS) was in effect for any asset placed into service after December 31, 1980.

For assets placed into service after 1986, the Modified Accelerated Cost Recovery System (MACRS) is the rule. This allows for rapid write-off of many assets, while restricting real property to unaccelerated depreciation over a longer term than was allowed with previous rules. Under MACRS rules, assets fall within a limited number of broader categories. These are explained later in this chapter.

The old system recognized part of a builder's investment as expense each year, until the full amount (less salvage value) was depreciated. Under the new rules, you can "recover" (write off as annual expense) part of your basis each year. This might seem a fine point, since the result is the same: a depreciation deduction. But there is a significant difference. The newer MACRS system doesn't require a reduction for salvage value, and the period of time isn't related to the actual useful life of the asset.

Intangible assets don't qualify for depreciation, and neither does land. Intangible assets have no value by themselves. Instead, they're rights and obligations like goodwill, covenants not to compete and contract rights. Some intangible assets can be amortized over a specified period. While amortization is similar to depreciation, MACRS rules do not apply.

Personal Property Depreciation

Under MACRS rules there are six recovery periods for personal property, and two periods for real property. The periods for personal property are:

3-year property: This category includes your automobiles and light-duty trucks and miscellaneous assets with less than five years of useful life, as defined under the previous Asset Depreciation Range (ADR) rules.

5-year property: This category includes most office equipment such as computers, and copy machines and fax machines, as well as heavy-duty trucks.

7-year property: This includes office furniture, fixtures and any property not assigned a useful life under previous ADR rules.

10-year, 15-year and 20-year property: Most contractors won't have any assets in these groups. They include specialized assets used in specialized industries, like agricultural buildings and sewage treatment plants.

The personal property categories (that is, all assets except real estate) are depreciated under what is called the *half-year convention.* That is an assumption that all property is acquired and disposed of at the mid-point of the year. This makes uniform the calculation of depreciation during the first year and the last year of depreciation. So in the year that you place an asset into service, you are allowed to claim one-half of the year's depreciation, no matter when you actually buy it.

❏ Accelerated Depreciation

You can claim *accelerated* depreciation for personal property classifications. "Accelerated" means that you can claim a higher deduction in the first few years and a smaller deduction in later years. The alternative is *straight-line* depreciation, which allows the same deduction each year. For 3-year, 5-year, 7-year and 10-year property, you can claim 200 percent declining balance depreciation. For 15-year and 20-year property, the 150-percent method is used.

To explain how each of these forms of depreciation works, we must first explain straight-line depreciation. Let's say you bought a trenching machine for $10,000. It belongs in the 5-year property classification. Straight-line depreciation would be $2,000 per year. Simply divide the cost of the property by the number of years in the depreciation period. That's straight-line depreciation.

Accelerated depreciation is also called *declining balance.* To figure 200-percent declining balance, just double the depreciation for the first year. That would result in a depreciation deduction of $4,000. In subsequent years, you reduce the basis by that amount, and then compute 200-percent depreciation on the remainder. In our example, the $10,000 asset is reduced to $6,000 at the end of the first year. Divided by five years, the straight-line would be $1,200. And 200 percent of that is $2,400. Here's how it looks:

Year	Basis	200% DB Depreciation
1	10,000	4,000
2	6,000	2,400
3	3,600	1,440
4	2,160	1,440
5	720	288

The same method is used for 150-percent declining balance depreciation. But instead of doubling the straight-line rate the first year, you multiply it by 150 percent. As you can see from the table, strictly applying this method completely writes off the entire value. In practice, MACRS depreciation applies a declining balance for a number of years and then reverts to straight-line.

The IRS publishes detailed tables showing the percentage to use each year, taking the half-year convention into account. Figure 2–1 summarizes the percentages you use under the first three time classifications. (The 10-, 15-, and 20-year classifications haven't been included, since most contractors won't have any assets in these classifications.) To use this table, locate the class of assets. Then multiply the asset's value by the percentage shown for each year. The result is the dollar amount you are allowed to depreciate under the standard method.

❏ The Alternative Depreciation System

If you prefer, you can depreciate assets under these classes using another method. This is called the Alternative Depreciation System (ADS), and provides for straight-line rather than accelerated depreciation. Suppose you expect to have operating losses during the earlier years of the asset's recovery period. You would prefer to increase depreciation in later years when the tax reduction will probably be of greater value.

Under the ADS system, you can use alternate recovery periods and the mid-year convention might be replaced by a mid-quarter convention. In some situations, ADS is required. Check with your accountant to see whether or not ADS would be an advantage to you.

Another caution: Some property is not qualified for MACRS depreciation. If you have transportation assets, computers, cellular phones, and some other types of assets that are used less than 50 percent of the time for business (called *listed property*), you have to use special tables. If this applies to

Recovery Period			
Year	3-year	5-year	7-year
1	33.33	20.00	14.29
2	44.45	32.00	24.49
3	14.81	19.20	17.49
4	7.41	11.52	12.49
5		11.52	8.93
6		5.76	8.93
7			8.93
8			4.46

Figure 2–1

Declining balance depreciation

you, check with your accountant for the rules and the special tables you have to use, as well as limits on depreciation you can deduct.

Real Estate Depreciation

There are two classifications for real estate: residential and non-residential. If you own the building where you do business, you're allowed to depreciate its value, as well as any improvements you make. But you can't depreciate the land itself. The values of land and buildings are usually set by dividing the total basis by the percentage of assessed value for each. Your county assessor will determine the assessed value for property tax purposes. Use this same value for dividing between land and building for depreciation purposes.

Let's say you bought the building and land for $200,000 last year. The assessed value is $108,000: $40,000 for the land and $68,000 for the building. The land value is 37 percent (40/108), and the building's share is 63 percent (68/108). Applying these percentages to your purchase price, the land is worth $74,000 (37 percent of $200,000); and the building is worth $126,000 (63 percent of $200,000). So only $126,000 of your purchase price would be subject to depreciation.

It's worth noting that land can't be depreciated, regardless of how you use it. But you can still depreciate all improvements that add value to the land, such as excavation, grading, removal of existing buildings, paving, tunnels between buildings, adding sidewalks, gutters, and drainage.

The straight-line method is always used for real estate depreciation. The two classifications are:

27.5-year property: This recovery period can be used only for residential real estate. To qualify, a building has to have 80 percent or more of its rental income from dwelling units.

31.5-year property: This is for non-residential real property.

For real estate depreciation purposes, you don't use the mid-year convention. Rather, the amount of depreciation allowable during the first year is based on the month it was acquired. Figure 2–2 shows the first-year percentage of depreciation to be claimed based on the month the asset was acquired. The figure shows the breakdown both for residential and non-residential property. In subsequent years, divide the building's value by 27.5 (for residential) or 31.5 (for non- residential) property.

Here's an example of how you might use the percentages in Figure 2–2: You purchase a building to be used exclusively for business in July. The building's value is $150,000 (without land). In the column headed *Non-residential*, find the percentage for the seventh month. That would be July if your fiscal year coincides with the calendar year. Multiply the percentage in that column by the building's value:

    1.455% x $150,000 = $2,182.50

This is the amount of depreciation you're allowed the first year. In following years, divide the value by 31.5 (years) to determine annual depreciation. The amount in this example is $4,761.90. After 31 years, the total depreciation claimed will be $149,801.40. So in the 32nd year, the final depreciation will be $198.60. After that, the building will be fully depreciated.

Expensing Assets

You are allowed to "expense" part of assets you place into service each year. Rather than claiming depreciation over a period of years, you write off the asset (or part of it) the first year.

The maximum you can expense each year is the smaller of either $10,000, or your taxable income for that year. Or, if the total qualified assets in a particular year are below either of these thresholds, then the maximum is the value of the asset itself. If your taxable income is lower than

Month	Percentage	
	Residential	Non-residential
1	3.485	3.042
2	3.182	2.778
3	2.879	2.513
4	2.576	2.249
5	2.273	1.984
6	1.970	1.720
7	1.667	1.455
8	1.364	1.190
9	1.061	0.926
10	0.758	0.661
11	0.455	0.397
12	0.152	0.132

Figure 2–2

First-year real estate depreciation

$10,000, you are allowed to carry over the excess to be used in future years as expensing deductions.

If you expense only part of an asset, the balance can be depreciated under MACRS rules. However, the expensed part is treated as depreciation already claimed. And you're subject to several limitations in the use of the expensing provision:

1. Whenever personal property placed into service during any one year is higher than $200,000, the allowable expensing limit is reduced one dollar for each dollar of value above that level. So if you place $210,000 or more into service next year, none of it can be expensed.

2. Controlled corporations and married couples are restricted to only one $10,000 limit each year.

3. If you execute a like-kind exchange, the old asset's basis has to be deducted when you compute the expensing deduction for the new asset. For example, if you exchanged an asset that had originally cost $15,000 for a like-kind asset valued at $20,000, only $5,000 (the difference) could be expensed.

4. Property held for investment does not qualify for expensing. Only property used in your business can be expensed.

5. You can't expense any property that is inherited or given to you as a gift; or that is sold to you by a relative.

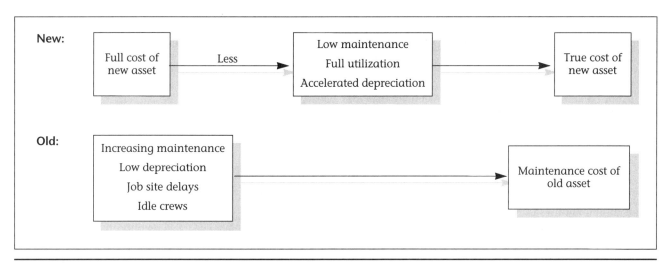

Figure 2–3

Calculating the true cost of an asset

6. You can't claim an expensing deduction for any property used less than 50 percent for business.

Capital Asset Tax Benefits

The rules for depreciation of capital assets can help minimize your tax liability. With the combination of accelerated depreciation and expensing, you can get a nice deduction in the year you acquire property.

The tax benefits have the effect of discounting the cost of acquiring capital assets. For example, if you purchase a qualified asset worth $10,000 and expense it all this year, you reduce your taxable income by $10,000. So if your effective rate is 29 percent, you save $2,900 in taxes — a 29 percent discount on your purchase.

Even for assets you don't expense, the rules for accelerated depreciation reduce taxes, especially in the early years of the recovery period. The rapid recovery rules are designed to encourage the replacement of aging equipment.

New equipment is usually more productive and requires less maintenance than older assets. For example, as machinery or trucks age, the repair

costs tend to rise. More idle time is needed for repairs. At some point, the higher maintenance cost, lost depreciation, and idle time make replacement the cheaper alternative. This idea is summarized in Figure 2–3

The benefits under today's MACRS rules are:

1. Tax advantages provide an incentive to buy more productive equipment.
2. Your after-tax profit is higher during the early recovery years.
3. Your working capital is improved because the tax liability is lower in early recovery years.
4. Bookkeeping and depreciation computations are simplified by use of the published IRS tables.
5. A lot of guesswork has been removed because there's no need to compute the useful life or salvage value of equipment.

Faster depreciation under MACRS makes purchase a more attractive alternative than leasing in many cases. In the past, leasing was more attractive because lease payments are deductible immediately. But in many cases, the depreciation allowance during the earlier years of the recovery period will exceed the lease payment write-off.

3

The Ordinary and Necessary Rule

Businesses pay tax on *net* income, the money left over when expenses are paid. But not all expenses are deductible from income. To be deductible, an expense *must* be both *ordinary* and *necessary*, as defined by the Internal Revenue Code and regulations enacted under that code. The ordinary and necessary rule is also used to distinguish between expenses that are deductible in the current year and capital assets that have to be depreciated over several years.

Ordinary

To be considered ordinary, an expense must be business-related. It can't be personal, and it must be related to the purpose of the operation.

You can write off an ordinary expense in the current year, rather than capitalize it. Investments in equipment with value beyond twelve months are considered capital assets. Some expenses which must be capitalized, even if they're associated with general overhead, are discussed later in this chapter.

Ordinary expenses must also be customary and normal to your type of business. For example, the cost of this book for use by your construction company would be customary and normal. A subscription to an antique collecting magazine probably would not.

Expenses such as telephone, office supplies, and postage are ordinary to the builder because they are customary and normal. But his leasing a motor home to take family vacations would not qualify because there is no business connection.

You can't consider an expense as ordinary just because you've been deducting it for many years. For example, it's not proper to deduct as a business expense the cost of framing pictures that hang in your home, even if you've done that on every tax return since 1983.

Ordinary refers to what is accepted in the industry, and how directly it's related to the conduct of business.

Necessary

Expenses must have a direct business *purpose* and the expense must be incurred to meet that business purpose.

For example, installing a car phone in a company truck would be directly related to business if the phone is used for company calls. Buying a set of golf clubs would be difficult to justify as a business expense for a construction company because there is no business purpose.

The cost of keeping a pet canary at the shop may or may not be necessary. But if you keep a dog to discourage break-ins at night, the care and feeding would be necessary. But if you took the dog home each night, there would be no relationship between the expense and the purpose of the business.

A synonym for "necessary" is "appropriate." A good test to determine whether an expense is ordinary and necessary is to ask, "Would a prudent business owner have incurred a similar expense in similar circumstances?"

Deciding to Capitalize Expenses

An expense which is not ordinary and necessary may still be allowed if capitalized (set up as an asset and written off over a period of years).

This rule extends to expenses directly related to acquiring long-term assets as well as the asset itself. For example, your construction shack erected during the construction of an office complex is probably a capital asset. The temporary structure contributes nothing permanent to the final building and the IRS might not consider it an ordinary and necessary current expense. It's part of the capital asset, and must be included in the building's cost.

If you purchase a used bulldozer and are required to invest heavily in maintenance and repairs to make it operational, these costs may not be ordinary and necessary expenses in the year of purchase. But they can be treated as part of the acquisition cost and depreciated over a period of years.

❏ Organizational Costs

Expenses related to preparing to go into business are organizational costs. They're not directly related to the cost of *doing* business, only to preparing to do business. As such, these costs must be capitalized and amortized over several years.

Organizational costs include expenses such as buying fixtures and getting licenses, market research, and ordinary overhead expenses incurred prior to opening for business. Leasing an office, installing a telephone, advertising for employees — these are all organizational costs.

Organizational costs are not properly classified as current assets (cash, receivables, inventory), nor as long-term assets (machinery, equipment, trucks). They are "other assets," and are amortized (similar to depreciation) over a reasonable life. If you write off organizational costs over 60 months, you would be allowed 1/60th of the total each month. This amortization expense reduces the asset until its value is zero.

Expenses Not Allowed

❏ Bribes and Fines

No deduction is allowed for some types of expenses under any circumstances. These include fines paid for violations of law (such as traffic tickets, fines for criminal violations or code violations), and illegal bribes or kickbacks.

There are cases where certain bribes could be considered ordinary and necessary. For example, if you're working on a contract in a foreign country where bribes and kickbacks are not illegal, such payments may be deductible. This is especially true if you can establish that such payments are both ordinary and necessary to the conduct of business. They would be reasonable if:

1. The amount was in line with similar bribes.
2. Circumstances dictated that the bribe was related to the successful pursuit of business.

You may also be required to pay finder's fees, commissions, or rebates. These are payments to achieve a business purpose, which are not illegal. Consider the case of a builder seeking a top-notch estimator. He may locate one through an executive employment agency. This agency requires a

$5,000 fee for locating the right man for the job. In addition, the builder takes the prospective estimator for dinner and drinks. He also pays his moving expenses as an added inducement.

Are the agency fee, entertainment, and moving expenses deductible?

They're certainly ordinary. Such payments are made in virtually every type of business. Without such payments, it would be harder to find quality employees.

They're necessary because the builder needs to fill this position to do business. Without a good estimator, he may lose or underbid key contracts, ending up out of business or spinning his wheels.

They're also reasonable if the level of each payment is in line with common practice. It would probably be considered unreasonable to give a prospective employee a new speed boat as an inducement to employment.

The distinction between a bribe and a finder's fee or entertainment expense is sometimes one of appropriateness. Buying a car for a prospective estimator is unreasonable and is a form of bribery, even though it isn't a bribe in the legal sense. Paying for a dinner consumed during an interview, however, is normal interviewing practice and therefore completely acceptable.

Drawing the distinction can be difficult. Intent is the determining factor. If it is your intent to influence above and beyond normal business practice, the expense may not be reasonable. If a payment is illegal, the expense is definitely unreasonable and you can't deduct it.

❏ Personal Expenses

Expenses must be business-related to be deductible. Many corporations have tried to deduct expenses for officers and executives that were, in fact, forms of compensation. These include buying fixtures for an employee's home, legal or tax preparation services for personal matters, large expense allowances, and direct payment of some personal expenses (utilities, telephone, home maintenance costs). Even if these are helpful to business, they can't be deducted.

Unless special circumstances exist, corporations can't deduct living expenses for its executives. Some executives receive such benefits and don't claim them as taxable income. However, if such

an expense is deducted by the company, it will commonly be taxed to the individual.

No deduction is allowed for lobbying costs or for political contributions. These are non-business expenses.

High-Visibility Categories

Several categories of expense are especially troublesome due to past abuses. For these, special deductibility and limitation rules apply.

❏ Travel

If travel involves both business and personal activities, you have to allocate your expenses between the two. Only the business part is deductible.

Special rules apply if you attend a foreign convention, which is defined as one outside the "North American area." Deductions are allowed only when:

- The meeting is specifically and directly related to your trade or business.
- It's reasonable to have such a meeting outside of North America, to the same extent that it would be to have the meeting in the North American area. For example, if all the attendees are from the Midwest, it would be difficult to justify a convention in Tahiti.

You won't be allowed to deduct travel for meetings held on cruise ships in general, although you could be allowed a deduction up to $2,000 per year under some circumstances. A seminar cruise would be subject to the same stringent rules: it has to be ordinary and necessary. You can't deduct any expenses for attendance at investment seminars.

When it comes to travel expenses, the most important rule is also an exception to the general rule about what is required to document business expenses. You have to prove the money was spent, but you also have to prove the business purpose and intent of the expense.

You have to prove the amount, the time and place, and the business purpose. In addition to producing receipts, you also need to keep adequate travel records, including a log book.

❏ Entertainment

Like records for travel, entertainment expenses have to be documented through a log or other written record. Only 80 percent of ordinary and necessary entertainment expenses can be deducted as business expenses.

To be considered ordinary and necessary, entertainment has to produce a specific result or benefit related to business. For example, if you depend on other contractors for referrals, entertaining them would be ordinary and necessary. But if all of your jobs come from competitive bidding, taking a fellow contractor to lunch might not have any specific business purpose.

You also have to hold business discussions during the course of entertaining someone. Three conditions have to be met for the expense to be considered as ordinary and necessary.

1. You have to expect to gain income as a result of entertaining the other person.
2. You have to discuss a transaction or negotiate conditions for a transaction.
3. The principal character of entertaining the other person has to be business-related. That means that talking about business in general is not enough; you have to discuss the idea that you believe will lead to producing income.

To prove an entertainment deduction, you have to prove several things:

- The amount and date of the expense.
- The name and address of the place where entertainment took place, including the type of business establishment.
- The business reason for the entertainment, or the type of business benefit you hoped to receive.
- The name and title of the person or people who were entertained, and their business relationship to you.

❏ Home Office

You can claim expenses for an office in your home, but only if a specific part of your home is set aside and used exclusively and on a regular basis for the conduct of business. This must be either your principal place of business, or a place you use to meet with customers, or a separate building not attached to your home. Also, if you are a sole proprietorship, you have to compute the business use deduction on a special schedule, Form 8829.

The deduction is usually calculated based on square feet. The number of square feet used exclusively for business, as a percentage of the total area of your home, is the percentage you can deduct.

If you own your home, the deduction consists of depreciation of the building's value, and the deduction is allowed at the applicable percentage. If you rent, the percentage of your rent used exclusively for business (based on square feet) is deductible. You can also deduct a percentage of utilities by the same rules.

❏ Auto Expenses

You can deduct auto and truck expenses when they are ordinary and necessary. The difficulty is that most vehicles aren't used exclusively for business. For most small contractors, the truck used to get to the job site and to pick up materials is the same truck used to go fishing and pick up the kids at school. You have to be careful here, as there has been much abuse of this deduction. The IRS may be particularly watchful.

If your automobile is used 100 percent for business, you are allowed to deduct all your expenses. There are two methods available in computing deductible expenses for business vehicles.

The first method is to deduct actual expenses. These include depreciation, gas, oil, tires, repairs, insurance, interest (if you are financing the vehicle), property taxes, license fees, parking and garage rental, and tolls. If you lease the vehicle, lease payments are also deductible. All actual expenses are legitimate deductions, but only to the extent that the vehicle is actually used for business.

When you use an automobile partly for business, you have to break down all actual expenses. This is based on mileage. For example, if you put a total of 34,000 miles on your truck last year, and 19,000 of those miles were for business, you can deduct 19/34ths, or 56 percent of all actual expenses.

The second method is to use the standard mileage rate. The rate per mile allowed as of 1995 was 29 cents per mile. Using the same example as above, if you drove 19,000 business miles during the year, you could deduct $5,510 as automotive expense (19,000 x 29 cents). You could also claim an additional deduction for parking fees.

Your actual expenses per mile will probably be less than the standard rate, especially if you can prove extensive business use of your car. The higher the mileage, the greater your standard mileage deduction. That's because the mileage rate is calculated to include depreciation. Using the actual mileage rate, you are limited by the actual cost of operating your car. But if you put on a lot of business mileage, using the standard mileage rate might be an advantage. Keep good expense records, then calculate your vehicle expense both ways to see which one works out best.

To qualify for the standard mileage rate, you can use only one car for business during the year. If you use two or more vehicles for business, you must use the actual expense method. You must also own the vehicle. A leased car or truck doesn't qualify.

4

Compensation

There are many ways to compensate employees and consultants. Salary and wages are only two. No matter what form compensation comes in, it's an area the IRS watches closely.

For tax purposes, employee income is anything that provides a financial or economic benefit, regardless of the form it takes.

Payments to a third party may be considered compensation to the employee. These fringe benefits may include payment of home costs, income tax preparation, legal fees, or of income taxes. Even if the company pays an employee's child or spouse, it's still income to the employee in some cases.

Reasonable Payments

Every employee is taxed on compensation received. The employer is allowed to deduct that compensation in the year paid if that compensation is *ordinary and necessary*. The test for ordinary and necessary compensation is the same as applied to expenses in Chapter 3.

"Ordinary and necessary" compensation is often hard to establish. The value of any individual's service is largely a matter of opinion. But the burden of *proving* that compensation is at an appropriate level rests with you, the taxpayer. Here are some grounds on which higher-than-usual compensation has been judged to be ordinary and necessary:

1. Relative value of an employee's services to the employer

2. The employee's contribution to the company's profits

3. Comparisons to similar circumstances in the same industry

4. Expert witness testimony as to the employee's value

5. The employee's indirect contribution (an individual who developed a computerized estimating system used by the builder) while self-employed

6. The total time dedicated to the business (such as overtime), whether in or out of the office

7. Testimony from a competitor as to the special value of a specific type of service

8. Favorable results in volume or profits influenced directly by the employee

9. The previous earnings record of the employee

10. The employer's difficulty in finding qualified people for the job

11. The company's compensation policy (a documented policy is preferable)

12. Working conditions. For example, an employee may be required to live in a hazardous or undeveloped area to be close to a job site.

13. Unusually low pay to the employee in previous years (such as an employee who was with the company since inception and stayed on the job with low pay and the promise of rewards later)

14. Unusual physical dangers such as exposure to hazards

15. Extremely specialized talents of an employee, especially valuable to the builder

The question of ordinary and necessary comes up most often for executives and other highly-compensated employees, especially in closely-held corporations where those same individuals are shareholders.

A valid contract between you and the employee doesn't make the amount of compensation appropriate by itself. Neither is an impressive title justification for a higher salary. The only standard is the reasonable value of the services to the builder.

Dividends

When an employee is also a shareholder in the corporation, the question of whether compensation is ordinary and necessary is of special importance. For shareholder employees, the IRS will try to show that the compensation is really a distribution of profits and should be taxed both to the corporation as profit and to the individual as a dividend. That's the double taxation that most employers and employees try to avoid. But it's also a tax law the IRS is trying to enforce. Paying employees in proportion to the amount of stock they own is usually a dead giveaway that profits are being disguised as compensation rather than being distributed as a taxable dividend.

In corporations where one or more salaried employees are controlling stockholders, it's especially important that you can justify the level of compensation. Controlling stockholders set their own compensation.

In some cases, high compensation to a non-shareholder employee based on incentives (such as annual bonuses) is held to be reasonable, while an identical payment to an employee-shareholder is not. Compensation isn't the same incentive for an owner as it is for a non-shareholder. An owner gets the benefit of excellent performance even without high compensation.

If the compensation is considered unreasonable by the IRS, there is a way to avoid double taxation: the employee can reimburse the company by the amount asserted to be unreasonable. This doesn't reduce the employee's income in previous years, but it does offset his income in the current year. The IRS will usually allow this repayment if the company has an agreement with the employee requiring repayment of any compensation which is unreasonable for tax purposes.

Salaries and Wages

Salaried employees don't generally qualify for overtime when they work more than the designated number of hours per week. They may receive compensating time off or, in recognition of their extra duties, they could be paid an annual bonus. Within reasonable limits, salaried employees are not docked for taking time off work, since they are paid a fixed sum to perform the job.

Wages, on the other hand, are payments per hour. You have to keep time records, and compensation is based on actual time worked. Wage earners have benefits such as paid sick days and holidays. Beyond these, absences are docked. Overtime is paid at rates set by agreement and by state and federal labor laws.

Payroll taxes apply to all income of both salaried individuals and wage earners. Included in this deductible expense are all taxes paid by the employer, such as his half of Social Security (FICA), state disability insurance, and federal unemployment insurance (FUTA).

Payroll taxes will be lower in the last part of each calendar year when withholding for highly compensated employees has passed the maximum required by law. Once that point is reached, the employer's liability ceases.

Salaries, wages and payroll taxes are all deductible and can be included on the builder's tax return in several ways:

Direct costs: Salary and wage costs that can be associated directly with generating revenues.

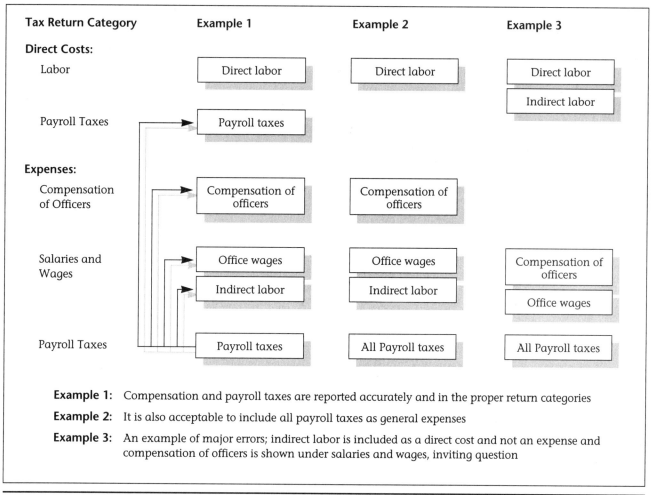

Figure 4–1
Tax return classifications

Salaries and wages: Office, clerical salaries and wages, and indirect labor costs (those not identifiable as belonging to specific revenues).

Compensation of officers: (Corporate returns) These are the salaries paid to each officer. Information must also be included on the amount of stock owned, the time the officer spends on company business, and the amount of expense allowances paid during the year.

Payroll taxes can be included on your tax return as a general expense. In fact, a large portion of these should be included as a direct cost since payroll taxes for direct labor are a part of the total cost of goods sold. Although this is a matter of individual interpretation, the important thing is consistency. Labor is a major part of your total expense and should be classified and reported the same way each year.

Inconsistencies in such a large deduction will distort year-to-year comparisons and raise questions during a tax audit. Figure 4–1 shows the various methods of classifying compensation and payroll tax expenses and costs.

Bonuses

Like other forms of compensation, bonuses are deductible as long as they're reasonable. They invite close IRS examination when paid to major shareholders of a corporation.

Bonuses paid when profits are high look even more like a dividend. Protect yourself by writing into the corporate minutes some objective measure of salaries that grants higher compensation when sales are higher.

Stock Options

An incorporated builder can compensate employees with incentive stock options. These are rights to purchase the company's stock at reduced rates. This is an attractive form of compensation because it gives employees a big incentive at low cost to the corporation. In addition, the tax code provides favorable treatment of stock option profits when they are exercised. When an employee exercises the option (purchasing the stock), no income is reportable. By holding the stock for at least one year, the employee can treat profits as long-term capital gains taxed at a lower rate than salaries and wages. Unfortunately, the stock of most closely held corporations has little market value and can't be sold to the general public. But stock options can be a major incentive in a company that's growing quickly and may be publicly held at some point.

Remember, the option itself is not taxed, only the profits from the sale. But to qualify as a long-term capital gain, there is also a combined holding period rule. The employee must have held the option and the stock for a total of at least two years. (This is not applicable in the case of the employee's death.) For example, the option can be exercised after one month and the stock held for 23 months; or the option can be held twelve months and the stock held twelve months.

Incentive stock options must be exercised within ten years. To qualify for favorable tax treatment, the option plan must be approved by the shareholders. Stock options are not transferable (except at death) and can be exercised only by the employee.

To participate, the employee can not own more than 10 percent of the corporation's voting power or total stock value. Options must be exercised in the order in which they were received. Figure 4–2 illustrates the holding period rules for long-term gains and the exercising of options.

Consulting Fees

Many construction contractors use the services of consultants or independent contractors who are not paid a wage. This consultant is self-employed and not entitled to any benefits such as sick leave, vacations, holidays, or paid health insurance. Further, you are not required to withhold taxes or

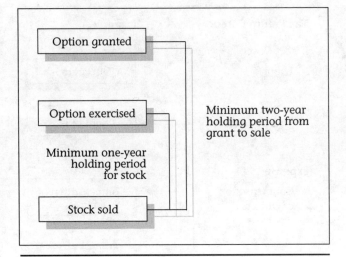

Figure 4–2

Long-term capital gain qualifications for incentive stock options

pay insurance premiums on self-employed individuals or consultants. That's a major advantage to the employer which invites abuse of the tax law. Many builders have yielded to the temptation to pay their workers as independent contractors rather than employees. There's no loss to the IRS, of course, so long as the independent contractor complies with the tax code. The problem is that many don't. So the IRS finds it easier to enforce the law against employers paying wages than employees receiving wages.

There's no single test that can be used to distinguish between employees and independent contractors (non-employees). Having a contract with someone or paying by the job doesn't make that person an independent contractor. Instead, the courts (and the IRS) weigh several factors:

1. Non-employees have their own office or work from their home.

2. The consultant has other clients besides the builder.

3. The agreement can't limit the consultant's practice or dictate whether or not other clients can be served.

4. The consultant must not be supervised as other employees are.

5. The consultant sets his own hours and isn't subject to the working hours of employees.

Figure 4–3 compares independent contractors to employees.

The Independent Contractor	The Employee
Has his own office	Works in the builder's office
Has other clients	Works only for the builder
Is not limited to working for only the builder	Not allowed to perform work for other employers
Is not supervised directly	Is supervised directly
Establishes his own working hours	Works the hours set by the builder

Figure 4–3
Comparison of the independent contractor and the employee

Be cautious when someone offers to work as an independent contractor. The risk is that they will claim later that you failed to withhold taxes and that they were, in fact, an employee. You may have to pay both back taxes and a fine. To avoid this, have a contract or agreement that specifies that the individual is an independent contractor.

As an employer, you're required to provide workers' compensation insurance for employees. An independent contractor injured on the job may claim to be an employee. You could be held liable for medical costs and civil damages. Independent contractors working on your jobs should provide their own workers' comp coverage and supply you with proof of coverage. Putting that in your subcontract agreements can save a lot of grief.

Payments for consultants must be reasonable. It isn't a good idea to compensate a shareholder as an independent consultant because it's hard to justify. Employees can't also be consultants. An individual must fall into one category or the other.

There are many ways you can pay a consultant. Common among these is the retainer, a fixed monthly amount for services. This allows both you and the consultant considerable flexibility in budgeting and cash flow, but makes it hard to see whether you're getting your money's worth.

Some consultants are paid on a "per project" basis. The consultant quotes a specific fee for a specific task. He or she may want progress payments, advances, or half before and half upon completion. You can budget a progress billing easily, and shouldn't be concerned with overruns.

Many independent contractors charge an hourly fee. This may be the most economical way to pay consultants. But the actual expense might exceed estimates. Hourly fees are convenient for work of fairly limited scope. But this arrangement can make the consultant an employee without the builder or the consultant realizing it. Remember the key differences: consultants qualify as non-employees by being essentially unsupervised and independent. This can't be the case if the individual works for you continually.

❏ Fringe Benefits

Many fringe benefits can be tax-free to employees but deductible to your company.

Not Taxable to the Employee

1. Group health insurance in a plan available to all qualified employees
2. Officer liability insurance (covering acts of officers during employment duties)
3. Gifts not given as a form of compensation for services rendered

Taxable to the Employee

1. Group life insurance above $50,000 and provided entirely by the builder (unless the employee is disabled or retired)
2. Individual life insurance on employees
3. Discount sales to employees (the difference between the fair market and the discounted price)
4. Lock-out benefits paid to union members
5. Awards for suggestions or referrals
6. Reimbursements of moving expenses
7. Sick pay, vacation pay and holiday pay
8. Salaries and wages paid without the return of services

❑ Deferred Compensation

Employees are generally cash-basis taxpayers. This means that income they receive in a given year is taxed in that year, regardless of when it is earned, promised or awarded.

Pension and profit-sharing plans (see Chapter 5) are common forms of deferred compensation. They accumulate in the current year but are not received or taxed until later. Deferred compensation is any amount earned now and received (thus, taxed) in a later year. Figure 4–4 shows the tax treatment for several forms of compensation.

Promises of payment aren't compensation. If you say to an employee, "I promise to pay you $1,000 for what you have done this month," and the payment isn't received until the following year, it won't be taxed until the following year.

There's one situation where an employee can be taxed without receiving any money. There are three parts to this exception:

1. The payment is available to the employee.
2. The company is prepared and ready to make the payment to the employee.
3. The employee chooses willingly to delay receiving the payment.

Suppose you owe a certain amount to an employee on December 31 of the year. You say to that employee, "Can you wait until next month?" The employee answers, "I guess so."

Is the payment available? It may be. It isn't clear in the example, and the employee didn't insist on immediate payment.

Is the company prepared to make the payment? In this case, probably not. The builder asked the employee to wait.

Did the employee choose to delay receipt? No, the builder asked for a delay. In this example, the payment wouldn't be taxed until the following year.

Suppose you had said, "I'll have the book-keeper cut a check today," and the employee said, "That's all right. Let's wait until after the end of the year." The income is rightfully taxable in the current year. The payment is available. You are ready and prepared to pay. The employee has delayed receipt voluntarily, so he will be taxed this year, even though he hasn't received the money.

Corporations can establish a program of deferred compensation for cash-basis employees.

Type of Compensation	Tax Treatment
Salary paid	Taxed in current year
Additional salary promised	Taxed when paid
Incentive bonus declared, paid in following year	Taxed when paid
Retirement plan contributions	Taxed when distributed
Bonus available for payment, but delayed by employee's choice	Taxed in current year
Note given to employee in lieu of salary	Taxed when paid

Figure 4–4

Comparison of the independent contractor and the employee

An incentive bonus earned in the current year can be paid over several periods. But have the program well documented in advance.

The question of when compensation is to be taxed is troublesome for small corporations and partnerships. It's your responsibility to compensate employees fairly and avoid unpleasant surprises. No one likes to find out that funds are taxable in a different year than expected. The rule of availability and ability to pay is clear enough that you can avoid most potential problems.

Payments to Subcontractors

Do payments to subcontractors fall under the same rules as compensation to employees? In most cases, no. Compensation is generally limited to your direct employees and consultants.

Your subcontractors are employers. Your payments to subcontractors are business income to a contracting company. But what if your subcontractor is an individual, working alone, doing specific work for several general contractors?

Have a written understanding that absolves you from the liabilities associated with employment. Mention in that agreement each of the points that define an independent contractor. Your agreement won't change the tax law. There's a risk that the "subcontractor" will be classified as an employee by state or federal enforcement personnel. But the written agreement prevents a subcontractor from claiming later to be an employee.

Contracts With Employees and Consultants

Any time you hire someone to work for your organization, you enter into a contract — even if you have no written agreement. Usually your agreement is verbal. The employee agrees to do certain work, and you agree to pay a certain wage and provide certain benefits.

Usually a verbal contract will be enough. As long as all conditions are satisfactory on both sides, the contract remains in force. It may be amended from time to time. For example, you may promote an employee or agree to an increase in salary as the employee's productivity improves or responsibilities increase. For key employees you may want a written contract that describes in great detail the understanding you've reached with an employee. That may help prevent misunderstandings and expensive disputes.

❏ Consultants

Consulting agreements are not as simple as most employment agreements. Your liability and the liability of your consultant are potentially much greater. If the agreement is verbal and a dispute arises, both parties will insist on carrying out the agreement as *they* understand it. An incomplete written contract is almost as bad. To protect everyone, many builders use comprehensive written consultation agreements.

Here are some points that a consultation or employment contract may cover:

1. Terms of payment
2. Liability protection
3. Taxation
4. Scope and performance of duties
5. Hours of work
6. Length of the contract and expiration date
7. Level of authority

We'll discuss each of these points in some detail.

Terms of payment: Disputes arise most commonly over the amount you agree to pay a consultant. A contract should specify how often and how much a consultant is to be paid and what expenses will be reimbursed. The contract should also set a limit on the amount that will be paid within a certain

period. If the agreement specifies only a cost per hour, you may be surprised by the hours expended during the first pay period. *Always* set limits.

Liability protection: Who's responsible for injuries a consultant suffers on your premises? The contract should specify. Since consultants are not generally covered under standard workers' compensation policies, the contract should state that the consultant is an independent contractor and is not covered by workers' compensation insurance.

Taxation: Be sure to specify that the consultant is responsible for payment of his or her own income taxes and that you won't deduct or deposit taxes for the consultant. Without this provision, a discharged consultant might claim to have been an employee. That could make you responsible for all back taxes, together with interest and penalties.

Scope and performance of duties: Again, be sure to *set limits,* and *be specific.* The consulting arrangement should describe clearly the scope of the consultant's duties and the manner in which they are to be performed.

Hours of work: One of the characteristics that identifies a consultant as an independent contractor is the ability to set work hours and the place of work. Without these options, a consultant looks more like an employee than an independent contractor. To be on the safe side, the contract should provide for both the consultant's independence and willingness to provide services when you need them.

Length of the contract and expiration date: All agreements must have a beginning and an end. Be sure to specify the dates on which the agreement starts and expires. Include a clause allowing for cancellation of the agreement by either side and the amount of notice required (30 days, for example) for such cancellation. The contract should also have a clause allowing for extension of the agreement with or without negotiated modifications.

Level of authority: Consultants usually have more authority than employees. But questions of abuse of authority come up quite often. Be sure to define exactly how much authority the consultant has, both as your agent in negotiating agreements with others and in dealing with employees. But avoid situations where the consultant would be acting like an employee. For example, don't let a consultant hire or supervise your employees. A consultant may interview and screen prospective employees and advise you to hire them. A consultant can also train employees.

But don't try to use a consultant as a supervisor on a job, for example.

Figure 4–5 is a sample consulting contract which covers all of the issues discussed above.

Consulting Agreement

This is an agreement between *Smith Construction Company,* a New Jersey Corporation, and an independent construction estimator who is referred to as "Consultant" in this agreement.

I: Background

Smith Construction Company is a licensed contractor engaged in construction activities; this extends to the contracting with general and subcontractors on projects under contract and awarded to Smith as "general contractor" or "subcontractor." It extends as well to the hiring of employees under the terms of agreements with the following labor unions:

Carpenters Local _____

Laborers Union Local _____

Plumbers Union Local _____

Other employees are retained for estimating, general clerical and accounting duties within the organization. Smith bids on a variety of public projects with total budgets as high as $750,000 and, as such, much depends upon the accuracy of its submitted estimates. In that regard, the organization will retain Consultant to provide professional services as an estimator.

II: Fees

Smith agrees to pay Consultant a fee of $ _____ (_____ dollars) per month, to be paid one-half on the fifteenth day and one-half on the last day of each month, beginning April 1, 19___ and ending on September 30, 19___. This six-month agreement is provided for services in connection with:

1. Research and documentation of current system used for estimating by Smith

2. Establishment of forms and new procedures and full documentation of the new system

3. Documented project estimates to be compiled in time for submission by deadline on as many as ten projects per month

4. Training of other estimating employees in proper use of estimating procedures

In addition, Consultant shall be reimbursed for his documented expenses reasonably incurred during the course of Smith's business, provided that such expense exceeding $300 (three hundred dollars) per month shall not be incurred without prior written approval from Smith.

Consultant shall be compensated the agreed retainer based upon an average commitment of 20 (twenty) hours per week and shall be compensated for all hours exceeding 86 (eighty-six) hours per month at the rate of $45 (forty-five dollars) per hour. Consultant shall exceed 86 (eighty-six) hours per month only with written approval for specific tasks from Smith.

Figure 4–5

Sample consulting contract

In the event that total consulting hours during a month are fewer than 86 (eighty-six) hours, Consultant's compensation shall be reduced in proportion to the hours actually spent on Smith Construction projects.

At or prior to September 30, 19___, this agreement may be extended for an additional six months, to be confirmed in writing via acknowledgment letter to be signed by Consultant and an officer of Smith. At the time of extension, Consultant and Smith may negotiate monthly retainer amount, hourly fee, and all other terms of the agreement.

Billings shall be submitted to Smith in writing by Consultant and include an itemized list of excess hours with copies of written pre-authorization for such hours.

III: Terms

The term of this agreement shall be 24 (twenty-four) months with stipulated six-month extensions. However, either party may terminate this agreement upon 30 (thirty) days written notice for cause. Cause shall be defined as gross neglect of duties specified herein, insolvency, conviction of a crime involving moral turpitude, incapacity for a period exceeding three weeks, or the inability to meet a mutually satisfactory fee or compensation base.

IV: Consultant's Duties

Consultant shall make himself available to the Smith organization for a minimum of 86 (eighty-six) hours per month, to be allocated on an average of 20 (twenty) hours per week, or as mutually convenient, or as the company may reasonably require to accomplish the goals and objectives of activities as outlined in Section II, Fees, and in accordance with the terms and conditions of this agreement.

Of the total weekly commitment specified above, Consultant agrees that no less than two full days per week shall be committed to the performance of duties in the organization's headquarters offices at:

_____

_____

V: Enforceability

It is expressly acknowledged and agreed that the covenants and provisions of this agreement are separable, that the enforceability of one covenant or provision shall in no event affect the full enforceability of any other covenant or provision hereof, and that in the event any such covenant or provision shall be for any reason found not fully enforceable in accordance with its terms, it shall be enforceable to the fullest extent permitted by law and equity.

Consultant is a self-employed consultant who makes his services available to other organizations. He will, at his discretion, disclose to Smith the terms of other consulting contracts in force, specifying organization name and scope of duties. In the event a conflict of interest is disclosed or discovered, the terms of this agreement may be re-negotiated or canceled.

Consultant establishes his own schedule of work within the terms of this agreement, to be agreed on in advance as to mutual convenience and satisfaction.

Consultant does not work under company supervision, establishes his own working hours, and may perform some duties at his own office, located at:

_____

_____

Figure 4–5
Sample consulting contract (continued)

Consultant is granted a level of authority necessary to the performance of duties as defined in this agreement, and is not an agent of the corporation who would otherwise be authorized to submit documents in bid, accept contracts, hire employees or other consultants, or otherwise act as an agent. Any activities involving commission for Smith will be completed only upon written consent from an officer of the corporation.

VI: Assignment

Neither party shall have the right to assign this agreement or any of its rights, obligations or duties without prior written consent of the other party.

VII: Modifications

This agreement constitutes the entire agreement between the parties and supersedes all prior understandings and agreements, both written and oral; this agreement may not be amended except in writing and upon signature of both parties.

VIII: Applicable Law

This agreement shall be governed by and construed in accordance with the laws of the State of New Jersey.

IX: Notes

All notices, requests, consents, demands, reports and correspondence required within this agreement shall be mailed to Smith and Consultant, at the address given in this agreement.

Either party may change the address provided, by giving written notice of such change to the other party.

X: Litigation

It is agreed mutually that controversies arising out of this agreement shall be satisfied by application of the procedures and standards of binding arbitration. Upon identification of a controversy, each party shall appoint an agent responsible to themselves, and those agents shall appoint a third arbitrator. The decision of this board, upon hearing both sides of the issue, shall be binding upon both parties. Each party agrees to be bound fully by the decision and shall waive all rights to further appeal.

XI: Captions

The headings and captions used in this agreement are for convenience and reference only, and do not constitute a part of this agreement.

IN WITNESS Whereof, the parties hereto have executed this agreement on

this _____ day of _____ 19 _____

_____
Smith Construction Company

_____
Consultant

Figure 4–5
Sample consulting contract (continued)

5

Profit Sharing and Pension Plans

Pension and profit sharing plans are used by many construction contractors to retain good employees, shelter income and provide substantial income after retirement. If your company is making good money and you're paying substantial taxes, consider setting up both a pension and profit sharing plan.

This chapter will only suggest how a pension and profit sharing plan would work for you. The law is far too complex to cover thoroughly in even several volumes this size. A number of companies specialize in setting up pension and profit sharing plans. Look in the yellow pages of your phone book under "Pension - Profit Sharing Plans" for companies and consultants that specialize in this work. Many of the larger life insurance companies, banks, savings associations and stock brokerage companies have pension and profit sharing plan specialists on staff. In return for an agreement to keep at least a portion of plan assets invested with the company, the specialist will help you set up a company plan.

Solicit offers from several different firms. Compare them and the features of each proposal. But be careful. Some charge heavy commissions. Others are less competent and a few are less than completely honest. Select as carefully as you would a doctor or lawyer.

Why Have a Plan?

Many attractive incentives have been built into the profit sharing and pension regulations. Contributions made to a qualified plan within specified limits are deductible to the corporation and are not taxed to the employees until distributions are taken. The plan helps both you and your employees save a substantial amount of money for retirement.

In some plans, the company contributes all funds on behalf of the employees. In others, employees can contribute. Contributions in some plans are pooled and invested by a committee of employees. Other plans are self-directed (employees make investment decisions on their portion of plan assets). When the participants retire or leave for other work, some or all of that money is available to them.

Contributions to a "qualified" plan are fully deductible in the year contributions are made. Qualified plans have to meet strict requirements under the tax code. Benefits include:

- Immediate deductions for contributions (money paid in) to the plan

- Deferral of tax on contributions made by the employer for the employee, which continues until money is withdrawn. (Employees can't usually reduce taxable income for voluntary contributions they make for themselves except their contributions to 401(k) plans, which we'll discuss below.)

- Deferral of any interest on earnings in the qualified plan. That means the employee doesn't have to pay tax when the value of his or her assets increase. Taxes are due only when money is withdrawn from the account.

- Favorable tax treatment when the money is withdrawn. When the employee finally does take out money, he or she might be able to reduce taxes through special income averaging rules.

Qualified retirement plans usually allow deferral of income tax. It's generally better to defer paying tax as long as possible. That maximizes the value, accumulating more earnings in the plan.

There's another reason to defer tax on retirement funds. Usually this money is paid and taxed after you retire when you're in a lower tax bracket. If you (or an employee) are taxed on earnings while working full time, your tax bracket is likely to be much higher. The higher your tax bracket, the larger the tax bite on each dollar earned. But if you retire with only a pension and Social Security benefits, you'll be paying tax at a much lower rate.

Qualified Pension and Profit Sharing Plans

Qualified plans come in two varieties, defined benefit or defined contribution. A defined benefit plan fixes permanently the amount of the benefit each employee will receive at retirement. The amount is based on retirement age and years of employment. The employer makes a contribution to the plan for each employee that's enough to provide the future benefit goal. Under a defined contribution plan, the annual contribution is fixed, usually based on

a percentage of salary for the year. The actual benefit at retirement depends, then, on how investments made in the account actually fare, and whether or not the employee makes any voluntary contributions. With this type of plan, each employee gets a separate account.

A qualified plan can include a variety of plans set up by employers for the benefit of employees. Qualified plans can exclude employees who are members of a labor union that has bargained for retirement benefits on behalf of union members.

A qualified plan can take one or more forms. A *pension plan*, for example, offers fixed benefits for a number of years. Defined benefit plans are always considered pension plans. A *profit sharing plan*, however, doesn't force you, the employer, to make any specific annual contribution as you would have to under terms of a pension plan. This is an important feature, considering the nature of your business. When money is tight and the contracts just aren't there, you don't want to be forced to dig up the cash to contribute to a retirement account. You have the option of making smaller contributions when profits are smaller.

A *stock bonus plan* allows a corporation to make distributions in the form of company stock. The typical form this takes is an Employee Stock Ownership Plan, or ESOP. This can be used to gradually transfer all or part ownership of a corporation to employees, or simply to provide them with incentives to stay on the job, and to take a keener interest in producing profits.

You can also offer employees a *target benefit plan*, which combines features of defined benefit and defined contribution alternatives. Although targeted benefits and contributions are fixed, actual distributions depend on investment performance within the retirement account.

Under a *thrift plan* or *savings plan* the employer agrees to match voluntary employee contributions to a retirement plan. Some employers offer to match contributions dollar for dollar, up to a maximum per employee per year.

Employees have to be allowed to participate in the plan if they meet the qualifications. You can't offer a qualified plan only to certain employees, and exclude others. You also have to be sure that your plan doesn't discriminate in favor of more highly compensated employees. Qualified plans also have *vesting* rules. Employees have to be fully vested in the money accumulated in their account within seven years. Until then, they may lose all or

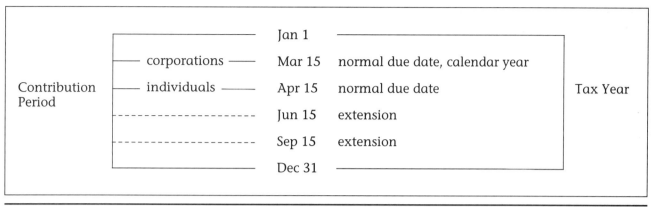

Figure 5–1
Retirement plan contribution period

some portion of the money accumulated in their account by leaving the company. Vesting rules prevent long-term employees from forfeiting plan benefits if they happen to leave the company before retirement age. Employers have several options in meeting these vesting rules.

Other Retirement Plan Options

The rules for setting up and administering retirement accounts can get very complicated. For most small businesses, a full-blown pension or profit sharing plan is just too costly. Administrative cost will usually be at least $2,000 a year for nearly any qualified retirement plan.

❏ SEP

A practical alternative is the *simplified employee pension*, or SEP. You make contributions for your employees, and employees don't have to pay tax on the amount you contribute, or on the interest and other earnings that accumulate in the plan. So the features of the other plans are available to everyone, but the administration is much easier.

If you have a SEP, you can deduct contributions made for your employees. The deduction is $30,000 or 15 percent of each employee's income, whichever is smaller. All contributions have to be made for each year by the time that year's tax return is due. But the due date for the tax return can be extended for at least six months under the law. This same rule is used to identify the due date

for most retirement plans. Figure 5–1 demonstrates how the due date for contributions compares to the due date for tax return filings.

The rules for participation in a SEP are simplified as well. You have to make the plan available to all employees over the age of 21 who have been on the payroll at least three out of the last five years, and who have been paid at least a certain amount. This amount is adjusted each year for inflation.

❏ 401(k) Plan

Another popular choice is the 401(k) plan, also known as a cash-or-deferral salary reduction plan. In this type of plan, you agree with an employee to reduce the pay to that employee and put the difference into a qualified plan. So part of the employee's pay is tax-deferred, along with any earnings that money accumulates. Either way, the employer gets a deduction for the business expense.

Under terms of a 401(k) plan, employees can qualify for a hardship deduction, meaning they can take withdrawals before retirement without penalty. In order to qualify, the employee has to show that there is an immediate, heavy financial burden, and that no other resources are available to meet the need. Included under this test are medical expenses, the purchase of a primary residence, and tuition for a family member.

❏ IRA

Most people have heard about the *individual retirement account*, or IRA. These were extremely popular a number of years ago. But then the rules changed and people with higher incomes can no longer qualify for the tax deductions. The IRA might still be a valuable retirement option for some people. To qualify for contributions to an IRA, you have to earn compensation during the year, and you have to be under the age of 70 at the end of the year. You can contribute up to $2,000 per year ($2,250 if your spouse doesn't work).

You're allowed to set up an IRA even if you're covered under other retirement plans. But if you or your spouse actively participate in other plans, you can't deduct your contribution to an IRA account that year. This is a very important limitation. You can still put money into the IRA, but you can't claim a deduction of that amount on your tax return. The money is still yours and, most important, you still defer taxes on earning in the plan. This makes the IRA a valuable savings account, even if you aren't allowed a deduction for contributions.

Deductions are limited for taxpayers with higher incomes. If you have adjusted gross income above $50,000 (joint return) or $35,000 (single) for the year, you're not allowed any deduction for IRA contributions, even if you don't participate in another plan. Any time you make a nondeductible contribution, you have to file an information form with your tax return, Form 8606.

Distributions from IRAs can begin after age 59, and must begin by the time you're 70. You're taxed on the amount withdrawn, in the year it's withdrawn. All contributions, plus earnings, are taxed; but voluntary contributions not deducted from gross income are not taxed as they are withdrawn. You are taxed on an allocation between taxable and nontaxable contributions. For example, let's say you contributed a total of $50,000 over 25 years. Of that, eight years' contributions, or $16,000, were nondeductible. All withdrawals would be treated as 16/50ths nontaxable, up to the point that withdrawals reach $16,000. All other withdrawals are taxed as they are withdrawn.

❏ Rollovers

The rules also allow rollovers from one account to another. Suppose Jane Smith is leaving Company A to take a job at Company B. Both A and B have retirement plans. The law allows Jane to roll her retirement plan assets at Company A into the plan at Company B or into an IRA account without paying any tax. But be careful. Get competent advice

before accepting a payout from the plan you're leaving. The rules have to be followed exactly.

A rollover is tax-free if you transfer retirement plan funds to an IRA you set up. Or, in another type of transaction, you simply move funds from one IRA to another. For example, let's say you set up one IRA in your bank, investing in certificates of deposit. Later, you open a new IRA with a mutual fund. Rather than having a lot of different IRA accounts at the same time, you simply do a tax-free rollover when the CD matures.

You can actually receive funds from one account before establishing a new one, but all of the money has to be put into the rollover account within 60 days. However, if the rollover isn't made directly, 10 percent is withheld upon distribution as a tax penalty deduction. You can do only one tax-free rollover per year. Any part you don't reinvest will be taxed that year, without the benefit of any averaging. In addition, you'll have to pay a 10 percent penalty, besides the tax, if you keep any of the funds and you are under age 59.

❏ Keogh Plans

Self-employed individuals can set up plans for themselves that are more flexible than IRAs and allow them to invest more money. A Keogh plan, also called an HR-10 plan, is designed for this purpose.

Sole proprietors and partners can invest in such plans based on their net earnings from self-employment. However, the net earnings are reduced for purposes of computing the allowable contribution, by one-half of the amount paid for self-employment tax. That is treated as an additional business deduction, effectively reducing taxable income and earnings from self-employment.

The maximum annual Keogh deduction for defined contribution plans is the lesser of 25 percent of net earnings, or $25,000 per year. But because the Keogh contribution is itself included as a business expense, the actual deduction maximum is 20 percent of net earnings. You also reduce your net earnings by one-half of the amount paid for self-employment tax.

Social Security Retirement

Many people now question the value of Social Security in their retirement planning. They're waiting for the system to go broke. But that system is more than just a monthly check for retired people. It includes disability and medical insurance as well.

There are four parts to Social Security:

1. Retirement benefits consisting of monthly allowances, which currently are partially taxed
2. Disability benefits for workers unable to work for extended periods of time, and for the dependents of disabled workers
3. Survivors' benefits for spouses and children of deceased workers
4. Medicare insurance for retired and disabled people

All these benefits are subject to changes, not only in tax treatment, but also in rates, which may be adjusted each year for inflation.

❏ Other Retirement Benefits

Social Security was never intended to meet the entire financial needs of retired workers. But retirement checks from the government are a nice supplement to your own retirement account. If you didn't have the foresight to plan for retirement, Social Security may help ease the burden in old age. At one time, Social Security benefits were tax-free, making them especially valuable to retired people. But as the government has searched for new sources of revenue, retirement benefits, unfortunately, are no longer exempt.

Social Security retirement benefits are partially reduced by your "earned" income after retirement. There is a maximum amount that can be earned before benefits are affected. Beyond that limit, benefits are reduced. Check with the Social Security Administration for current rules. Earned income includes salaries and wages, consulting fees and income from self-employment. It does not include interest, dividends, capital gains, pensions, or rental income. So if you have substantial income from an IRA, Keogh or corporate retirement or pension plan, this will not affect Social Security benefits.

Income from IRAs, self-employed plans (Keogh) and corporate retirement and profit sharing plans are taxable. Minimizing taxes on retirement usually means planning for withdrawal over a period of years to avoid high income years when a larger proportion of income is taxed.

Tax planning for retirement involves one additional uncertainty: The tax law changes every year. It's hard to say what the law will be next year, much less in 20 years. All you can do is base your planning on the existing law. Generally, existing plans are allowed to remain intact. It's a good bet that even if benefits or retirement plans are curtailed or eliminated in the future, funds placed in a tax-deferred program currently will remain tax-deferred until retirement.

Tax Shelters

A tax shelter is an investment that reduces taxes in the current year and almost certainly increases taxes in later years. It's also known as a tax deferral.

When you hear the words "tax shelter," you probably think of a limited partnership formed to deal in real estate or oil and gas programs. Today these types of investment are usually called "tax advantaged" investments. Tax shelter is a much broader term that covers many types of tax deferral plans.

Not every tax deferral is truly a tax shelter. For example, a six-month certificate of deposit can delay payment of taxes, though it isn't a tax shelter. If you purchased a CD in early July, with a maturity date of January 3, most of the interest is earned in the current year. But it's taxed on maturity in the following year. This is a way you can defer income taxes, but it isn't really a tax shelter.

Tax Shelter Features

Here are some of the common features associated with tax shelters in the past:

- Investment of cash plus signing of a note (usually "non-recourse," meaning you didn't really have to pay off the note)

- Accelerated depreciation
- An investment tax credit

Usually losses on these investments exceeded the actual investment. In some cases the tax saved was more than the amount invested. Those were the good (?) old days. Now, the law has changed. With some very extensive and healthy tax reform, abusive tax shelters like these are no longer available.

Two important limitations have been created under the law. First, you can take a deduction only up to the amount you actually have "at risk." That's the amount you are liable for personally. No non-recourse notes are allowed. Second, contributions have to be based on an item's cost. This is an important change.

For example, assume your effective tax rate is 33 percent. Let's say you come upon an offering of rare art prints. Here's how these tax shelters used to work: You buy the prints for $25,000. One year later, the prints are to be donated to a qualified tax-exempt organization. The promoter promises you the prints will be appraised higher than your cost. Usually the appraisal was arbitrary or predetermined just to make the deal work. So for purposes of this example, let's say those $25,000 prints are "appraised" for $100,000 a year later.

Tax value (33 percent of $100,000)	$33,000
Less: cost of prints	-25,000
After-tax profit	$ 8,000

The idea here is that you deduct the contribution at its current market value, or $100,000. That reduces your taxes by $33,000, even though your real cost is only $25,000. The obvious abuses in this scheme led to reform. Today you're allowed to deduct only the *cost* of the item contributed. As you might expect, the market value of art prints has taken a nose-dive since the law changed. Here's the result under current law if the same prints are donated to a charity:

Cost of prints	$25,000
Less: tax deduction	
(33% of your actual cost)	-8,250
After-tax loss	$16,750

The promoters of tax shelters such as these have moved on to other schemes.

At-Risk Limits

Losses are always limited to your actual investment plus amounts for which you are personally liable. These rules apply to all investments except real estate. Especially strict limits are applied to:

1. Oil and gas exploration
2. Geothermal deposit exploration
3. Motion picture and videotape ventures
4. Business equipment leases
5. Farming ventures

"At-risk" investments consist of:

1. Cash invested
2. Property you contribute to a program
3. Borrowed finds for which you are personally liable

Real Estate Investments

Real estate investments have always had many tax benefits because they usually involve heavy borrowing and heavy interest payments. The interest paid is usually deductible in the current year. But there are limits in the total amount deductible. Any excess is carried over to the following year.

The example below shows how an investment in a commercial building can produce significant tax losses and result in a positive cash flow.

Monthly note payment is $2,740,	
including interest of	$2,667
Insurance	418
Maintenance (average)	150
Total monthly cash-basis expenses	$3,235
Depreciation, first year ($155,000 basis, 15 years, 150% declining balance)	235
Total tax basis monthly expenses	$3,470
Monthly rental income	3,400
Monthly net loss, tax basis	-$70

Cash Flow:

Note payment	$2,740
Insurance and maintenance	568
Total payments	$3,308
Income	$3,400
Monthly positive cash flow	$92

This assumes that occupancy remains consistent all year, that expenses are fixed, and that there will be little or no variation in depreciation or interest expense. In real life, all these factors vary.

Admittedly, these numbers are very close. If there are any vacancies, that thin margin of positive cash flow vanishes quickly. The point of this illustration is that there's a difference between what is reported for tax purposes, and what you actually have in cash flow.

You also need to consider the tax advantage of depreciation. In the example above, the monthly loss for tax purposes of $70 represents a loss of $840 per year. If your effective tax rate is 33 percent, that's an after-tax savings of $277. If you expand these numbers for larger properties or for a number of properties, it's quite possible to gain a substantial tax savings with minimal effect on cash flow.

But be careful. Real estate, like any investment, comes with risks. Vacancies, unexpected maintenance, and increased property taxes will all affect the after-tax profitability and the cash flow of any investment. There's more about real estate investments in the next chapter.

Consider the Tax Consequences

Every major investment can have important tax consequences. Consider deferrals, non-cash expenses such as depreciation, credits, and all future tax consequences when you compare possible investments. If you don't, the comparison isn't valid. Often, present advantages could be wiped out by future unfavorable consequences.

❏ Taxable vs. Tax-Free Investments

Which is better, a 6 percent yield that is taxable or a 4.2 percent yield that is tax-free? Assume you're in the 33 percent bracket:

	Sheltered	Unsheltered
$5,000 placed in an account currently paying 6%	—	$5,000
$5,000 placed in a tax-free account paying 4.2%	$5,000	—
Income per year (not compounded)	$210	$300
Less: Income taxes, 33%	$0	$99
After-tax value of account	$5,210	$5,201

While these outcomes are close, it's easy to see that in some cases, less is more. Given the assumptions about effective tax rates, the 4.2 percent yield is a better deal than the 6 percent yield.

❏ Tax-Deferred Retirement Accounts

Qualified retirement plans such as IRAs and Keoghs (see Chapter 5), are tax-deferred accounts. They provide the following advantages:

1. Contributions are deducted from gross income.
2. Contributions earn interest or dividends which are not taxed until retirement.
3. The accumulated funds are taxed at a lower rate at retirement.

As an example of tax-sheltering benefits, let's assume your tax rate is 33 percent. If you place $15,000 in a Keogh plan, the immediate, current-year tax saving is $4,950. If your account earns an average yield of 5 percent, your real first-year yield is 38 percent (tax savings plus account yield). It's very unlikely that you'll ever find another investment to match an after-tax yield of 38 percent. Even if you could get 52 percent before taxes, your real after-tax yield would be lower.

	Keogh 5%	Taxable 52%
Yield on $15,000	$ 750	$ 7,800
Plus: first-year tax savings in 33% effective rate bracket, 33% of $15,000	4,950	—
Less: tax on earnings, 33%	—	-2,574
First year after-tax yield	$5,700	$5,226
	38.00%	34.84%

❏ Prepaid Expenses

Cash-basis taxpayers can generally deduct expenses paid in the current year even if they aren't actually due until the following year. But there are limitations. For example, interest prepayments can't be deducted in the current year. They must be amortized over the life of the loan. Similarly, rent payments can't be deducted when they are prepaid.

Expectation of Profit

A legitimate tax shelter must offer a reasonable expectation of future profits. The IRS takes the position that an investment made solely to avoid taxes doesn't qualify for deductions because it lacks a profit motive. Real estate investments meet this rule. A positive cash flow (cash-basis receipts exceed cash-basis payments) can coincide with a tax-basis loss (with depreciation). Yet tax losses in real estate are seldom questioned because there's nearly always an expectation of profit when the property is sold.

Many tax shelters have been offered which promise deductions but not a profit in future years. If these are judged to exist only to produce write-offs, the IRS will disallow the deductions.

In addition to the expectation of future profits, tax shelters should include the following:

- *Current deductions* or credits to offset other income
- *Income deferrals* so that investments made this year produce profits that will be taxed in later years at lower taxes. (Keogh and IRA are excellent examples.)

■ *Leveraging,* which is the investment of a minimum amount of cash, the balance to be covered with borrowed funds. Deductions are limited to amounts "at risk," so you must be fully liable for borrowed funds.

Tax Shelter Checklist

Here are the questions you should ask before you make any investment promoted as a tax shelter.

Who is promoting the venture? Seek additional opinions on a proposed tax shelter, even if it's presented to you by your accountant or attorney.

What is their past experience? Have the promoters been involved in this type of investment in the past? What is their credit rating? Do they have a possible conflict of interest in offering the program to you? For example, do they own the property or asset that you plan to buy? Even if you don't make a dime on the deal, they'll make plenty.

How much do the promoters get? If they tell you they don't get a commission or a fee, beware. There's always a payoff for those who organize and promote these programs. These aren't the type of people who do good deeds for the pure joy of it.

How are the promoters paid? Are they to be compensated in cash, shares or both?

Are any guarantees given? Beware of sales pitches offering a low-risk "sure thing." Also watch out for salesmen claiming that they have invested in the program themselves, or those who pressure you by claiming you must act immediately or lose the opportunity. Stay away from programs which claim celebrated persons as investors.

Did you receive a prospectus? This is required. Believe *only* what is in the prospectus. Disregard verbal assurances.

Does the program offer first-year write-offs? Don't rely solely on the tax opinion in the prospectus. Review the tax treatment for each year you'll be involved. You could lose in the long run.

What is the IRS position on this type of program? The IRS may have ruled that these deductions aren't allowed. Check this out independently before you sign up. The risk of disallowance by the IRS is yours, not the promoter's. Your neck will be on the line long after the promoter has moved on to some other scheme.

What are you liable for? Will you lose your original investment? What about debts? Are you required to make additional payments (capital calls)? Will you be liable for any claims filed against the partnership?

What will you get for your participation? Will you be a limited partner, sole owner of an asset, or a shareholder in a corporation? Is there a reasonable expectation of profits?

Do you know this field of investment? You should be familiar with the industry's terminology, trends and market history. For example, if you're investing in business equipment, have you determined it won't be obsolete in a short time? Did you know that over two-thirds of all exploratory oil wells are unprofitable? Research thoroughly before investing.

Can you afford to invest? How long will your capital be tied up? Getting in is often much easier than getting out. Be sure you can afford to tie up your money, and that you know how long it will be committed. Are you subject to transfer limitations? Find out how you can get out of the program later.

How will you be taxed in the future? Find out how future taxes will be affected by the program. In some shelters, you might be required to pay taxes on paper profits ("phantom gains"), while you receive no funds in that year.

What are the chances of an IRS audit? There is the chance the IRS will rule against the deductions. In general, the larger your tax benefits in a sheltered program, the greater chance of an IRS audit.

Remember, if it's worth someone's time to sell you a tax shelter, it's probably a bad deal.

7

Real Estate Transactions

Most larger construction contractors buy and sell land as a part of their construction program, for investment purposes, or to provide office and yard space for their business. Because so many builders own land for one purpose or another, it's appropriate to look at the tax aspects of real estate transactions in some detail.

Real estate can be both a profitable investment and a versatile tax shelter. The right investment can yield a good return with little chance of loss. For example, you could buy an industrial building suitable for your office and with enough land for your storage yard. You could rent out any extra space. Then you could gradually take over this extra space as your needs grow.

There are significant advantages to investing in real estate. Among them are sheltered income on the rentals, depreciation on the full property, appreciation in the value of the land and building, and the chance to expand without the high expense of moving.

Tax Advantages

The special tax advantages of real estate are:

1. Losses on the sale of real estate held for business are deductible.

2. Profits on the sale of real estate are considered capital gains. There's a ceiling on the tax rate for capital gains.

3. Security deposits you collect from tenants aren't taxed as income, and only become taxable if the amount is retained or converted to rent at the end of a lease.

4. Investment costs can be depreciated along with the basis in buildings and improvements.

5. You are allowed to deduct interest on mortgages, which is higher in the early years and lower in the later years.

6. Your property values can be improved tax-free in some circumstances when tenants make their own improvements.

7. Repair and maintenance expenses maintain or even increase property value while providing you with a current deduction.

8. Real property can be owned by individuals, partnerships, or corporations.

9. Proceeds of real estate sales are taxed as they're received. Gains can be reported and taxed on the installment method if you receive payment over a number of years.

10. Profits from trading investment real estate for like-kind property are tax-deferred.

Depreciation is taken in all cases on a straight-line basis for real estate. Residential property is depreciated over 27.5 years, and non-residential property over 31.5 years.

Interest is fully deductible in the year it is paid. So in the earlier years of a mortgage loan, when most of the payment is for interest, the deduction is substantial. If your effective tax rate is 33 percent, that means 33 percent of all the interest you pay reduces taxes. So a $1,000 monthly interest bill discounts your tax liability by $330.

Before investing, take the time to compute the true return you're likely to earn from real estate. Otherwise, it will be very hard to judge whether or not the decision to buy real estate will meet your personal investment goals. Budget for the rate of return you can realistically expect to earn.

❏ Two Types of Investment Return

You should be concerned with two types of investment return: true yield and return on cash invested.

True yield is the actual appreciation of property, after deducting all costs related to improvements, acquisition and maintenance. If you net exactly twice the amount of a building's original cost, your return is 100 percent. Over five years, that's a return of 20 percent per year (ignoring compounding and taxes). Calculating the true yield in percent per year will help you compare the investment choices available.

Return on cash invested is a way of comparing depreciation levels and mortgage amortization. Depreciation provides a deduction for tax purposes but no cash outlay. It's an especially valuable part of every capital investment.

Over the life of a property, its depreciation value decreases. More depreciation is allowed in the first years than in the last. And once the building is fully depreciated, the annual deduction for depreciation is gone. But your mortgage payments may continue to be high even after the high depreciation years have passed.

When you make mortgage payments, part of the money paid covers interest and part reduces principal (the mortgage balance). The amortization portion (principal payment) is not deductible: It's repayment of a loan. As depreciation decreases, mortgage amortization usually

increases. The final payments on a fully amortized note will include little interest.

If depreciation expense exceeds principal payments, the difference is a tax sheltered cash return. When principal payments exceed depreciation deductions, your cash return is reduced.

Once depreciation has been all used up, your tax advantage is greatly diminished. The loss of depreciation write-offs is only part of the picture. At that point, you'll probably also have your original mortgage paid off. Once the mortgage is paid off, you'll have virtually no deductions left. And you'll probably be charging higher rents by then.

This argument assumes that you'll hold onto your investment property for 30 years. Many people get into real estate and trade up after a few years. Trading up re-starts the depreciation and interest schedules all over again. Remember, too, that although you'll have less interest to write off after 30 years, you'll also have a much better cash flow. Not having to make a mortgage payment means income from rents that might be virtually free and clear (except for maintenance, insurance, and property taxes). That gives you more spendable income — and higher taxes.

Here's how to compute the amortization of a fixed-rate interest mortgage payment. Let's assume that your original balance is $200,000 and your annual interest rate is 8 percent. Your monthly payment in this example is $1,672.90:

First, divide the annual interest rate by 12 to get the monthly interest rate:

$$\frac{8\%}{12} = 0.006667\%$$

Second, multiply the monthly rate by the previous month's mortgage balance forward to get this month's interest:

$$.006667 \times \$200,000 = \$1,333.32$$

Then subtract the interest from your total monthly payment to get the amount that goes to principal, or reduction of the loan balance:

$$\$1,672.90 - \$1,333.32 = \$339.58$$

Finally, subtract principal from the previous balance forward to get the new balance forward:

$$\$200,000.00 - \$339.58 = \$199,660.42$$

Repeat this procedure each month. Remember though, the balance forward decreases each month as principal payments are applied. An

Month	Total Payment	Interest	Amortization (Principal)	Balance
				$200,000.00
1	1,672.90	1,333.32	339.58	199,660.42
2	1,672.90	1,331.07	341.83	199,318.59
3	1,672.90	1,328.79	344.11	198,974.48
4	1,672.90	1,326.50	346.40	198,628.08
5	1,672.90	1,324.19	348.71	198,279.37
6	1,672.90	1,321.86	351.04	197,928.33
7	1,672.90	1,319.52	353.38	197,574.95
8	1,672.90	1,317.17	355.73	197,219.22
9	1,672.90	1,314.79	358.11	196,861.11
10	1,672.90	1,312.41	360.49	196,500.62
11	1,672.90	1,310.00	362.90	196,137.72
12	1,672.90	1,307.58	365.32	195,772.40
Total	20,074.80	15,847.20	4,227.60	

Figure 7–1

Mortgage amortization

example of one year's loan amortization is shown in Figure 7–1.

In this example, out of payments of $20,074.80, only $4,227.60 went to paying off the loan. The rest is tax-deductible interest. So if your effective tax rate is 33 percent, that $15,847.20 in interest payments reduces your taxes this year by $5,229.58. Another way of looking at this is to say that your "after-tax net interest cost" is $10,617.62, or that your after-tax interest rate is reduced from 8 percent to 5.36 percent. That's 67 percent of the full interest rate, or the amount you end up paying after tax benefits.

The tax benefits of deducting interest are important when you consider the cost of borrowing. That $200,000 loan used in the example would require a total of payments over 30 years of more than three times the loan balance. You'll pay out $602,244 for a $200,000 loan if interest at 8 percent is calculated every month on the outstanding balance.

Of course, the interest paid doesn't really matter very much if rental income is enough to cover interest payments. You actually get the tenant to pay your mortgage for you. And during that entire time, you are allowed to claim interest and other expenses, plus depreciation. So your net cash flow and tax benefits make the investment worthwhile. And, with any luck, the market value of the property will appreciate.

Buying and Selling Property

By itself, buying business property has no tax consequence. But, of course, there's a substantial cash or financing commitment, usually for a long term. So a variety of tax benefits and consequences can arise. Any increase in property value while you own the property will not be taxed. The tax laws don't consider change in value until the property is sold. But the increase in your equity lets you borrow cash without liability for income taxes.

Consider the advantages of borrowing against the increased equity in your property and using the proceeds to make improvements in the property. The improvements increase property values. So, you may borrow your own inflated values without paying taxes, and use the money to increase the values even further. The benefits of real estate as a tax-sheltered investment are attractive. See Figure 7–2 for an example.

The advantages of investing in commercial property are available even if you operate out of a building used partly for business and partly as a

	Current Value	Estimated Future Value
Original property cost	$200,000	$275,000
Less outstanding loan	135,000	
Equity	65,000	
Second mortgage - to invest in property improvements	50,000	68,000
Remaining equity	$15,000	
Plus basis of improvements	50,000	
Current equity balance	**$65,000**	
Current value / future estimated basis	$250,000	$343,000
Less balance of current mortgages	185,000	185,000
Current equity / estimated future equity	**$65,000**	**$158,000**

Figure 7–2

Improvements and equity

residence. This happens when you have living quarters in an office building or run a business from your home. Of course, you have to determine the portion of the property used for business.

The most dependable way to calculate the business use is based on square feet of space:

Total cost of property	$200,000
Less value of land	45,000
Depreciable portion	$155,000
Total square feet	16,400
Actual business footage	11,800
Business portion (11,800/16,400)	72%
Depreciable basis of business portion	$111,600

Only 72 percent of other expenses such as fire insurance, external repairs, and general maintenance are deductible. Shared expenses can be taken for the business only in proportion to the percentage of business use.

If you run your business from your home, deductions are allowable, but the rules are strict:

1. You must use an area *exclusively* and all the time for business purposes. For example, if you also store old clothes or furniture, no deduction is allowed.
2. The home office must be necessary. If you also have an outside office, you must establish the absolute necessity of having a home office as well.

The deduction for a home office has been abused and has become an audit target. Be prepared to support it.

You get one more tax advantage when the property is sold: Any profit is taxed at capital gains rates. To determine the profit, you must compute the *basis* of the property, compare it to the adjusted selling price, and arrive at a tax-basis gain or loss.

Basis consists of the original cost (including fees that were capitalized when the property was purchased) plus any improvements, less depreciation taken to date. So a property that has been fully depreciated will also have a reduced gain. This results in a higher profit or a lower loss. Net gains are taxed at much lower rates than your ordinary net income after depreciation. An example of basis and adjusted sales price is given in Figure 7–3.

Who Should Own the Property?

Before buying real property, consider the tax advantages for each way title can be held.

❏ Individual Ownership

If you own the property as an individual, all income received is added to your personal taxable income. There are several forms that personal ownership can take.

A joint tenancy allows two or more people to own a single piece of property. Each joint tenant owns an undivided share of the entire parcel with the right of survivorship. When one tenant dies, title passes to the other tenant or tenants automatically.

Under a tenancy in common, two or more owners own an undivided share of the parcel but there is no right of survivorship. If one owner dies, that person's portion of ownership goes to his or her beneficiaries.

Basis:	Original cost[1]	$200,000
	Plus improvements	50,000
		250,000
	Depreciation (fully depreciated)	205,000
	Adjusted basis	$45,000
Sale:	Sales price	$343,000
	Less commission and closing costs	31,800
	Adjusted sales price	$311,200
Gain on Sale (sales price-basis):		$266,200

(1) Original cost includes $45,000 for undepreciable land.

Figure 7–3
Basis and adjusted sales price for real estate

❏ Partnerships

Partners own a share of all partnership property in proportion to their share of the partnership. Thus, a 30 percent partner will earn 30 percent of the appreciated values, and will be entitled to only 30 percent of depreciation write-offs.

A partnership that exists for another purpose can buy property as an investment. Or, partnerships can be formed exclusively to buy real estate, even if only one piece of property is involved.

The partnership is not taxed. Each partner is responsible for taxes on his share of income. Other partnerships or corporations can participate as partners themselves. Figure 7–4 shows several partnership possibilities.

Capital contributions made to a partnership to invest in property don't affect taxes. Only actual profits and losses are passed on to the partners, regardless of how much capital is withdrawn. Money can be taken out of the partnership at any time without tax consequence to the partners. This isn't profit, just a reversal of the investment process. But all profits flow though to the partners and are taxable to them, even if the money actually stays in the company and the partners receive none.

❏ Limited Partnerships

In a general partnership, partners have a voice in management, participate in operations, invest,

and are usually compensated. A limited partnership is quite different. There are two classes of partners, general and limited. General partners have control over management and operations, and are liable for acts of the partnership. Limited partners are liable only to the extent of their investment in the partnership and usually don't have a voice in management. In fact, a limited partner who does participate in management and operations could lose his limited liability status.

When a general partner dies, the partnership is reorganized. But with the death of a limited partner, ownership passes to the beneficiaries.

Limited partnerships can be set up for a limited time, and then be continued. This allows a great deal of flexibility. A limited partnership may be formed to buy, improve, and resell a property. Once this is done, it may dissolve or repeat the process.

A major disadvantage is that limited partners may find it hard to sell their interest. If none of the other partners wants to buy that share, the share value in a quick sale may be very small.

Here's a checklist of questions to ask before you invest as a limited partner:

Will the partnership be involved in development? Projected income might not allow for increased construction costs, labor problems, and the effects of inflation. Be sure the general partners have allowed for reserves.

What are market conditions? Check for overdevelopment in the proposed area, social and economic conditions, and potential environmental objections.

What are the management fees? Are these reasonable? Compare the general partners' compensation in agreements. Reputable general partners will reveal both management fees and commissions.

Is the general partner competent and honest? Does this proposed partnership involve properties he currently owns or has interest in? Is it stipulated that sales commissions won't be taken until after the limited partners have recovered their investment costs?

What is the general partner's real estate experience? Be sure the proposed manager knows how to manage property of that type.

What is the IRS position? Be sure that the limited partnership will be taxed as such. If not, you won't receive the tax-shelter benefits.

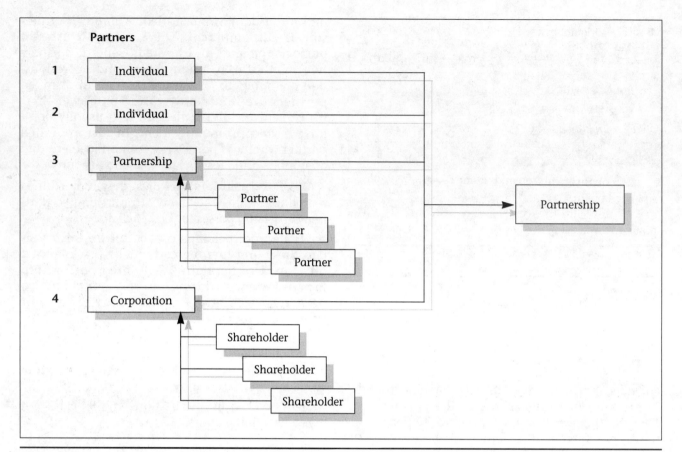

Figure 7–4
Partnership possibilities

Corporations

Unlike partnerships, corporations are not dissolved when a shareholder dies. This is important because investing in real estate is often a long-term commitment.

Corporate shares are usually more marketable than the interest held by a limited partner. Also, there is no need to transfer title to the land or to recognize a gain or loss on the land when stock is sold. Of course, a gain or loss on stock sold will have tax consequences. But there's a major disadvantage to corporate ownership of real estate: Shareholders don't receive the benefit of sheltered income.

Capital for the purchase can be raised by selling additional stock or borrowing in the corporate name. It's often less complicated for a corporation to take out a loan than it would be for a partnership. The partners probably have widely varying credit status.

Partnerships are potential tax hazards for individuals. In good years when the partnership is profitable, the partners are taxed on high net income of the partnership, even if they receive little or none of the profit earned. If the partners are in high tax brackets, the tax burden can be crushing. The partners have no choice in delaying income from the partnership. Compare that with stockholders in a corporation. A corporation can protect shareholders by delaying distribution of income until shareholders can use the money. Of course, there are limits to how long this income can be delayed, and corporate income tax has to be paid on net income in the meantime.

The advantage of having a corporation own the real estate is the option to delay income. The disadvantage is that the shareholders can't take advantage of the depreciation, as partners could. Sometimes timing or receipt of income is more important that lost depreciation.

Also, a corporation is usually better able to plan ahead and anticipate tax liability. Earnings can be sheltered in a pension or profit-sharing plan for employees. In a real estate corporation, the employees may be the only shareholders.

Contributions to retirement plans are deductible by the corporation and not taxed to participants until benefits are distributed, usually after employees have reached 60 years of age.

The corporation can also provide medical benefits, group insurance, and other benefits. These are deductible, but not presently taxable to the participants.

❏ S Corporations

You will recall that shareholders in an S corporation are taxed like partners. Individual shareholders can sell their shares when they wish and still enjoy the limited liability of the corporate form. And, of course, pension and profit-sharing plans as well as other corporate benefit programs are also available as in any other corporation.

❏ Syndication

Syndicates are formed to pool capital to buy land and buildings. The advantage is that risk of loss can be spread among a larger group of people. Many larger builders organize syndicates to raise capital for the purchase of land that can be developed. Usually the syndicate organizer does all the direct management, record-keeping, reporting and coordination (for a fee).

There are many advantages to syndication. If properties are paid for in full, risk of loss is all but eliminated. With no mortgage payments to make, the syndicate can survive any downturn in the real estate market or any spike in interest rates. Of course, the cost of professional management may be higher. But all tax benefits will usually be available to investors.

The manager may be one or more individuals, a partnership, or a corporation specializing in the organization and management of real estate investments. Or management could be a combination of these. Syndications can also be organized as Real Estate Investment Trusts (REITs).

A REIT is treated the same way as an open-end mutual fund. This means that the number of investors isn't limited. The organization itself doesn't pay taxes. Profits are distributed to its members, who are taxed individually. With a REIT, losses aren't deductible.

Be sure to check the scope of a REIT's operations. It might be involved in activities other than purchase and sale of real estate. Understand the market conditions as well as the expectation of profits before you invest.

Real Estate Income

Income from real estate is treated like other income for tax purposes. For cash basis taxpayers, income must be reported as it's received. If your company is on an accrual basis, income is reported when it's due.

Advance rentals are taxed when they're received, regardless of your reporting basis.

Security deposits aren't taxable if they're held solely to ensure that the tenant lives up to the terms of his lease. They are taxed when applied against rentals due, and when a lease expires or is broken. Tenant payments made to cancel a lease are taxed like rental income.

If a tenant pays your taxes, interest, mortgage amortization, insurance, repairs, or other operating expenses, these payments are really rental income and must be reported as such.

Insurance claim settlements for loss of rents resulting from fires or other casualties are taxed as income.

Tenant improvements are not taxable as income unless there is a reduced rent payment. Improvement costs paid in this case are taxed as rents. There is no tax on the improvements even if you move in later. But you can't depreciate more than your actual cost. As a result, your "basis" in the improvements is zero.

Deductions

These are the most common deductions for real estate ventures:

- Interest expenses are deductible as paid, but no deduction is allowed for advance payments of interest.

- Real estate taxes are deductible as operating expenses when they are paid.

- Depreciation
- Management expenses
- Cost of rent collections such as commissions
- Maintenance expenses
- Salaries for employees such as janitors, security guards, maintenance personnel and property managers
- Travel expenses to check on your investment
- Legal fees
- Insurance premiums for fire, liability and glass breakage are deductible over the term of the policy. Advance premium payments are not deductible. Nearly all casualty insurance is payable in advance. So you usually can't deduct the full premium when paid. Deductions are reported over the period covered by the policy.
- Demolition losses may be deducted if you did not purchase the property with the plan to demolish it.

❏ Deduction Limitations

Local improvement assessments (like a fee for street repairs on your block) can't be deducted or depreciated. They're not considered a form of property tax. But they are added to your cost basis for the land.

Capital improvements must be capitalized as structural additions and depreciated. Lease expenses must be written off over the period of the lease.

Loan fees add to the cost of the property and must be depreciated. Acquisition fees paid to acquire real estate are capitalized.

If real estate is acquired with the intention of demolishing it, demolition costs can't be deducted or depreciated. The cost is added to the basis of the land.

Interest and taxes paid during construction have to be capitalized and depreciated.

Maintenance and repairs are deductible as current year expenses. Improvements and replacements must be depreciated over a period of years.

The distinction is permanence. Is the item an actual addition to the building that ultimately increases its value? Or is it a recurring expense that only maintains conditions or fixes something that has broken down? Figure 7–5 lists typical expenses and capital improvements.

Typical Expenses	Typical Capital Improvements
Patching floors	New floors
Repairing foundations	New foundations
Stairway supports	New stairways
Roof repairs	Roof reshingling or replacement
Plastering	New walls
Papering	New wall decor (paneling, etc.)
Mending leaks	
Replacing defective wiring	New electrical wiring
Termite work	Rat-proofing
Enameling furnace	Relining furnace
Insulation	
Replacing defective plumbing	Placing new type of piping
Cleaning or repairing walls	
Restoring damaged property to normal condition	Restoring damaged property for a new use
General maintenance and housekeeping	Building alterations
	Heating system conversion
Repairing fire escapes	New fire escapes
Replacing run-down front	Installing new front
Grounds maintenance	Architect's fees

Figure 7–5
Expenses vs. capital improvements

The cost of maintaining property and making needed repairs is deductible. But any permanent change is a capital item.

If a cost is a permanent improvement, but is below a minimum amount, you might be able to deduct it as a current expense. Some maintenance expense items are so large that they should be capitalized and amortized over a period of time.

Record Keeping

If you invest in a property that you occupy, be sure to keep two sets of records — one set of books for the business and another for the property. Separate books provide several benefits. Some involve taxes and some involve your business:

- Sources of income and categories of expenses are segregated.

- Profits and losses and cash flow can be seen easily.

- Expense levels, trends and ratios of costs and expenses or profits are isolated from unrelated sources.

When real estate operations are kept in separate books, report results as in the sample below:

Real Estate Activities

Rental income	$50,000
Rental expenses	28,000
Net rental income	$22,000

Building Operations

Gross receipts	$1,815,000
Cost of goods sold	1,265,400
Gross profit	$549,600
Other income:	
Rentals	$22,000
Interest	4,000
Total income	$575,600
Operating expenses	484,100
Net income before taxes	$91,500

Suppose you're a builder and own your office. You also rent out space in the same building. My advice is to separate income and expense into categories. You need a separate bookkeeping system and checking account for each. Your real estate operation is like a subsidiary company and should be run entirely separate from the building business.

Assume you establish an account to manage the investment in your own building. If you transfer $15,000 to this account, make the following entries:

	Building Operations	Rental Account
Cash	$(15,000)	$15,000
Investment in r.e. (asset)	15,000	
Equity account		(15,000)

All rental income and expense will flow through the rental account, keeping building operations separate. Rent is collected from the other tenants and deposited in this account. Rent for the builder is handled by a journal entry as follows:

	Building Operations	Rental Account
Equity in r.e. (net worth account)	$(750.00)	
Equity account		$750.00
Rental (income)		$(750.00)
Rent (expense)	$750.00	

This keeps tax reporting and financial analysis simple. Net income for the building company will be inflated if the company isn't charged rent by the real estate company. To keep company results comparable, books for the building company should reflect rent paid and maintenance expense met. That way ratios on your tax return will be in line with standards for the industry.

The building operation's balance sheet carries two accounts: *investment in real estate*, which is an asset; and *equity in real estate*, which is equity account. Eventually, as rent expenses are recorded and the equity account builds, the asset account can be eliminated. Report the net difference between asset and equity as an equity amount.

If accumulated funds are transferred from the real estate account back to the building operations account, a check should be issued and deposited in the regular checking fund.

	Building Operations	Rental Account
Cash	$10,000	$(10,000)
Equity in r.e.	$(10,000)	
Equity account		$10,000

Note that the building operations *equity in real estate* account (combined with the original investment in real estate balance) will always equal the rental account's *equity* account. This keeps both sets of books in balance. When financial statements are prepared, the two bookkeeping functions can be combined, greatly simplifying reports and their preparation. Detailed results of the real estate investment can be reported separately or identified in a footnote to the financial statement.

Here is an example of consolidated reporting:

	Building Operations	Rental Account	Consolidated Report
Cash in bank	$8,416.08	$2,401.76	$10,817.84
Investment in r.e.	15,000.00		-0-
Equity accounts	(7,405.80)	7,594.20	-0-

Since the net balance of the building operation's investment and equity accounts equals the rental account's equity balance, they can be eliminated in consolidated reports. Only the cash balance is added and included. It isn't necessary to alter the format of financial statements because of the segregation.

It is important, however, to note significant profits on the financial statement. Management should always know what profits can be anticipated for tax planning.

Within the real estate accounting system, records should be kept separately by property. Individual differences in investment return, spendable cash, and cash yields will be obvious. When computing capital gains for the sale of a property, this separation is helpful.

Real Estate As a Tax Shelter

Tax consequences are always important when you buy, sell or just hold real estate. In many transactions, tax savings may be the best part of the deal.

The actual return on improved property is usually higher when tax savings are considered. For example, it's possible that a real estate investment could leave you with spendable dollars at the end of each month (after paying property taxes and insurance and making principal and interest payments) and still show a loss that can be used to reduce your taxable income. There aren't many such properties for sale, but you'll see some that come fairly close.

Improved real estate reduces your taxes because interest payments on loans used to buy real property are generally deductible from your income. And, of course, the new accelerated depreciation rules let you deduct from income the cost of improvements to the land over a relatively few years.

A good real estate investment has the four primary advantages of any good tax shelter. First, it brings in more money than you spend each month. Next, it shows a tax loss (due to interest cost and depreciation) that reduces your taxable income. Third, it has a tendency to appreciate in value over time. That gain isn't taxed until the property is sold, and even then any gain is taxed at lower capital gains rates. Finally, it has loan value that can be used when needed to provide cash.

Depreciation is a major advantage in owning real estate. You can depreciate the value of buildings and capital improvements, but not, of course, the land itself. Depreciation is a non-cash deduction. You're writing off the amount invested over a period of time. Expenses such as maintenance, management fees, real estate taxes, insurance and record-keeping costs are deductions that can be taken in the year paid.

Here's a summary of how depreciation and interest shelter income from the tax collector. Suppose you put up a warehouse for your construction company on land that you already own. The cost of the building is $150,000. The depreciation deduction each year is $4,762 (divide the building's cost by 31.5 years). You lease the warehouse to your construction company (or to another tenant) at the market rental rate of $26,000 per year. Interest payments on the loan you took out to finance the building come to $24,500 per year (on average). At year-end, your typical year's income and expenses look like this:

Rental income	$26,000	
Less expenses		
Interest	$24,500	
Depreciation	4,762	$29,262
Net loss		$3,262

You see that the real annual cash flow is positive by $1,500 — the amount rental income exceeds interest payment. So you have tax benefits through depreciation that reduce your taxable income.

This example doesn't consider other expenses, such as maintenance, insurance, and property taxes. But it does make the point: Property can show a loss for tax purposes while providing you with positive cash flow, or at least with a tax benefit that reduces the outflow of cash. In this example, you could shelter $3,262 of additional income while actually receiving $1,500 per month in cash.

The same logic applies to any depreciable property. It's true whether you purchase a property yourself, buy with others in a partnership or a corporation, or place investment money in a REIT or other investment program.

Real estate offers tax advantages you won't find in other forms of investment. It shelters income, is relatively safe, and, if you manage it properly, may yield a positive cash flow.

8

Write-Offs

All businesses have losses. Some are sudden and unexpected. Others result from someone's intentional act. A few are the result of obsolescence.

In this chapter we'll discuss bad debts (someone refuses to pay you), casualty losses and thefts (unforeseen, sudden events), abandoned property (worthless to you from obsolescence or damage), and intangibles like covenants not to compete (rights bought and solid to limit competition).

Bad Debts

A bad debt must be proven before it is deductible. Four conditions must be met to prove the bad debt.

The debt must be valid. You must have a right to payment. The agreement can't depend on an event that might not happen. For example, if you loan money to someone and tell him he must repay only if he has a profit, the debt isn't valid. A debt is not valid if you charge interest above the legal rate. This makes the debt voidable (cancelable by the borrower).

A debtor-creditor relationship must exist. There must have been an enforceable promise to repay the debt. Gifts can't be written off as bad debts. Loans to family members are not debtor-creditor agreements.

The amount you want to deduct must have been reported as income. If you report on the cash basis, no deduction is allowed for unpaid receivables. These are income only when they are paid. If you're on an accrual basis, you record the income when the receivable was established.

Accrual Entries:	Debit	Credit
Accounts receivable	—	
Income		—
Bad debts	—	
Receivables		—
Cash Basis Entries:		
Cash	—	
Income		—

The debt must become worthless during the year. The bad debt is deductible *only* in the year it is reasonably deemed to be worthless. To claim the deduction this year, you must have had some hope of collection at the end of the previous year. It must have no value at the end of the year in which the deduction is claimed.

As long as you have a "reasonable expectation" that the debt is collectible, it can't be considered worthless. A truly worthless debt is one that can in no way be collected.

A debt doesn't have to be due to be written off. For example, a business that owes you money next year may go out of business now. If there's no chance of collection, the debt is worthless, even though it isn't due for payment.

If you cancel a debt, that doesn't make it worthless. You must establish that a canceled debt met the rules to be called worthless before you can take a deduction.

Some common events that justify bad debt deductions are:

- Insolvency during the year without hope for recovery
- Bankruptcy
- Receivership
- Liquidation of the business
- Debtor goes out of business, without a reasonable expectation that you'll be able to collect the debt

There are two ways to claim bad debts: The first is the reserve method. A specific amount is added to a reserve each year. The second is the actual loss method, in which specific debts are written off as they become worthless.

❏ The Reserve Method

Under the reserve method, you claim a deduction by anticipating bad debts for the year and establishing a reserve. This reserve is reported as a reduction to accounts receivable. The reserve must be based on experience in sales or accounts receivable in the past.

Reasonable yearly additions to the reserve can be deducted as bad debts. If you have lower bad debts than expected, you must reduce or eliminate the addition to the bad debt reserve.

Reserve Based on Receivables

A reserve based on receivables may be calculated as:

- Average bad debts expressed as a percentage of total average outstanding balances
- Average bad debts experienced as a factor of average receivables collected per year
- Average bad debts as a percentage of total credit granted
- Average bad debts as a percentage of balances outstanding more than 30 days

Other *reasonable* and consistent methods can be used. But, if your volume in credit sales or outstanding balances is changing significantly, be certain your method allows for these changes.

Reserves Based on Sales

Reserve additions can be based on your sales experience in relation to bad debts, but this is only reliable if you have mostly credit sales.

Reserves Based on Outside Information

Your current bad debts could be higher than average if you have reliable information that a debt is going to be uncollectible.

For example, suppose an employee of a client of yours tells you that his employer is going into bankruptcy and the amount you are owed will not be paid. That would make it reasonable to increase your current reserve. The burden of proof is on you to justify a higher-than-average reserve addition.

You can change your method of calculating bad debts by filing Form 3115 with the IRS within 180 days of the year of change. This form asks your reason for making the change. Have a qualified accountant or tax consultant assist you with this form.

❏ The Specific Deduction Method

While the reserve method is probably best for accrual-basis builders, the specific deduction method is also acceptable.

Specific bad debts are written off as they become known. This method's disadvantage is that you don't get the deduction as soon. It does provide accurate reporting and timing of the bad debt deduction, however.

Cash-basis builders can't use the reserve method at all. You have to use the specific deduction method because receivables aren't recorded as income until they're collected.

But cash-basis builders do have bad debts. For example, you receive a check and record the income. If the check isn't good, you may reverse the income entry, arguing that you never really received it. Suppose you recorded the income in late December but didn't find the check wasn't good until January of the following year. You make an effort to collect and find that the debt is not collectible. At this point, you can take a bad debt deduction if you recorded the income.

The two methods, reserve and specific deduction, can't be combined. If you report on the reserve method and find that the client is going into bankruptcy, you can increase your reserve but you can't write off the specific income.

You can deduct the unreimbursed loss of business property due to theft, damage by fire, storm, flood, earthquake or other natural catastrophe. Progressive deterioration such as termite infestation doesn't qualify for casualty loss treatment. Damage from an unusually severe frost does.

Casualty Losses and Theft

Losses from theft are deductible if the act was illegal in your state and you can prove that it occurred.

Casualty and theft losses are treated in much the same way for income tax purposes. You are allowed to deduct the net value of assets that would normally be capitalized and depreciated over a longer period of time. Casualty loss deductions must be reduced by the amount of insurance coverage.

You must be able to prove the following to qualify for casualty and theft deductions:

1. That the casualty actually occurred. Save newspaper stories, photographs, and other documents that tend to prove the casualty.
2. The value of property both before and after the loss. These can be provided by experts. For motor vehicles, use the Blue Book value.
3. The cost of repairing damaged property. Actual repair bills are the best proof. The repairs must be reasonable. Repairs that improve the property can't be deducted as casualty losses. Also, if you repair the property and add safeguards against future casualty losses, you can't deduct the extra repair cost.
4. The original cost of the property. A deduction can never be more than the original cost.

Natural causes or damage from:	Fire losses to:
avalanche	autos and trucks
blizzard	equipment and furniture
cave-in (from unknown causes)	office building and facilities
cyclone	warehouses
drought	inventory
dust storm	uniforms
earthquake	
extreme cold, dry, or wet	**Thefts of:**
flood	inventory
freezing	capital assets
hurricane	other business property
ice and sleet	
ice pressure	**Other losses:**
landslide	from vandalism, riots or civil disorder
lightning	
quarry blast	damage caused by a plane crash
rain, if heavy or sudden	icy roads
sinking (such as bedrock after a heavy rain)	faulty driving, except willful negligence
one-day damage from polluted air	falling through ice
sonic boom	boiler explosions
storm	severe blasts
thaw	
tidal wave	
tornado	
volcano	

Figure 8–1
Deductible casualty and theft loss

Invoices, bills of sale, and canceled checks prove the original cost. If improvements and additions are involved, be prepared to prove these as well.

Figure 8–1 is a list of deductible expenses under the casualty and theft loss rules.

While casualty losses may be provable by general knowledge (a natural disaster occurring over a wide area), thefts are sometimes harder to document. Prove theft loss with witness statements, a police report and any news articles reporting the theft.

Report a suspected theft to the police. This provides documentation even if there is little or no hope of actual recovery. If you don't report the incident, the IRS may assume that you regarded the event as something other than a theft.

The amount of a theft loss can't exceed the original cost. A piece of equipment or machinery that has increased in value (high replacement cost, rarity value) can only provide a deduction of the original cost. Protect yourself against this with insurance coverage up to the replacement value.

Embezzlement losses are deductible in the year the loss is discovered. If you use cash basis accounting, you can take a deduction only for cash received and recorded as income.

Losses resulting from riots, vandalism, or civil disobedience are deductible. Document your losses with repair cost invoices, photographs and police reports.

❏ Inventory Losses

Inventory losses are not usually taken as a separate deduction. But they are reflected in a lower ending balance. Thus, the actual change in physical inventory includes the amount lost by casualty or theft. Assume you have $5,000 worth of lumber and plywood stolen from your yard:

	Without Loss	With Loss
Beginning inventory	$147,800	$147,800
Purchases	635,055	635,055
Other direct costs	36,310	36,310
Total	$819,165	$819,165
Less:		
Ending inventory	163,850	158,850
Cost of work done	$655,315	$660,315

Note that by reducing the ending inventory to account for the $5,000 casualty loss, the cost of work done is increased by the same amount. This has the effect of reducing taxable income. That's the same as deducting a separate loss.

The deduction may be claimed by adjusting either the beginning or ending inventory, depending on when the loss occurred. The method shown above is more practical in most circumstances. And it's easier to document.

Inventory losses must be reduced by the amount of any insurance reimbursement. If you use the recommended method (reflecting the loss in inventory changes) and receive an insurance reimbursement, report the amount received as miscellaneous income. It is also acceptable to use the net loss to offset the cost of goods sold. Starting with the beginning inventory, add your direct cost and deduct any insurance collected for casualty loss and the ending inventory. The result is the cost of work done.

In the case where $5,000 was lost, costs were increased from $655,315 to $660,315. If $4,000 was recovered from an insurance reimbursement, actual costs would be $659,315.

The IRS may disallow the loss if you have insurance coverage and don't file for reimbursement. If actual insurance reimbursements are greater than the basis of lost property, the net difference must be reported as income. This gain can be avoided if you invest the proceeds in similar property.

❏ Timing of Deductions

There are two times when you can recognize and claim a casualty loss:

1. When the casualty occurs.
2. When the insurance claim is settled or denied.

It's most common to deduct a casualty loss when it occurs. In some cases, such as embezzlement, the loss is deducted in the year of discovery.

Accrual-basis builders can't claim a deduction until the insurance reimbursements are payable. A claim settled or denied in the year after a casualty loss will delay the tax deduction.

To compute the actual amount of loss, establish the loss of market value. Next, figure the adjusted basis (cost, plus improvements, less other casualties and depreciation). Finally, figure the amount of loss. If property is totally destroyed and the market value is lower than the adjusted basis, your loss is the adjusted value less any salvage value. Computation of casualty losses is shown in Figure 8–2.

Abnormal Obsolescence and Abandonment

You have abnormal obsolescence when property is withdrawn from service prematurely. The schedule for normal retirement is disrupted. This can be the

1) Loss in market value:
Market value before loss
Less: market value after loss
= Loss in market value
2) Adjusted basis:
Cost
Plus: Improvements
Less: Previous casualty losses
Less: Accumulated depreciation
= Adjusted basis
3) Amount of loss:
Lower of loss in market value or adjusted basis*
Less: Salvage value
Less: Insurance proceeds
= Casualty loss

* Note: If property is totally destroyed and the market value before the loss is less than the adjusted basis, use the adjusted basis to compute the amount of loss.

Figure 8–2
Computing casualty loss deduction

result of unexpected development of more efficient models or methods, or casualty losses.

To claim a loss for abnormal obsolescence, the property must be totally abandoned. A deduction for abandonment will not be allowed under any of the following circumstances:

1. The property is still in use
2. Insurance coverage on the property continues in force
3. The asset is kept on your books and depreciated

While depreciation is a write-off of an asset over an established period of time, abnormal obsolescence is a write-off of assets *not* in use. To claim the loss, you must be prepared to establish:

1. The year that the property became obsolete
2. When the asset's status changed to little or no value
3. The time that the asset became permanently unusable

To claim this deduction you must prove you have no intention of using it again. Idleness is not abandonment; the asset must be disposed of.

Cost (building only; exclude land)	$85,000
Plus: Closing costs	2,485
Adjusted cost	87,485
Less: Accumulated depreciation	63,000
Adjusted basis	24,485
Sale of scrap metal and wood	4,000
Demolition loss deduction	$20,485

Figure 8–3
Calculating a demolition loss

Machinery for specialized work that is unused for several months is not necessarily abandoned. But if it's given away because you're no longer doing that type of work, you have abandoned it.

Demolition is another type of loss. No deduction can be claimed if you buy property with the intention of demolishing it (such as purchasing land and buildings, tearing them down and developing the land). But if property is purchased with no intent to demolish, demolition losses can be claimed. The calculation of deductible demolition losses is shown in Figure 8–3.

Inventory Write-Offs

Inventory can become obsolete. This happens when:

1. It can't be sold at normal prices
2. It can't be used due to damage, shop wear, discovered flaws, or change in utilization
3. New and improved material becomes available

The deduction allowed is the actual cost less the salvage value.

Suppose you buy $7,500 worth of air conditioning equipment for a future job. The job is then canceled. During the year, that line of equipment is discontinued and replaced by a new line, making your equipment obsolete. You can't use the equipment and can't return it to your supplier. You try to sell it for scrap. At year-end it hasn't been sold, but the market value for salvage is estimated to be $3,000. That estimated value is carried as part of ending inventory. The balance,

$30,000 Original Value 60-Month Amortization		
Month	**Asset Value**	**Amount of Expense**
January	$29,500	$500
February	29,000	500
March	28,500	500
April	28,000	500
May	27,500	500
June	27,000	500
July	26,500	500
August	26,000	500
September	25,500	500
October	25,000	500
November	24,500	500
December	24,000	500
Balance at beginning of term	$30,000	
Expense written off during year		$6,000
Balance at end of term	$24,000	

Figure 8–4
Amortizing organizational costs

$4,500, is "abandoned" as worthless, representing the portion of inventory that can't be recovered.

Defective goods: Inventory can be revalued when defective goods are discovered (such as warping or rot caused by exposure to the elements, leakage, or handling damage).

Shortages: Losses from theft, waste or unexplained shortages are deductible. These losses are reflected by lower ending inventories. They are deductible when found, at inventory time.

Involuntary Conversions

When government takes property through legal process, it is called an *involuntary conversion.* Your property is converted to cash without your permission. Any tax on the gain can be deferred by reinvesting the compensation in replacements (as long as the replacement costs at least as much as the amount of compensation).

Involuntary conversions occur and qualify for deferred treatment when the property is completely or partly destroyed, stolen, or condemned or seized by a governmental agency for public use.

If insurance proceeds or condemnation awards are reinvested, you *must* postpone any gain. But in some cases, you might be better off paying tax on the gain than deferring it. This can happen in low-income years. To avoid postponement, you can:

1. Fail to replace the property
2. Replace it with dissimilar property
3. Replace it for a lower cost
4. Let the time limit expire before replacing it

Deferring gains on involuntary conversions establishes a lowered cost basis. As a result, any capital gain will be greater.

Intangible Asset Write-Offs

Intangible assets in a construction business include covenants not to compete and goodwill. These two intangibles are often closely related. If a covenant not to compete is given to protect goodwill, the covenant is taxed as a capital gain. But a covenant not associated directly with goodwill is treated as ordinary income.

The buyer of a business who pays the old owner for a covenant not to compete has legal protection and a tax advantage. The new owner can write off the cost of the covenant over the term of the agreement. The seller who received the money is taxed on the amount received.

Covenants not to compete may not involve a transfer of money. A seller may induce a buyer to accept his terms by offering to sign a noncompetition agreement without receiving any compensation. In this case, no deduction is available to the buyer, but he still has legal protection. No taxable income is received by the seller.

Goodwill is the value of the business reputation among customers, suppliers, associated companies, and the community in general. When a business is bought, a value may be placed on goodwill. This may be associated with the company name, motto, logo, or general reputation. Goodwill is an intangible. You can't see it or feel it, but you know it's there. Goodwill proceeds are taxable to the seller (who received cash) but can't be written off by the buyer. Goodwill is carried on the books as an unchanging intangible asset.

Description	Organizational Cost	Expense	Direct Cost (Inventory)	Capital Assets
Before opening business:				
Furniture and equipment				—
Legal fees	—			
Accounting fees	—			
Rent expense	—			
Merchandise (for resale)			—	
Telephone expense	—			
Salaries and wages	—			
After opening business:				
Rent expense		—		
Telephone expense		—		
Salaries and wages		—		
Merchandise (for resale)			—	
Machinery and small tools				—

Figure 8–5
Identifying organizational costs

Organizational Costs

Costs for starting a business, or for reorganizing a phase of business, are called organization costs. They must be amortized over a period of time, usually five years or more. If the business is discontinued before the amortization period, the balance of organizational costs can be deducted at the time business ceases. See Figure 8–4.

Organizational costs include practically all items except fixed assets and inventory. Included are:

- Legal fees to enter the business (partnership agreements, lease negotiations, incorporation)
- Accounting fees (to set up books, controls or procedures; to consult on accounting methods, fiscal years, tax planning)
- Filing fees (permits, licenses, etc.)
- All overhead expenses until the time the business becomes active

Figure 8–5 shows how to treat costs, expenses, and investment of capital before and after business begins.

9

Accounting Methods

There are two common ways to keep your books: cash and accrual. Each has advantages and disadvantages. If you choose accrual accounting, you have to make one other decision. Do you want to follow percentage-of-completion or completed-contract rules for reporting income? This chapter explains these terms and what they mean in your business.

Cash Accounting

The cash accounting method is the simplest. But it doesn't let you see the true financial condition of your company. And you can't use it if you maintain any substantial inventory. Very few larger businesses use cash basis accounting. It usually isn't practical if a company issues more than a few invoices or gets more than a few bills each month.

With cash accounting, income is recognized (recorded on the books) only when it is received. Expenses are deductible only when they're paid. All the money due you and all your unpaid bills are ignored until money changes hands. All individuals and proprietorships use cash basis accounting.

Technically, this is an accurate way to keep books. But it doesn't account for all your credit sales that will become cash in a month or two. A large sale in the current month won't show up on your books until it's paid. Costs and expenses are distorted too. Suppose you have the following activity:

Gross sale	$125,000
Direct costs	65,000
Gross profit	$60,000
Related expenses	48,000
Net profit	$12,000

If the income was received this month but all the expenses were paid next month, you would have the following results:

	First Month	Second Month
Income	$125,000	—
Costs and expenses	—	$113,000

Cash basis accounting doesn't provide a very good picture of how your business is doing. But it's simple because no accruals are made and there are no accounts receivable or payable.

The major weaknesses of the cash accounting system are:

- Poor control for tax purposes. Unusually large fluctuations are likely from one year to the next. That makes tax planning harder.

- Accounting and tax controls must be established outside of your bookkeeping system. Cash flow is difficult to control from the financial records.

- Financial statements are never accurate. They don't reflect what income was earned and what liabilities were incurred. They paint an unrealistic picture of results.

But cash accounting offers one tax advantage. You defer reporting income until it is actually in hand. Few larger builders find this enough of an advantage to justify its use, however.

The IRS accepts cash accounting but may want to review details of how your system operates. For example, you can be taxed on income *constructively* received but not in your accounts. Suppose you receive a check near the end of your fiscal year and delay depositing it. On audit by the IRS, this amount will probably be added to your income. The delay is usually easy to find if your records are audited. Unusually large deposits in the first month and small deposits in the twelfth month show that someone is trying to manipulate income and expense.

You also have constructive receipt of income if funds are available to you. If some accounts are ready and willing to pay, but you ask that payment be delayed, you've probably got that income for tax purposes.

❑ Hybrid Accounting

You can't change accounting methods back and forth to benefit from differing circumstances. But some changes in accounting systems are permitted.

- *Contributions* are made on the cash basis, and are deductible only in the year actually paid. But corporations declaring contributions can get a deduction without making payment. To qualify, the payment must be made within 75 days after the close of their fiscal year.

- *Insurance premiums* covering more than one year can be deducted only over the period of the policy. Thus, even on the cash basis, a three-year insurance premium can be deducted only one-third per year.

- *Social Security taxes* (federal) are always deducted on the cash basis. So an accrual-basis builder who has a payroll on the first day of his fiscal year can't accrue Social Security taxes on the payroll, even though they were for the previous year's wages.

Accrual Accounting

Accrual accounting assumes that income, costs and expenses become "fixed" at a certain point, even though cash may change hands much later. You accrue (report as income) all amounts which you have the right to receive. In other words, you have income when you are owed the money. Costs and expenses are deductible when you owe the money.

Accrual accounting is better for many reasons. First, it places income and the cost of earning that income in the same reporting period. Second, financial statements allow you to judge your tax liabilities, see how well your cash flow controls and budgets are working, and plan ahead with solid and accurate information.

Accrual accounting requires a higher level of accuracy in record keeping. But the result is worth the trouble. Figure 9–1 shows a comparison between cash and accrual reporting. Since the work was completed in February, it makes sense that all income, costs, expenses, and profits should be reflected in that month. The cash basis causes inaccurate results in at least two months.

Income (the right to receipt) and liabilities (the obligation to make payment) relate only to real results that are known and computed. You can't accrue estimated future values until they are earned (income) or incurred (costs or expenses).

To compare cash and accrual accounting methods you must consider the impact on reportable profits. Cash accounting obscures the monthly and yearly profits of your business. Tax liabilities can jump wildly. If your receipts are unusually large, and related costs and expenses aren't paid until the following year, your tax consequence would be devastating. Although losses can be carried back to prior years or forward to future years, you'll have to wait for a year to correct the error.

	Cash Basis		Accrual Basis	
	February	March	February	March
Sales	—	85,600	85,600	—
Cost of goods sold	41,300	—	41,300	—
Gross profit	(41,300)	85,600	44,300	—
Expenses	28,100	—	28,100	—
Net profit (loss)	(69,400)	85,600	16,200	—

Figure 9–1
Comparing cash and accrual accounting

Figure 9–2 shows the treatment of business transactions under each method. Note the reference to constructive receipt. If funds are totally available to you, you can't defer the income by delaying deposit or recording of the receipt.

❏ Deferrals and Accruals

Unearned income is money received but not yet earned. It's treated as deferred income under the accrual method. You put the money in the bank and have the use of it, but it appears as a liability on your books. Deferrals increase the cash available to you without raising taxes.

Assume you received $4,000: $3,000 for work completed and $1,000 toward work that won't be done until next month. You would make the following journal entry, assuming the $3,000 has been reported as income previously:

	Debit	Credit
Cash	$4,000	—
Account receivable (asset)	—	$3,000
Deferred income (liability)	—	$1,000

The following month, as the $1,000 becomes earned, the following entry will be made:

	Debit	Credit
Deferred income	$1,000	—
Income	—	$1,000

This demonstrates that income is reported in the period it's earned. Usually you complete the work and then bill it out. It's then a receivable which can be expected to be paid later. But the same principle also applies to funds received before the work is done. Obviously, deferrals are very desirable in almost any business.

Completed-Contract vs. Percentage-of-Completion Rules

If you're using accrual accounting methods, you have to decide whether to accrue income when the work is completed and billed to your client (completed contract), or monthly, according to your estimate of how much of the job has been finished (percentage of completion). The two will produce about the same result if your clients get monthly bills for work done or have a progress payment schedule that nearly matches the proportion of work already finished. If you get two or three lump sum payments on a job that lasts more than three or four months, your choice of completed-contract or percentage-of-completion rules may be very important.

The problem of deferred income doesn't come up when the completed-contract method is used. No income is recorded until the job is finished. Deferred income may be a problem under the percentage-of-completion method.

Long-duration work (lasting one year or more) must be accounted for by one of the two methods. But you can use both methods in one business. Short-duration work will probably be paid in one installment — upon completion of the job. This would be completed-contract accounting. Either method can be used on longer jobs.

	Cash Basis		Accrual Basis	
	Income	Costs and Expenses	Income	Costs and Expenses
Billing sent out			—	
Payment received	—			
Payment received, check not cashed*	—			
Invoice received				—
Invoice paid		—		
Social Security taxes paid:				
For this period		—		—
For prior period		—		—
For future period		—		—
Two-year insurance premium paid:				
Current portion		—		—

*Constructive receipt

Figure 9–2

Comparing the treatment of business transactions

In choosing percentage-of-completion or completed-contract accounting, the major considerations should be:

- Record keeping
- Tax consequences
- Financial reporting
- Type of work performed

❏ Percentage-of-Completion Accounting

Under this method, income, costs, and completion schedules are directly related. Reporting for tax purposes depends on the percentage of a specific contract that is finished. Thus, a delay due to weather, labor problems, or material shortages affects your income, profit and cash flow.

If you receive progress payments that are less than your estimate of what you've earned at that point, accrue the difference by setting up an account receivable. If payments exceed your estimate of percentage of completion, record the balance as deferred income. Here are two examples:

$100,000 contract:

40% total payments received	$40,000
Job is 35% complete:	
Booked income	$35,000
Unearned (deferred) income	$5,000

$50,000 contract:

40% total payments received	$20,000
Job is 48% complete:	
Booked income	$24,000
Accrued income (receivable)	$4,000

Your direct costs are handled the same way. Figure the percentage of job completion. Record estimated costs that match this percentage. If costs are in line with your job estimate, recorded costs should parallel income, not receipts. In the second example, some income has been accrued. This indicates that it's appropriate to accrue part of direct costs. Subcontract payments may be withheld until the earned income has been received in total.

This method reflects earnings, costs and expenses in the months that the work is performed. It offers you several benefits:

- Project controls can be established and coordinated within the accounting system.

			Gross Income				
				Accrual Methods			
Month Received	Amount Received	Cash Method	Completed Contract Method	Percent Complete	Gross Income	Accrued Income	Deferred Income
January	50,000	50,000	—	20%	40,000	—	10,000[1]
February	50,000	50,000	—	50%	40,000	—	—
March	—	—	—	60%	20,000	20,000[2]	—
April	100,000	100,000	200,000	100%	80,000	—	—
	200,000	200,000	200,000		200,000		
		Booked as received	Booked only when 100% complete		Booked as contract progresses		

[1] 20% earned, 25% received; the balance must be deferred.
[2] 60% earned, 50% received; the balance is accrued.

Figure 9–3
Reporting income

- Tax planning is easier. You can see results to date and the expected profit.
- Financial records are realistic.

The major drawback of this method is that income and costs are estimated. Your books are only as good as your estimates. Some accountants like to keep estimates off the books as much as possible. But it's unrealistic to ignore the impact of jobs in progress. It's better to include your best estimate than to ignore the facts altogether.

❑ Completed-Contract Accounting

This method recognizes income and related costs only at the end of the contract. All income and costs are recorded accurately, but the timing is unrealistic. No estimates are included. All significant income will be taxable at once.

Tax planning, cash control, and project controls are important on every construction project. Under completed-contract accounting your record keeping system doesn't provide these features. As a result, you'll need to create other job control methods that don't rely on accounting records.

Completed-contract accounting is realistic for use in work to be completed within the current year, but presents problems on longer-term projects.

Consider the tax consequences of each method as shown in Figure 9–3. Under the percentage-of-completion method, gross income is received over a period of time. But under completed-contract accounting, it's recognized all at once. The impact in a single year of a large contract is significant. If, for example, you finished six long-term jobs in the same year and were under the completed-contract method, you would have unusually large income.

Financial statements prepared on the completed-contract method aren't realistic. In a period of high activity, you could report no business whatsoever.

Cash or Accrual Accounting: Other Considerations

You can keep your books on one method and pay taxes on another. But you have to record adjustments at year-end. You could maintain accurate financial reporting and controls with the accrual method, but pay taxes by the cash method.

Both cash and accrual accounting methods are consistent in their treatment of capital assets. An asset can be depreciated with either method from the time it's placed into service. Purchasing machinery in the last month of a fiscal year qualifies it for the beginning of a depreciation program, even if that asset is not paid for in that year.

Similar rules apply to the advance receipt of income. Under the accrual rules, income received before it's earned is deferred. But advance payments may be taxed if there aren't any restrictions on your use of the funds.

❏ Tax Consequences

Cash-basis accounting is simpler than accrual accounting, but the disadvantages outweigh the advantages in most cases. First, of course, you can't use cash-basis accounting if you have any supplies in inventory. For most contractors, reducing inventory to zero to change to cash-basis accounting would be foolish.

Next, cash-basis contractors are limited in the year-end tax planning they can do. To deduct expenses during the year, the money must actually be spent in that year. This can put a strain on cash reserves that may cause problems during the first quarter of the following year. And if you don't have any ready cash at year-end, you won't be able to take advantage of deductions that could be taken under accrual accounting.

Under cash-basis accounting, any cash received before year-end must be included in income for that year, even if the payment is not yet earned. If accrual-basis customers prepay their bills to create additional deductions at year-end, the cash-basis contractor will be stuck with added taxable income in that year.

Accrual accounting allows far more planning for taxes. Expenses can be deducted as long as they are for goods received. The bills may not be paid until mid-March, but the deduction will be allowed for materials received in December. The accrual-basis contractor has a better chance to spend at year-end to create deductions through timing. Every dollar spent on legitimate business expenses is one less dollar of income and part of a dollar less in taxes for that year.

Under accrual accounting, income isn't taxed until it's earned. So for the accrual-basis system, early receipt of income is deferred for tax purposes. Tax isn't paid on the income until it's reportable. On the accrual system, taxes may be calculated and planned far in advance, an advantage not shared under the cash system.

Contractors using the accrual system have the option of recognizing income only when the job is completed. Most accrual-basis contractors follow the percentage-of-completion method. The completed-contract method is limited because it recognizes all income from a job only when the job is complete. New laws make the completed-contract method all but obsolete for most contractors. But short-term jobs can probably continue to be treated under this method.

Under the completed-contract method, builders had a relatively simple system for reporting income. Income was documented by the record of jobs finished. As each job was finished, all income, costs and expenses were reported at once.

This might seem attractive because it defers income to the last possible minute. But if several profitable jobs "hit the books" in one year, the sudden tax liability could cause chaos in the reporting, paying and depositing of taxes and in the operation's cash flow.

Some builders used the completed-contract method to defer income — sometimes with devastating consequences. It interfered with careful tax planning because it's usually not possible to judge the precise completion date of every contract. Percentage-of-completion accounting requires a more detailed system but makes good tax planning possible.

Under percentage-of-completion accounting, the accrual-based builder recognizes that part of income, costs and expenses which corresponds to the degree of completion on each job. This allows for accurate reporting of results, assuming a good estimate of the level of completion on each job.

For percentage-of-completion accounting, you need to identify stages of project completion. Usually these stages are based on the billing schedule agreed upon between the contractor and owner or the subcontractor and the general contractor. If these stages are well-defined, it should be easy for anyone concerned to examine the project and see what stages are complete and what stages remain to be finished. Definition of these stages should be documented in both the construction contract and the payment schedule. This supports your calculations made for tax purposes.

It's relatively easy to recognize income and expense as a job progresses. But what about the profit? The profit you expect may fluctuate as the job progresses. But on most jobs you'll have a reasonable estimate at the beginning. This estimate can be adjusted as appropriate several times before the job is complete. Use your same breakdown of stages of completion to estimate the expected profit.

The Importance of Record Keeping

No matter what accounting system you use, good record keeping is crucial. Eventually you'll be asked to prove a deduction, document all income, and provide worksheets for calculations.

Under the percentage-of-completion method, every calculation of completion must be documented completely. This is especially true at year-end. Be as careful to show why your calculations are correct as you are to show that a certain progress payment is due from your customer.

Your original estimate, progress payment schedule, and daily log of work done and materials received are all the documentation you'll need. Inspection reports will also be helpful in proving that your level-of-completion estimates are accurate and fair.

The more complete your file, the less likely you will be challenged during a tax audit. Expect your IRS auditor to be as concerned with the accuracy of your estimates of completion as the bank officer who loans you money.

Documenting Tax Deductions

T he tax code requires you to maintain records which support the information reported on your tax return. Your records are the invoices and receipts that document each transaction you make.

You won't have much trouble documenting most expenses like materials, bills from subcontractors and labor costs. Just save the invoices from vendors, the bills from subcontractors and payroll records. Don't pay bills until you have an invoice that explains exactly what you're paying for. That's the easy part. Rules for travel and entertainment require more detailed records. Finally, this chapter will cover record retention (how long you have to keep these records).

The Need to Document

If your tax return is audited, the IRS will probably require you to produce records that support deductions. If the records don't support the claim, or if you've lost or discarded them, the IRS will determine your tax liability based on whatever records are available or can be made available.

This invariably works against you. It's far better to keep accurate records. If your tax liability is prepared by revenue agents, many legitimate deductions will be lost. Unfortunately, your word isn't enough. You need to preserve written records.

The law doesn't specify exactly what records must be kept, only that they must be permanent, accurate, and complete. Records must be kept a specific number of years, in most cases three years from the filing date for that return, to satisfy the statute of limitations for verifying data on your tax return.

Accurate books help you take advantage of benefits allowed by law and safeguard your transactions against errors. Your system should both meet IRS requirements and meet generally accepted bookkeeping standards.

Your files should include sales vouchers, invoices, receipts, canceled checks, and other documents that prove your transactions. A bookkeeping system begins with the detailed records of each event. These are summarized in a series of journals and ledgers. The general ledger is the final summary record, from which your tax return is prepared.

Keeping records is required by law. But even if it weren't, you would still have to record each transaction. Your office records provide eight important benefits:

1. Without business records, you can't do any effective tax planning

2. They make it possible to deduct every legitimate expense

3. They let you track costs and use of assets on each project

4. They help control cash flow

5. They provide information needed for monitoring general expense budgets, and improving the accuracy on future budgets

6. They help you track repairs and maintenance costs, depreciation, and replacement programs

7. They let you make income projections based on past performance

8. They help you spot trends, track receivables and bad debts, and anticipate potential problems before they arise

The flow of money is at the heart of every business. Looking at each transaction individually tells nothing of the future or the past. But a summary of transactions, like a profit and loss statement, is like a road map showing where you are and how you got there. Everyone running a business needs a financial road map to make business decisions that affect the jobs you take, taxes you pay and the use of company assets.

The Burden of Proof

The burden of proving each deduction is entirely on your shoulders. You must be prepared to prove any item of income or deduction claimed on your tax return.

Proof consists of a series of documents. Your canceled check plus an invoice is usually proof enough for a deduction. It helps to have a purchase order if the invoice isn't detailed enough to describe the items purchased. Very often, a single piece of documentation isn't enough by itself. Two documents may be needed to describe the total transaction. For example, here are some

common pairs of documents that would be used together to document a single expense:

- Canceled checks and invoices
- Your sales invoice and bank deposits
- A payroll tax return and employee's record
- Airline and hotel bills, and an expense report

Often, one item proves the occurrence of a liability and the other offers proof of payment. Simply proving that a payment has been made (a canceled check) doesn't answer the more important questions:

- What was it for?
- Was it ordinary, necessary, and reasonable?
- Was it business-related?
- Does the payment apply to the correct tax year?

If the IRS decides your income has been understated or that expenses have been overstated, they are free to compute your tax liability. It's your responsibility to prove otherwise.

For example, if you claim a deduction for a home office, and the IRS decides you claimed too much, you must prove that the computation was reasonable. You must also establish that it was ordinary and necessary in your business.

You can see that the documentation problem doesn't stop with just keeping receipts. You must be able to defend the extent and scope of each deduction.

Even if a specific type of expense is considered acceptable for the type of business you're in, you must still prove the accuracy of what you claim. It could be clear that you needed to spend money for a certain item. But, because of your failure to keep proper records, your deduction could be lowered to less than the entitled amount.

Poor records can result in losing legitimate deductions. You could also be assessed a negligence penalty.

If your records aren't enough to prove what you claim, the IRS may reconstruct your income. They often use the Net Worth method. If your net worth increases, it will be assumed it is due to taxable income. You may have received loans or tax-free gifts, but the burden of proof is on you to prove the loans or gifts.

Deposits made to your bank account may be assumed to be income unless you can prove otherwise. If you have negotiated a series of short-term loans and deposited this money in your account, be prepared to document the loans. If you have transferred funds from one account to another, keep good records of each transfer. These problems are easily overcome with proper documentation.

Travel and Entertainment

Special rules apply to travel and entertainment expenses. Reasonable estimates are not permitted. If you don't have the documentation, you can't deduct the expense.

If you reimburse employees for travel or entertainment expenses, pay special attention to both the treatment of payments and to the type of records you keep.

You may reimburse employees for business-related expenses: entertaining business associates, travel for business purposes, or transportation (other than commuting, which is not a business expense) for business.

Expense allowances are general payments to cover a range of expected expenses. These must be reported as wages on the employee's W-2. It's up to the employee to offset expense allowances with detailed actual expenses. Any balance is taxable as income. If expenses are more than the expense allowance, a net reduction to gross income is allowed. If your company takes a large deduction for "employee business expenses," a tax audit of employees becomes quite likely.

Expense reimbursements are repayments for specific expenses. The employee is required to submit an expense report. This report must summarize expenses in broad categories: transportation, meals, telephone expense, entertainment, auto expenses, etc. Attach to the expense report the receipts and vouchers which support the expenses. The expense report should also include an explanation of the business purpose and the people involved.

Keep these reports. If you don't require proof from employees for travel and entertainment expenses, the amounts you pay have to be included as compensation on the annual W-2 form.

Corporate officers reimbursed by the corporation must be able to *prove* that the expenses were business-related.

There are special, specific rules for three categories of expense: travel, transportation, and entertainment.

❏ Travel

Travel, for tax purposes, occurs while away from home on business. This means you are not close enough to return home and must arrange for other accommodations. You must be gone longer than an ordinary work day.

For example, suppose you are at a remote construction site for more than one day. You take a motel room for the night before another full day of inspections. You'll have no problem with that deduction if you have records of how much was paid, for whom and why.

But suppose you're on the job site in the morning, have a meeting in the client's office in the afternoon and return home that night. Can you deduct the cost of a hotel room so you could shower and change clothes before the afternoon meeting? Conceivably, it could be necessary to take a room in the middle of the day. But the burden would be on you to prove that this room was necessary.

Suppose you put in a full work day and could have returned home that evening. But you just didn't feel like making the drive. Instead, you take a hotel room. Since there isn't a good business reason for taking the room, the cost isn't deductible.

Document deductible travel expenses carefully. Establishing the business purpose and necessity is as important as the vouchers.

Travel expenses include:

- Air, rail, and bus fares
- Cost of using your own car
- Taxi fares between airports or terminals and hotels, from one customer to another, or from job site to job site
- Transport between hotel and job site
- Baggage charges
- Meals and lodging while away from home on business
- Cleaning and laundry expense
- Telephone expense
- Tips related to travel activities
- Other expenses directly related to travel

These expenses are deductible only as far as they serve a business purpose. If you combine travel with a vacation, only that portion relating to business is deductible. The trip must be primarily business or you get no deduction.

❏ Transportation

Transportation is local travel. Your principal transportation expense will be the cost of automobiles. But it can also include rail, bus, or taxi expenses.

The cost of commuting from home to work and back is not deductible. If you carry tools, any additional costs (such as renting a trailer) are deductible. Trips from a union hall to a job are not deductible for your employees.

If you work away from your regular or permanent base on a temporary assignment, transportation costs are deductible. But if the temporary assignment becomes more permanent, the expense will not be deductible.

For cars, the business portions of gas and oil, repairs and maintenance, tires, insurance, road and bridge tolls, and parking fees can be deducted. In addition, you are allowed to depreciate a business auto and may qualify for an investment credit.

The *standard mileage method* lets you deduct a certain amount per mile. In addition, all business-related road tolls and parking fees can be expensed. Only business mileage, fully documented, can be used.

The *actual expenses method* allows you to deduct all business costs, including depreciation (but only for the months the car was used for business). Once you compute all expenses for the year, you are allowed to deduct the business portion. This is expressed as the percentage of business use to personal use, based on mileage. For example, if you put a total of 10,000 miles on your car in one year, and 6,000 were for business, you can deduct 60 percent of all expenses.

Document automotive expenses in detail. You don't have receipts or any other solid proof for specific trips, so you must create your own record. Make daily entries in a diary.

Figure 10–1 shows how to document automotive expenses. This form is useful if you use the standard mileage method. But if you use actual mileage, you must still maintain a log. Note that space has been allowed for the "business purpose." Remember the absolute need to establish a business purpose.

A book published by Craftsman, *Construction Forms & Contracts*, contains a full-page Expense and Travel Report, along with over 100 other construction-related business forms, and comes with a computer disk that will enable you to personalize and alter the forms for your particular business. An order form for this and other construction manuals is bound into the back of this book.

❏ Entertainment

Any expense which is associated with providing amusement or recreation to business prospects, clients, or potential clients, is entertainment. Entertainment can take place at:

- Night clubs
- Sporting events
- Vacation resorts
- Social or sporting clubs
- Athletic clubs
- Theaters

Even furnishing living expenses to customers and their families is a form of entertainment.

A deduction will be allowed if the expense is directly related to business. Just having a business association does not meet this rule. You must establish that:

1. You had more than a "general" reason to expect income or other benefits in the future.
2. You had business dealings with the person during the period entertainment was provided.
3. The main purpose of the entertainment activity was the business purpose and the transaction that resulted.

A deduction is also allowed if the expense is associated with but not directly related to business. If you have a clear business purpose, such as getting new accounts or keeping up the relationship with existing customers, there is an associated relationship to business.

❏ Records Required

Keep travel, transportation, and entertainment expenses listed in a log or diary. Also keep all expense statements and other records. Always get receipts.

		Auto Expense Record					
				Other Expenses			
Date	Miles	Bridge	Parking	Amount	Description	Business Purpose	

Figure 10–1
Auto expense record

In some cases, you may need more documentation than you think. Entries in your appointment book are not enough to claim a deduction.

Keep records up-to-date. If you don't, you'll forget important details and shortchange yourself. Delayed recording may also undermine the credibility of your recording and documentation system.

Remember, no deductions are allowed for estimates, approximations, or "unreasonable" expenses. Everything must be fully documented.

You must document the location of the entertainment, the people entertained, and their business title or relation to your business. An entertainment log is shown in Figure 10–2.

❏ What to Prove

Your burden of proof for travel and entertainment is much heavier than with general expenses such as postage, office supplies, telephone, or rent. Deductions for travel and entertainment have been grossly abused. The IRS is in the business of stamping out these abuses. Any significant travel or entertainment expense is examined with extra care.

Here is a summary of what you must prove for travel and entertainment deductions:

❏ Travel

1. Each amount that was spent while away from home
2. Dates of leaving and returning home and the number of days spent on business
3. Travel destination
4. Business reason for travel or other benefit expected or received

❏ Entertainment

1. Each amount that was spent on entertainment
2. Date the entertainment took place
3. Name or address of place where the entertainment occurred
4. Type of entertainment provided
5. Business reason for entertainment and business discussions that took place
6. People entertained and their positions or titles (establishing their business relations)

A final note on travel expenses. If you choose a location too distracting, chances are a deduction will not be allowed. A noisy nightclub or lounge,

			Entertainment Log			
			People Entertained or Present		Expense Description	Amount
Date	Location	Business Purpose	Name	Title		

Figure 10–2
Entertainment log

which could make any discussion difficult, may be judged inappropriate to the stated goal of entertaining with a business purpose.

Documenting Other Expenses

The IRS is tough on travel and entertainment expenses. Many audits are confined exclusively to T & E deductions. But don't conclude that you can be casual about documenting other expenses. You're still required to prove several points:

1. That the expense was incurred
2. That it was ordinary, necessary and reasonable in your business
3. That the expense occurred in the tax year in which a deduction was claimed
4. To whom the payment was made
5. That the expense was strictly business-related

❏ Rent

The physical presence of your shop and offices proves this expense. Your lease provides additional proof.

Rent payments are ordinary. They are necessary to conduct business, especially if you have to store tools and equipment and hire employees. Unless you rent a lavish penthouse which has no connection with business activities, your rent deduction should be the easiest to prove.

That it was paid in the proper tax year can be established by your journal and supported by the canceled checks. The entry and check will also establish to whom the payment was made.

To establish a business relationship, be certain to use the office and shop facilities 100 percent for business. Don't store personal property or allow parking for the family car.

❏ Telephone

Document telephone expenses with itemized billings submitted by the telephone company. But be prepared to prove that long distance calls are business-related. Restrict nonbusiness use of company lines and, if necessary, keep a log of all calls made. This record both supports the tax deduction and discourages employees from improper use of the phone.

Telephone expenses can include more than just charges on company office phones. When on the road, calls can be charged to hotel rooms. If you make many calls from a pay phone, consider getting a company telephone credit card. That's an easy way to document calls made from pay phones. Each month you'll get a printed record of charge calls made during the month. Otherwise, it's too easy to forget to document those calls. If you estimate them and are audited, your estimate may not be accepted.

Your home phone bill can't be paid in full. But a part of it may qualify. Keep a record of business calls made from your home phone. Take a deduction for these. For many contractors this could be a considerable deduction over a year's time.

❏ Office Supplies

Establish a vendor relationship with one or more local stationers. Some have good catalogs that offer nearly all the office supplies you're likely to need. Keep the number of vendors small if possible. That makes record-keeping easier.

Documentation should include at least the vendor's invoice and your canceled check. These alone will usually establish that what was ordered was ordinary, reasonable and necessary. But in some cases you'll need additional facts. The most valuable document may be a purchase order which shows exactly what job or what department required the items ordered.

A simple purchase order system will help you keep expenses down while providing a chance for you to preapprove all purchases. It also creates good documentation for tax deductions.

The system can be very simple: The purchase order is completed, approved, and delivered to the vendor to fill. A copy of the purchase order or at least a reference to the purchase order number should be included with each delivery. Before you pay the bill, match the packing slip and invoice against the purchase order copy in your file.

The vendor's invoice, with a copy of a purchase order attached, is adequate documentation for office supplies. This is an account often reviewed during tax audits. Many construction contractors tend to dump a lot of miscellaneous expenses into the office supplies account.

Set up some guidelines that help keep this account free of expenses that belong elsewhere. An unusually high deduction for office supplies will trigger an IRS audit.

❏ Operating Supplies

Be sure you understand what expenses belong in this account. While almost all contractors have expenses that belong in an operating supply account, it's often abused. Keep capital expenditures, small tools, office expenses, and lease payments out of this category.

Operating supplies should include only materials that are consumed in the maintenance of your office and shop. Cleaning materials and supplies fall in this category. If the account is well-defined and reviewed regularly, it won't be corrupted with expenses that belong elsewhere.

Be especially careful to avoid coding capital assets to this account. Under the new tax law, you can "expense" a substantial portion of capital expenditures each year. But not if they're coded as operating supplies. Expensed assets have to be kept separate for depreciation calculation. Have a separate account for these items. A large deduction for operating supplies casts doubt on the tax return and could trigger an audit.

❏ Insurance Expense

Even for the cash-basis taxpayers, insurance premiums are deductible only during the period covered. So only one-third of a three-year premium can be deducted each year. Document insurance deductions by showing how the premium for each year was calculated. Identify each item of deduction by reference to coverage type, company and coverage period.

Prepaid insurance should be set up as an asset and amortized over the life of the policy. If this involves several different policies with different coverage periods, be sure to retain the policies even after expiration so you can support the entry for prepaid insurance.

❏ Interest Expenses

Many construction contractors make and repay several short-term loans during the year. Be sure to keep good records on each loan. Understand how interest is calculated on each so you can identify the interest part of each payment.

Interest can't be prepaid, even by a cash-basis builder. It's deductible only in the year in which it is earned. Pay all interest charges due up to the last day of the month, but don't try to prepay interest. It's fairly easy to show that interest has been prepaid.

Here's the information you need to record on your loans:

1. Amount of the loan
2. Source (name of the lender)
3. Interest rate
4. Schedule of interest expenses
5. Payment dates or demand date
6. Breakdown of monthly or quarterly payments between interest and principal
7. A copy of the signed note

❏ Salaries and Wages

Salaries and wages are relatively easy to document. You're required by law to keep records for each employee and for total payroll expenses. You routinely file both federal and state quarterly payroll tax returns and an annual unemployment insurance tax return. You also must report and pay workers' compensation insurance.

Be sure that payroll records are complete, in balance and up to date. On audit, be prepared to establish that all taxes withheld have been deposited with the bank or to the state agency. Failure to deposit payroll taxes is a serious mistake that can close down a construction company faster than any other business error.

Also be certain that all employees are completely identified in your records, by name, address and Social Security number. The IRS routinely investigates payment of salaries to nonexistent employees. Be prepared to prove that your employees are real people receiving payment from you for services rendered. And remember to save employee records even after they no longer work for you.

❏ Licenses and Fees

Most construction contractors pay substantial fees for city and county inspections, business licenses, state licenses and federal permits. Be sure your file notes what was paid and to which agency. Upon audit, the IRS is likely to review this file and may request full documentation. If your file of paid invoices is kept in alphabetical order, this file may be hard to reconstruct. Consider keeping a list of license fee and permit expenses. This list should show the date paid, amount, payee, and purpose of payment.

If you pay more than five or ten fees per month, set up an account in the general ledger with subsidiary listings. This helps explain the large number of transactions in the account. Finally, be aware that fines such as those assessed for traffic violations are *not* deductible. They should be coded as reductions of surplus.

❏ Repairs and Maintenance

This will be an important account if you own any heavy equipment. Be sure to check coding carefully so you don't include capital expenditures in this account. A common mistake is to put a down payment for new equipment in this category. If you write more than ten or fifteen checks a month against this account, break the account into sub-accounts. Explaining several smaller accounts is easier than explaining one big one. Remember, a single item could trigger questions from the IRS.

If your company owns and maintains six or eight trucks, your breakdown of expenses could be to the following categories: repairs and maintenance, parts and replacements, tires, accessories.

The division could also be made by creating a separate account for each class of equipment. Keep repairs and maintenance of office equipment (copy machine, typewriter, computer) separate from construction equipment. Be sure that rental or lease payments on equipment and machinery don't end up in the repairs and maintenance account.

❏ Small Tools

Many builders use this account to expense purchases of tools too small to capitalize and depreciate. Remember, you may expense part of your assets each year. But don't use the small tools account to write off capital acquisitions. Be sure to document the dollar amount that divides assets which will be capitalized from items that will be expensed.

❏ Taxes

This account should include nearly all taxes *except* federal income tax and payroll taxes. It covers diesel fuel tax, excise and gasoline taxes, property taxes, auto registrations (unless included under "licenses and fees"), local taxes and state income taxes.

Payroll taxes should be recorded in a separate classification. The taxes account, like licenses and fees, can accumulate a substantial balance and may be of special interest during an audit. Keep a good subsidiary record of this account and review it occasionally to be sure that everything included there actually belongs there.

❑ Payroll Taxes

This is the account against which your share of payroll taxes is charged. The amount withheld from employees is a liability which is subsequently paid by deposit or with the filing of your quarterly tax return. But employers are responsible for a matching amount of FICA, the FUTA tax (Federal Unemployment), state unemployment taxes in most states, and local payroll taxes.

As a rule, payroll taxes you owe can't be accrued. So it's wise to end payroll periods whenever possible at the end of a calendar month and avoid the loss of deductions in a tax year.

Payroll taxes are documented by referring to payroll records and tax returns. It's a good idea to prepare worksheets for the computation of taxes and to keep these in a payroll file for future reference.

❑ Depreciation Records

Depreciation under the MACRS (Modified Accelerated Cost Recovery System) has made this area of the rules uniform, and simpler than in the past. If you use the charts supplied by the IRS for the appropriate percentage each year, there is no guesswork or extra computation involved.

Depreciation records should document the date of purchase, the type of equipment, the purchase price, the classification for MACRS purposes, the amount depreciable each year, expensing (if applicable), and any equipment inventory number that you assign.

The MACRS system also simplifies depreciation in one other way. You no longer have to compute salvage value for assets. You depreciate the full amount (except land in the case of real estate).

Because there are a limited number of asset classifications, each with a set life, many decisions (and opportunities for abuse) have been eliminated. It's also less likely that an audit will adjust your claimed depreciation deductions.

❑ Advertising and Promotion

Most construction contractors don't spend heavily on promotion. But when you do have these expenses, be sure to document them fully. Note carefully that each was reasonable, ordinary and necessary.

Nearly anything that promotes the name and reputation of your company will qualify, unless the expense is way out of proportion to the expected benefit.

❑ Retirement and Pension Plans

Payments to qualified plans are deductible. But keep detailed records on all of your contributions. These records should include complete files on participating employees and must show the calculations of all contributions on their behalf. Contributions to plans based on net profits should be made in time to qualify for deductions. Generally, this will be the due date, plus extensions, of the tax return for that same year. For corporations, the due date is usually 75 days after the close of a fiscal year.

In case of audit, profits may be adjusted upward and an additional tax assessed. This may change the amount that could have been paid into a profit-sharing plan. Because audits are usually done after the filing deadline, the organization will lose the right to increase contributions to a qualified plan for the audited and adjusted year.

If profits are amended down in an audit, any contribution you made over the proper amount may be carried forward and applied to the next year.

❑ Employee Benefits

Employee benefits other than direct compensation are a sensitive area. Benefits can take many forms. Although it's difficult, it's important to document each benefit if you want to take the deduction for that benefit.

If you provide your employees with insurance such as health or disability coverage, be sure to keep copies of all premium calculations. Any allowance paid in cash to employees (for travel, automobile usage, or entertainment) must be supported by documentation in your file and reported as income to the employee. Employees then have to back up their receipt of cash with a record of how they spent the cash for a business purpose.

Code to employee benefits the cost of providing coffee to employees, employee luncheon or dinner meetings paid by the company, and other social events for the benefit of your staff. Office gatherings such as Christmas parties are deductible and are considered necessary as part of your employee package, provided that other similar businesses engage in like activities and the total expense is reasonable.

Many types of employee benefit programs are deductible. You can sponsor educational expenses, alcoholic rehabilitation programs, and savings programs among others. But be sure to document and be prepared to justify all such expenses.

❏ Union Welfare

Construction contractors can deduct union benefits that are paid during each tax year. These can be substantial, especially for a contractor with contracts with several unions. Office copies of union reports that are filed with the payments will document each payment. Be sure to keep your file of these reports up to date.

❏ Professional Fees and Outside Services

Almost every construction company retains the services of accountants, attorneys, and consultants from time to time. As explained earlier, it's a good idea to have a written contract with consultants who work with you on a regular basis and for extended periods. The agreement should specify all the conditions that make the relationship a consulting agreement rather than an employment contract.

Any invoice you get for professional services should establish the business purpose of the service. Usually you'll get a document from these professionals that establishes the deduction; for example, an auditor's report or an attorney's final draft of a contract. But a complete explanatory statement of billing is always advisable.

Before entering into an agreement with a professional firm or individual, be sure he or she agrees to provide you with detailed statements for your files.

❏ Equipment Rentals and Leases

Many contractors rent or lease equipment rather than buy it, especially when the equipment is needed for only a single project, for a short time, or on an irregular basis. Leasing often makes sense also for office equipment — computers, word processors, typewriters and copy machines. Regardless of what you lease, keep a file of lease or rental agreements and be certain that all payments are coded properly.

You'll probably want at least two accounts for rental expenses; one could be for rentals and the other for leases. But the distinction is sometimes hard to draw. It makes more sense to have accounts for each type of equipment rented or leased: one for office equipment, another for heavy equipment, a third for vehicles.

Maintenance agreements are often included in a lease and may be paid as part of each lease payment. You may include these expenses as part of the lease expense or break it out as a maintenance expense. In either case, be sure the coding is consistent.

❏ Dues and Subscriptions

Be prepared to document the ordinary, reasonable and necessary aspects of joining a group or subscribing to a service or publication.

Subscription to a service which updates prices of commonly-used building materials is easy to justify if you do any cost estimating. Likewise, subscriptions to industry publications can be justified. But magazines and periodicals with no direct connection to your business may be disallowed.

Membership in clubs that don't provide direct business benefits are questionable and should be avoided if possible. You can justify such an expense if you can prove that you regularly discuss business there with contractors and potential sources of future income. But a tennis club, for example, is primarily recreational, and may be a difficult deduction to support.

❏ Data Processing Expenses

Almost every business uses a computer directly or indirectly. And data processing expenses can be substantial. To claim a deduction, be sure to distinguish between capital investment and current expense.

If you purchase hardware, the acquisition must be capitalized. Deductions are taken through depreciation. Of course, no depreciation is possible on anything you expense directly.

Leases can be charged off as monthly expenses, as can the cost of time sharing on someone else's system. But software (the programs that make computers work) is more difficult because it may be either an expense or a capital investment. In most cases, if you spend any substantial amount on programming or writing software, you'll be required to capitalize the cost and depreciate it over a class life. But if you develop or purchase software at a relatively low cost, you can take it as a current deduction.

Supplies such as paper, ribbons and disks are current expenses. If this is a substantial item, create a new general ledger account called Data Processing Supplies.

❏ Inventory Adjustments

Document fully all adjustments made to ending inventory. This becomes an issue when you abandon useless or damaged property or suffer a loss from theft or vandalism.

If you abandon destroyed property, take photographs to establish the degree of damage. If vandalism is the cause, include a copy of a police report in your files. Keep a signed physical count of the loss in the file as well.

Document obsolescence by completely describing the material abandoned and the reason it became obsolete.

Another common adjustment to inventory is a write-down when material is sold at less than its original value. In this case, the write-down is the difference between the inventory basis and the sale price. Full documentation is important and necessary.

❏ Uniforms

If you require your crews to wear a specific type of uniform on the job, whether work shirts or protective gear, document expenses for cleaning, replacement and repair carefully. Be ready to show that all expenses were for the particular clothing required for the job and that no personal items were included. The cost of clothing other than uniforms and protective gear is not a legitimate business expense.

Proper Documentation

Documentation should establish both that the money was actually spent and that it was spent for a legitimate business purpose. For example, when charging gasoline in a company vehicle, it isn't enough to retain just the charge slip and receipt. You also have to show a business use for the vehicle. Your travel log or job records should show the travel that was necessary on that day.

A canceled check is not enough to prove a business expense. It's a common misconception that you only have to prove that the money was spent. The business purpose must also be shown through proper documentation. Be careful to save invoices and other papers that will prove the ordinary, reasonable and necessary nature of each expense.

A purchase order system will help for supplies, repairs and maintenance. When that's not appropriate, keep a work order or other voucher describing the business purpose for each expense.

If documentation for an unusual expense isn't available, supplement your files with a memo from others describing the circumstances, photographs, contracts or agreements, police reports (for losses from crimes), newspaper accounts (of a destructive event leading to a casualty loss), and any other means available to substantiate what you claim on your tax return.

Subsidiary Accounts

Subsidiary accounts help explain why deductions are legitimate. You'll find that many special accounts are easier to use and explain for tax purposes if there is a subsidiary system.

Use a subsidiary account system for the following accounts:

- Accounts receivable and bad debts
- Payroll and payroll taxes
- Accounts and taxes payable
- License and fee expenses
- Repairs and maintenance
- Equipment and depreciation records

A subsidiary account system is simply an organized way of keeping explanations of how the amount of the deduction was determined. It could be worksheets of the calculations your bookkeeper or accountant made. A formal subsidiary system is balanced back to the general ledger. But usually it's informal; only estimates made and supported by written calculations.

Another subsidiary system could be a monthly analysis of particular accounts, especially those with a large volume of activity. You might want to include a full explanation of expenses to prove proper handling of the expenses and to identify any expense charged in error. This also builds a documentation file in case a particular deduction is questioned later.

Account analysis doesn't take long to complete, even for several expense accounts, and can save a great deal of time and trouble later on. It's hard to develop some of the facts and documents you need months or years after the event, when current records have been filed away and must be retrieved and reconstructed.

Inventory adjustments, bad debts and casualty losses must be documented as completely as possible. They're considered extraordinary business expenses. Include everything in the file that will help prove the degree and the extent of a loss or an adjustment. For bad debts, be prepared to prove the debt became worthless in the year claimed. Include a record of all collection attempts: telephone and direct contact, letters, collection agency attempts, and bankruptcy notices.

For any extraordinary item, having more than you need is always a better alternative than having less. Keep these important documents as though you were sure to have an IRS auditor poring over them during your next audit. For most construction contractors, having good records takes only one or two more file drawers than having skimpy records. The space and time needed to keep good records will usually pay off several times over.

Tax Return Support

Whenever you have an extraordinary deduction on your business or personal tax return, anticipate questions that the IRS may have. The auditor sometimes makes an initial review. If you can satisfy the auditor right off the bat that the documentation is there and in order, the audit may stop short of a full scale review.

Here's a good example: If you have a large casualty loss or inventory adjustment, attach to your tax return copies of the police report or a newspaper account relating to the event. Also include a letter explaining the extraordinary item.

By drawing attention to the item, you will answer questions before they are asked. Strategically, it's wiser to disclose in full the nature of an unusual item and explain it at the outset. When the IRS is prompted by one unusual item to conduct an audit, they may inspect many other items as well. That's something that even the most conscientious taxpayer would rather avoid.

Record Retention Rules

How long must you keep your documents? In an active and productive business, you'll accumulate filing cabinets stuffed full of records each year. Once they're no longer needed for other business purposes, how long should they be preserved for tax purposes?

Generally, records that support your tax return must be kept until the statute of limitations runs out. This is three years from the date the return was filed (including approved extension periods), or two years from the time your tax liability was paid, whichever is later.

If your tax return omitted 25 percent or more of actual income for the year, the statute of limitations extends six years from the date the return was filed. For example, assume you reported income of $100,000. An audit reveals that you failed to report an additional $25,000 or more income. The limitation period would be extended to six years.

There is no statute of limitations on fraudulent tax returns or failure to file any return. These rules are summarized in Figure 10–3.

In some cases, it's necessary to keep documents and copies of tax returns even longer. For example, if you sell real estate that you bought years ago, you will need to establish your *basis*. That means you have to keep receipts from the date of original purchase. So if you bought a building in 1980, sold it in 1988, and traded up, and then sold your second building in 1993, you would need documentation of all improvements made over the years, closing costs, and reported deferred gains on your 1988 tax return — even though the statute of limitations on the return itself has expired.

1994 Taxes	Statute of Limitations Expires After:
Return filed April 15, 1995	April 15, 1998
Extension until June 15, 1995	June 15, 1998
Tax liability paid in full on August 10, 1995	August 10, 1998
25% or more taxable income was not reported on original return (filed April 15, 1995)	June 15, 2001
Fraudulent return filed	No statute of limitations
No return filed	No statute of limitations

Figure 10–3
Statute of limitations for tax records

Retain all the documentation needed to prove a claim made on your tax return. This includes:

- Income records and vouchers
- Sales slips
- Bank records: canceled checks, reconciliation worksheets, statements, and debit and credit vouchers.
- Records to establish credits
- Inventory records (requisitions, physical count worksheets, material purchases)
- Long-term asset purchases and sales, and depreciation records
- Employee records: name, address, Social Security numbers, dependents, marital status, rate of pay, gross pay, description of duties, and job title.
- Records establishing collection and payment of sales or excise taxes
- Copies of all tax returns: income, payroll, sales, federal and state employment, excise, and highway use

You can keep records on microfilm or a computer if you first get approval from the IRS. Consult your accountant before you establish an automated storage system.

The key to good record availability is separating current and non-current files. Let's start with the features your filing system for current files should have.

❏ Current Files

1. Should avoid unnecessary duplication of information
2. Should allow an audit of files to weed out duplication and misfilings
3. Should emphasize ease in locating needed data
4. Should place files close to employees who use them most frequently
5. Should include a procedure for moving older current files periodically to non-current status
6. Should include fire safety procedures (fire-resistant files, sprinkler system, smoke alarms, etc.)
7. Should allow room for expansion

❏ Non-Current Files

1. Should be safeguarded against damage or loss
2. Records and documents should be in clearly marked boxes or files
3. Should make use of uniformly-sized boxes specially designed for storage of records
4. Should be in a location from which records can be retrieved conveniently
5. Old files should be marked with a date for destruction
6. There should be some sensible file referencing system

Establish procedures to control the retention of documents and force yourself to abide by them.

Adequate records should meet your demands without producing logjams. Here's a checklist of points to make your system adequate:

- Make certain your records comply with legal requirements.
- Be especially alert to defects in travel and entertainment documentation.
- Create logs for travel and entertainment or auto and other transportation expenses.
- Keep copies of all tax returns long enough to meet minimum statutes of limitation.
- Write "file memos" (notes to your file) to remind yourself months (or years) later of important points (such as how deductions were computed or the basis for deductions).
- Check your systems: Do they produce data necessary for your business purposes, and necessary to comply with the law? If not, improve the system to produce needed results.

11

Taxes and Cash Accounting

All income (on the cash basis) or cash receipts (on the accrual basis) eventually flow into the cash account. This account should be your key control device for documenting business transactions, preparing tax returns and managing cash flow.

Cash: A Tax Control Account

Ideally, you should deposit all income into your cash account. But there are always exceptions. Accrued income and deferred receipts can't be deposited until they're collected. So it's a rare year when total income on your tax return equals the year's bank deposits. But get in the habit of depositing all income in your bank account. Make as few exceptions as possible.

It's important to reconcile your gross income to deposits. Unexplained differences could work against you. When your tax returns are questioned by the IRS, the burden of proof is on you to establish that surplus funds are not income.

Of course, there are many reasons why cash deposited to your account might not be income. For example, it could come from:

- Proceeds from the sale of a long-term asset
- Additions of capital
- Reimbursed overpayment
- Cash for canceled orders
- Journal entries adjusting cash for voided checks or for bank errors in your favor
- Tax refunds
- Returned deposits for telephone, utilities, or rent
- Transfers from savings accounts or other cash funds
- Transfers of funds from subsidiaries

Total deposits should equal total income plus other receipts if you are on a cash basis. On the accrual basis, total deposits equal total gross sales plus or minus the net change in receivables plus other receipts.

The same rules apply to cash payments. Of course, it's unlikely that the total of checks disbursed in a year will equal the expenses claimed on your tax return. A reconciliation must account for:

- Loan payments
- Deposits or payments of tax liabilities
- Payment of accrued liabilities

- Submission of duplicate payments for lost checks
- Journal entries adjusting cash for bank charges and other debits
- Purchasing long-term assets
- Deposits made for telephone, utilities, or rent
- Transfer to business savings or other cash funds
- Transfers to subsidiaries

In both accrual and cash-basis businesses, you make a series of journal entries that affect net profits. Some may occur every month, others only at the end of the year.

These include:

- Recording your portion of payroll taxes
- Recording depreciation expense
- Amortization journals:
     amortization costs
     covenants not to compete
     prepaid assets (insurance, etc.)
     deferred assets
- Reversing prior accruals for receivables
- Reversing prior accruals for payables
- Deferred income entries
- Recording bad debts
- Changes in inventory levels

Proper reconciliation requires that *all* income and *all* expenses on a cash payment basis be recorded in the cash account.

Figure 11–1 summarizes this concept. It isn't easy to record every item through the checking account. How do you handle spending your personal funds for local transportation costs?

The solution is to establish a petty cash fund. Although it may seem a waste of time to control minor payments, you should claim every deduction to which you're entitled. When the petty cash fund runs low, take the time to put together, classify and process the receipts and vouchers. A single check, covering many small expenses, re-establishes the balance, and provides documentation. This can add up to a significant deduction each year on your tax return.

Recording every expense on a check makes it simple to reconcile costs and expenses to total checks. In the cash-basis system, the total of cash costs and expenses, plus other payments and jour-

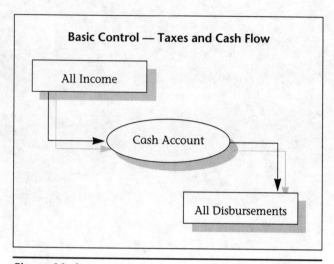

Figure 11–1

Recording income and expenses through the cash account

nal adjustments, should equal disbursements. In an accrual system, the formula is:

```
Total cash expenses adjusted by net change
   in accounts payable and other payments

     Plus or minus changes in inventory

Plus or minus the effect of journals (for
     depreciation, amortization, etc.)
```

Statement of Cash Flows

The best way to reconcile book entries to tax return results is to compare the cash flows of your business: where the money came from and where it went. The advantage of this is that it not only documents and reconciles but also gives you a tool for judging the effectiveness of your cash flow procedures.

Management of working capital is essential for every construction contractor. Good management makes cash available when it's needed without leaving large amounts idle. Poor management results in lost discounts, a poor credit rating, and the inability to plan for the future.

Working capital is the difference between current assets (all cash in within one year), and current liabilities (anything due and payable within one year). A generally acceptable ratio is two to one. You should have two dollars in current assets for each dollar of current liabilities. Anything above this (more than two) indicates a healthy

Statement of Cash Flows		
Sources of Funds:		
Net profit		$14,480
Non-cash expenses:		
depreciation	$3,180	
amortization	1,500	4,608
Cash basis profit		$19,088
Other additions:		
from sale of assets		6,000
from loans granted		14,000
from additional capital paid in		1,000
Additions to working capital		$40,088
Applications of Funds:		
Repayment of loans		$17,481
Reduction of accrued liabilities		4,653
To purchase long-term assets		21,406
Applications to working capital		$43,540
		$(3,452)
Changes in Working Capital:		
Cash	$(1,845)	
Accounts receivable	(14,520)	
Accounts payable	18,060	
Current notes payable	(2,866)	
Payroll and sales taxes	(128)	
Change in working capital	$(3,452)	

Figure 11–2
Statement of cash flows

situation. Anything below shows a problem in cash control. Several things may cause this:

1. Poor collection of receivables
2. High bad debts or delinquencies
3. High inventory
4. "Dead stock" included on the books
5. Heavy short-term borrowing
6. High payables

Cash flows analysis is a way to check your cash flow and reconcile changes in the value of assets and liabilities over the year.

Figure 11–2 is an example of a cash flows analysis. Notice that, although a net profit of $14,480 is shown for the period, the actual working capital decreased by $3,452. If this happened to your business, you'd probably ask your accountant, "If I showed a profit, where is it?"

Maybe the profit was invested in higher accounts receivable or inventories, or used to reduce liabilities (repayment of notes, for example). Or it could have been used to buy equipment and machinery. Your analysis shows where the profit went.

In Figure 11-2, long-term loans were reduced by $17,481 during the year. New assets were purchased for $21,406. To offset equipment investment, the builder received $6,000 from a sale and took a new loan of $14,000. A net pay-out of more than $19,000 resulted from equipment transactions alone.

The summary shows how working capital was influenced by cash flow during the year. Notice that a large reduction resulted from increased commitments to accounts receivable. This builder is permitting receivables to increase. There may be a valid business reason for this. Or, it may just be that someone isn't watching delinquent accounts.

This analysis becomes the reconciliation required for your tax return. The first line is "net profit." This figure, which agrees with the reported total on the tax return, is then adjusted through the "Statement of Cash Flows" showing increases and decreases to all accounts, including cash.

Reducing Expenses

Sometimes an expense item has to be reduced. For example, you'll have to reduce an expense category when you void a check. If you pay someone in the last months of your fiscal year, and the check is still outstanding six months later, you must make an entry to correct the problem.

When you contact the payee you may discover the check was never received. Or the check might have been destroyed. The payment could have been an error. If the item represents a major deduction, you'll have to file an amended tax return.

If it's for a minor amount, correct the problem in one of two ways.

1. Void the original check by reversing the entry, and replace it with another. The net effect of this is no change to cash (you remove an outstanding check with a new payment) or expense (you reverse and re-record the same amount to the expense category).

2. Write off the original check by crediting the expense account and debiting cash. This increases your cash fund and decreases a deduction, thus increasing net profits.

The right step to take depends on the circumstances, the time elapsed, and the nature of the payment.

Expenses can also be reduced by establishing and controlling cash flow and expense budgets. There is no advantage to having high expenses. You're money ahead paying 50 percent tax on each dollar earned than spending 100 percent on a deduction. Don't let your effort to reduce income taxes result in foolish spending. Excessive expenses reduce after-tax income and cripple your cash flow.

Multiple Accounts

Consider using two or more bank accounts to help you control disbursements. It's usually easier to reconcile two small checking accounts at the end of each month than it is to reconcile one large account.

And here's a simple trick that makes reconciliation even easier. The first month, write checks against account A. The next month, write checks against account B. At the end of the second month, reconcile account A. Nearly all checks from that account will have cleared, and the job of reconciliation should be simple. In the third month, write checks only against account A again. At month-end, reconcile account B. Continue alternating this way each month.

Remember also to make deposits only to the active account each month.

If your company has trouble reconciling its bank statement each month, one or both of the following statements probably apply:

1. Internal controls in your office are poor or nonexistent. Your employees may not understand the process, and they may need better direction. For example, they may be making math errors on checks, in carrying balances forward, or in totaling deposit slips.

2. Your bank makes it difficult to understand its system of debits and credits. Some banks have better systems than others. Check with other businessmen you know and ask for references to other banks.

While setting up two bank accounts can simplify reconciliation, there are some disadvantages to this procedure:

1. There are more places to look for information when you need to document tax deductions and deposits.

2. Your cost for printing checks will be higher because you'll be buying checks for two accounts.

3. More careful cash flow planning may be required if idle balances are left on deposit for a month at a time.

4. If the source of your problem is poor understanding among employees, multiple accounts won't solve it for you. If your employees are already confused, multiple accounts will only increase the confusion.

5. You'll need two disbursements journals, and you won't be able to see the flow of recordings without consulting both journals.

But there's another good reason to have two checking accounts. Suppose you pay most of your bills during the first ten days of the month following the month they become due. In most systems, this requires a monthly procedure for reviewing all unpaid invoices and recording a journal entry for payables. This can be a lot of posting and a great deal of work. And then you have to reverse the entry the following month.

Using two checking accounts, or one account with checks that have two separate series of numbers, can save time and trouble. Use one series of numbers for current expenses and costs, those paid within the month against which they apply. Use the second series only for payment of invoices that are for the prior month's activity.

At the end of the accounts payable period (approximately the 10th of the month), the accounts payable journal is added and footed, and an entry is made directly to the books from the journal. Meanwhile, current expenses and costs are paid from the "current" journal. This is a convenient alternative and a workable system.

It's simpler, however, to use two separate bank accounts. If you have two numbering systems and journals within one account, it's harder to keep a running balance of actual cash, because you make disbursements from two places. And when you reconcile the account, cash controls will be more complex because you'll need two separate lists of outstanding checks.

Specialized Accounts

Tax and cash controls are sometimes easier if you set up special-purpose accounts. Do this if you have a high volume of activity in one particular category, or if you need to document a certain type of expense.

Some contractors use a special account to deposit taxes that have to be paid at a later date. It's a "forced savings" program that guarantees the money will be there when needed.

Here are some specialized accounts that contractors might need:

General account: For the payment of current costs and expenses only, and for the deposit of *all* receipts. Then funds can be transferred from the general account to other specialized accounts.

Accounts payable account: For accounts payable only, as described previously.

Payroll account: For payroll and payroll taxes. This account may use checks that have a special stub showing the details of amounts withheld. Each payroll period, the builder deposits an amount equal to gross pay plus taxes payable (FUTA and all quarterly taxes).

Tax account: To pay sales tax, diesel excise tax, licenses and fees, and so forth. This account is a "forced savings" account. If, during the last year, you've paid an average of $600 per week in taxes, deposit this amount each week, whether any taxes are due or not. This could prevent a crisis when several annual taxes all come due in one month. Deposits of federal and state corporate taxes can be made from this account as well.

A specialized account is very useful for a high-volume expense category, such as taxes. It provides an excellent subsidiary system for documentation. The disbursements journal for the tax account has all the detail necessary to report on a tax return and, if necessary, respond to an audit.

A specialized payroll account is convenient for the collection and reporting of all deductions. And it frees up four or five columns in the general disbursements journal.

Many contractors set up a specialized account for every large project. If you've had trouble separating the costs and expenses for your various projects, this might be a good solution. Use a particular checking account exclusively to report all direct expenses and overhead for a project. Income from the project is also deposited into this account.

This account may ease the problem of separating the costs and expenses for your larger projects. But having a special account for each project may create other problems. For example, if you make one purchase of materials for use on two or more jobs, you'll have to pay for them out of two or more checking accounts. If you pay from a single account, you must transfer cash between accounts or make a journal entry so that disbursements accurately reflect the expenses for each job.

For most builders, the main objection to specialized accounts is the idle cash sitting in a multitude of small accounts. If cash is short, you'll have to transfer balances between special accounts to meet current obligations. That's a nuisance if it happens too often.

Before setting up specialized accounts and absorbing the cost of printed checks for several different jobs, consider the administrative and accounting burdens involved.

Specialized accounts make cost reporting and accounting much easier. But cash flow problems and the extra effort spent in reconciliation may not be worth the trouble. The more checking accounts you have to fund and control, the more time you'll spend on bookkeeping and accounting.

Try setting up one or two special-purpose accounts, and make sure they're saving you time and trouble before you open any more.

Petty Cash Account

The cleanest possible way to document business transactions is to have a single source from which all payments are made — one checking account. But this isn't always possible, because almost all businesses spend some cash.

One solution is to use a company credit card. This makes it easier to keep track of expenses. Most major expenses can be charged. And credit cards make it unnecessary to carry large amounts of cash. Using a credit card also simplifies expense reporting. You might, for example, use one credit card for travel and entertainment expenses and a different one for office supplies. But you'll always need some cash.

The biggest problem with cash purchases is remembering to ask for a receipt. This is true especially for cab fares, bridge tolls, and meals. But the receipt is essential for tax purposes. The IRS will disallow all expenses you can't prove.

If you spend cash for any business purpose, use money from a petty cash fund. Use it only for small expenses and incidentals. If any employee makes a purchase, instruct that employee to return with change and receipts equaling the amount advanced.

The amount in the fund should be enough so it needs to be replenished no more than once or twice per month. If you set up a $200 fund, keep it in a box that can be locked up each night. At all times, the total of all cash and receipts in the box should equal $200.

When the funds gets low, divide the receipts into general ledger categories and write a check for the total, payable to "Petty Cash" or to the name of the employee in charge of the fund. This check is cashed and the money put back into the box. Any overage or shortage should be insignificant. If large shortages occur each time the account is totaled, you have a control problem.

Petty cash should be controlled by only one employee. Make that person responsible for the fund. When the fund is reimbursed, the collected receipts should be filed in the paid invoices file. These receipts document cash expenses and bring the expenses into the accounting system.

This is the key to an efficient petty cash system—capturing the cash expenses and the receipts that back them up, and running them through the general account.

Petty cash can be abused. Someone might go through the paid invoice file and remove, for example, a postage receipt from a previous month. That person then submits the receipt for reimbursement from petty cash. Likewise, personal receipts for non-business expenses can find their way into the cash box.

Don't view petty cash shortages as insignificant. The amount of money taken may not be great. But someone who takes petty cash will find other ways to foil your system. Be sure that the employee in charge of the account can be trusted to fully document all uses of petty cash. Also, the approval of expenses, signing of checks, and reconciliation of accounts are responsibilities that should be split up between employees. Avoid having all these done by the same person.

A business owner who has assets stolen is often at least partially to blame. Poor controls are an invitation to losses. Sure, everyone suffers some losses, theft or accidents at one time or another. But many losses can be avoided with intelligent application of systems that both reduce exposure and provide good documentation for tax purposes.

Investing Fundamentals

Every construction contractor has wide swings in cash flow. Sometimes, money is scarce. At other times, there's plenty of cash. When cash is available, even for a relatively short time, it's sensible to take advantage of one of the many investment vehicles that are on the market.

This chapter summarizes the common investment alternatives and their tax advantages and disadvantages. But let's start with one of the most important of those investing fundamentals: compound interest.

Compound Interest

Let's say you're offered an investment that pays 8 percent per year. What does that really mean?

Simple interest shows the percentage paid on the amount held at the beginning of the year and for a one-year term. At 8 percent simple interest, $100 grows to $108 at the end of one full year.

Compound interest is different. An investment paying 8 percent, compounded quarterly, yields 8.24 percent. This is calculated by dividing the interest rate by 4 (for the four quarters), and calculating the interest earned each quarter. The rate grows because the base amount increases each period:

First quarter —
$100 × 1.02 (1/4 of 8%) is $102

Second quarter —
$102 × 1.02 is $104.04

Third quarter —
$104.04 × 1.02 is $106.12

Fourth quarter —
$106.12 × 1.02 is $108.24

Total earned, $108.24 (8.24 percent)

The calculation of 8 percent quarterly interest can also be summarized as follows:

```
$100 x 1.02 x 1.02 x 1.02 = $108.24
```

There are many ways to calculate interest. These include:

- Simple interest
- Daily compounding
- Monthly compounding
- Quarterly compounding
- Semi-annual compounding

Daily interest can be calculated on either a 360-day year or a 365-day year. The formula for calculating interest for a 360-day year is:

$$\left(1+\frac{\text{interest rate}}{360}\right)^{360}$$

	$100.00 compounded monthly at 8 percent, for one year:		
Month	Monthly Rate*	Monthly Interest	Balance
			$100.00
January	.00667	.67	100.67
February	.00667	.67	101.34
March	.00667	.67	102.01
April	.00667	.68	102.69
May	.00667	.69	103.38
June	.00667	.69	104.07
July	.00667	.69	104.76
August	.00667	.70	105.46
September	.00667	.70	106.16
October	.00667	.71	106.87
November	.00667	.71	107.58
December	.00667	.72	108.30

*Monthly rate: 8% ÷ 12, or .006677 per month
Annual yield: 8.30 %
Formula: $100.00 $(1.00667)^{12}$

Figure 12–1

Compounding illustration

Year	Annual Deposit	Interest Earned	Balance at Year End
1	$2,000.00	$166.00	$2,166.00
2	2,000.00	345.78	4,511.78
3	2,000.00	540.48	7,052.26
4	2,000.00	751.34	9,803.60
5	2,000.00	979.70	12,783.30
6	2,000.00	1,227.01	16,010.31
7	2,000.00	1,494.86	19,505.17
8	2,000.00	1,784.93	23,290.10
9	2,000.00	2,099.08	27,389.18
10	2,000.00	2,439.30	31,828.48
11	2,000.00	2,807.76	36,636.24
12	2,000.00	3,206.81	41,843.05
13	2,000.00	3,638.97	47,482.02
14	2,000.00	4,107.01	53,589.03
15	2,000.00	4,613.89	60,202.92
	$30,000.00	$30,202.92	

8% compounded monthly
(Deposits made at beginning of year)

Figure 12–2

Growth of annual deposits and interest

or, at 8 percent:

$$\left(1+\frac{.08}{360}\right)^{360}=1.08327744$$

The annual yield is 8.327744 percent

Your bank can probably provide tables that show true annual yield at various interest rates. Figure 12–1 shows the calculation of 8 percent interest on $100, compounded monthly.

Each period's interest, if left on deposit, adds to the principal and the interest earned in the following period. Figure 12–2 shows an example. Suppose at the beginning of each year you deposit $2,000 in an account paying 8 percent (compounded monthly). You never make any withdrawals and leave on deposit all interest earned. In the ninth year, the account will be increasing faster from credited interest than from your deposits.

But even the impressive returns shown in Figure 12–2 may be turned into losses when you consider the effects of income taxes and erosion in the value of the dollar.

Income Taxes and Inflation

Unfortunately, the more successful you are, the greater your tax burden. You must consider tax consequences, amortization and depreciation, capital gains rates, and tax deferral. For instance, if you paid taxes in a 50 percent bracket, 8 percent yield is only 4 percent, after taxes. (Your "tax bracket" is the percentage of federal and state tax paid on the last dollar earned each year.) If you invest in a year when your combined bracket is 50 percent, the *additional* gains on that investment are taxed at the 50 percent rate.

While income taxes erode your earnings, inflation reduces the real value of your principal. If you invest $100 on January 1, and inflation is 10 percent, your investment's value at year end is only $90. Imagine the effects of 10 percent inflation every year on a $100 investment:

Rate of Inflation	Tax Bracket								
	22%	25%	28%	33%	38%	42%	45%	49%	50%
6%	7.69%	8.00%	8.33%	8.96%	9.68%	10.34%	10.91%	11.76%	12.00%
8%	10.26%	10.67%	11.11%	11.94%	12.90%	13.79%	14.55%	15.69%	16.00%
10%	12.82%	13.33%	13.89%	14.93%	16.13%	17.24%	18.18%	19.61%	20.00%
12%	15.38%	16.00%	16.67%	17.91%	19.35%	20.69%	21.82%	23.53%	24.00%
14%	17.95%	18.67%	19.44%	20.90%	22.58%	24.14%	25.45%	27.45%	28.00%

Figure 12–3
Break-even yield for taxable savings

2nd year	$81.00
3rd year	72.90
4th year	65.61
5th year	59.05
6th year	53.14
7th year	47.83
8th year	43.05
9th year	38.74
10th year	34.87

When you combine the effects of income taxes and inflation, the yields may be very unsatisfactory. Figure 12–3 points out the importance of these considerations. The amounts shown are the break-even rates that must be earned in various tax brackets (combined federal and state) with various rates of inflation. These rates only show where you break even. When inflation is above 8 or 10 percent, you have to earn a very high return to provide any real after-tax income. Any investment with a return this high usually involves substantial risk of loss.

Figure 12–4 shows examples of break-even interest for an investment of $1,000. The effect of inflation at 12 percent is computed as principal times the inflation rate ($1,000 x 12% = $120).

In these examples, real earnings are zero. Earning 18.18 percent results in no growth if you are in the 45 percent bracket and inflation is 10 percent.

Investments that pay either tax-free or tax-deferred interest may be much more desirable. Interest earned on some bonds is free of either federal or state tax or both.

Interest earned or gains on many types of investments aren't taxed until you cash in or receive the proceeds of the investment. Qualified retirement accounts (IRA or Keogh), investments in real estate and common stocks fall into this category.

But tax consequences are *not* the only consideration. Your investments should match your own goals and interests. The goals you have may demand specific types of investment. Long-range financial planning is explained at the end of this chapter.

Dividends and Capital Gains

Individuals who receive qualified dividends can exclude part of those proceeds from income. Qualified dividends include those paid by domestic corporations and mutual funds.

Examples of non-qualified dividends are:

- Charitable corporation payments
- Dividends from mutual savings banks
- Dividends paid by foreign corporations
- Dividends from Real Estate Investment Trusts (REITs)
- Capital gains distributions
- Contributions from S corporations

If you receive dividends from public utility stock investments, and you reinvest in additional shares, you can exclude up to $750 ($1,500 on a joint return), subject to certain requirements. Check with your accountant for details.

A short-term investment offers liquidity (availability of your money) and current income. A long-term investment usually offers better long-term growth and income. You have to decide which is needed in your case.

Tax Bracket	25%	33%	45%
Inflation Rate	12%	8%	10%
Amount invested	$1,000	$1,000	$1,000
Break-even interest	16.00%	11.94%	18.18%
Gross interest	$160.00	$119.40	$181.80
Income tax	40.00	39.40	81.80
After-tax earnings	120.00	80.00	100.00
Effect of inflation	120.00	80.00	100.00
Net "real" earnings	-0-	-0-	-0-

Figure 12–4
Examples of break-even interest

Types of Investments

The following section discusses the main features, benefits and drawbacks of several popular forms of investment.

❏ Savings Accounts

Scope: Banks and savings and loan institutions offer a number of savings accounts. These are convenient and easily opened or closed. Yields aren't as attractive as some other types of accounts.

Tax treatment: Interest is taxed as earned, whether it is withdrawn or left in the account. There is no sheltering or deferral provision, unless the account is part of a sheltered plan (IRA or Keogh).

Yields: Yields on savings accounts vary with the method of compounding, type of account and term of investment.

Risks: Accounts are insured by an agency of the federal government and are essentially as safe as the dollar is sound.

Liquidity: Funds are available immediately or at the end of the investment term, depending on the type of investment. Some institutions charge a small activity fee on accounts with frequent withdrawals and all assess forfeitures for early withdrawal of term accounts.

❏ Certificates of Deposit

Scope: Certificates of Deposit (CDs) are available to you in many forms. They are offered by banks and savings and loans and are issued for specified periods, from a few months to several years. The most common CD offers a fixed rate of interest for the entire term.

Tax treatment: Interest is taxed in the years it is paid or becomes available for withdrawal. There is a limited tax deferral if you buy six-month Treasury Bills after July 1. The term falls mostly in the current year. But interest is not credited until the next year and is taxed at that time.

Yields: Longer-term accounts pay a higher yield in exchange for the promise to leave the money on deposit. Yields are fixed at the beginning of the period.

Risks: CD accounts are insured by a federal agency. The risk is that high inflation will reduce the real value of the investment.

Liquidity: Certificates of Deposit are not liquid. Funds are committed for the agreed term. An early withdrawal results in a loss of interest. This forfeiture penalty is tax deductible.

❏ Common Stocks

Scope: Publicly-traded stocks are bought and sold through securities brokers. Once you open a trading account, you can handle transactions by telephone. The stock of over 5,000 companies is traded daily. When requested, your broker can buy stock in nearly any of these companies for your account.

Most people who invest in stock are looking for dividend income and growth in value. There is no guarantee that any stock will continue to pay dividends or increase in value. Price quotations for nearly all stocks fluctuate daily.

Some investors sell shares of stock without having bought them first. This is called *selling short*. These people hope the stock will go down in value so that, at a later date, they can cover their position by buying the shares they sold previously.

To invest "short," the investor must have collateral, such as cash or other shares, on deposit with the broker. Selling "short" should be done only with a thorough understanding of the risks.

Tax treatment: Dividends are taxed in the year paid. For individuals, the exclusion rules explained earlier in this chapter apply.

Capital gains and losses on trades are taxed in the year of sale. The minimum holding period for long-term gains is one year.

Yields: Any change in the price of the stock is recognized only when the stock is sold. Prices can change very quickly as a result of favorable or unfavorable news about the company.

Some companies pay dividends of up to 14 percent of the value of the stock. Many companies pay no dividend but may still be good investments. Profits are used to expand operations, rather than to pay out to stockholders as current taxable income. The amount of dividend to be paid to investors (stockholders) is declared each year by the company's Board of Directors. It's usually paid four times a year.

Some dividends are paid in additional stock rather than cash. For example, suppose a company pays a 10 percent stock dividend. If you owned 100 shares, your post-dividend holdings would increase to 110 shares. Stock dividends are not taxed until the stock is sold.

Stock splits are like stock dividends. A split increases the total number of shares, so dividend income may increase as well. If a company declares a 2 for 1 split, the result is a doubling of the number of shares. But the value of the shares usually falls to about half the price of the old shares. For example, 100 shares, each worth $30, will probably be valued at about $15 after the 2 for 1 split. There is no immediate advantage, but the fact that the stock was split probably means that the company is doing well. That could tend to move the price back toward the $30 range.

Risk: Stocks may decline in value, creating a "paper loss." This doesn't become a capital loss until you sell.

A company going through bankruptcy may be wiped out completely, reducing the stock value to zero.

Liquidity: Stocks can be traded daily by telephone. When you sell, funds won't be made available for five working days. After that, your broker will send you a check for the amount due. Stocks should be considered as long-term investments unless you have enough knowledge to speculate. Few speculators are able to make a decent return on their investment.

❏ Options

Scope: There are two types of options: calls and puts. A *call* is the right to buy stock at a specified price (the striking price). Calls can be bought and sold from securities brokers.

A *put* is the right to sell stock at a specified price (again, the striking price). The price you pay for calls and puts is the *premium.* These change daily. Options have firm expiration dates. When an option is described as "40 Aug" it means the striking price is $40 per share and the month of expiration is the following August.

When you purchase an option, you buy the right to buy (calls) or sell (puts) at the striking price at any time before expiration. If you hold a "40 Aug" call and the stock is valued at $52 per share, you will gain $12 per share, or $1,200 total. Options are always for 100 shares. They are listed by the price for one option:

- 5 options will cost $525
- 7 options will cost $750

So if you buy one call and the stock value goes up, the option also increases in value. Options are bought and sold but rarely exercised. There are four types of option transactions besides exercising:

1. Buy a call, hoping stock (and call) will increase in value, to be sold at a profit.

2. Buy a put, hoping stock will decrease in value. When this happens, the value of a put increases, to be sold at a profit.

3. Sell a call, hoping the stock (and call) will decrease in value; the call will then be bought (covered), creating a profit. If you sell a call for stock of which you own 100 shares, the transaction is called "covered." If you don't own the stock, selling a call is referred to as "writing a naked call."

4. Sell a put, hoping the stock will increase in value. If this happens, the put will decrease in value, to be bought (covered) to produce a profit.

If you sell, you may wait for several things to happen:

1. The value of the option decreases and you can buy (cover) for a profit.

2. The value of the option decreases and you can take no action.

3. The call or put expires and your commitment ends.

4. The call or put is exercised and you are required to buy or sell stock. In doing this, you could produce a profit or loss, depending on the amount you received for the option,

whether or not you own the stock, and the price at which it was purchased.

There are a great number of strategies involved with option trading. Some investors buy stocks and puts, the latter as insurance in case the stock goes down in value. Short-sellers achieve the same result by covering their "sold" positions in purchasing a call.

Tax treatment: When you buy an option and later sell it, you have a short-term gain in the year sold.

When you sell (write) an option, there is no tax on funds received. You are taxed when:

1. You buy the option back.
2. It expires.
3. It is exercised.

Yields: Returns on option trading vary considerably. "In the money" options (for example, calls with a striking price at a point when the value of the stock is equal or higher) will normally increase or decrease $1 for each dollar of change in the stock itself. For example, assume a certain stock has a market value of $42. An August call with the striking price of $40 is worth $7. If the stock goes up $1, to $43, the 40 Aug. call value should increase to $8. In this situation, sizable gains and losses can occur quickly.

The option market is volatile. You can double your money or be wiped out fairly quickly.

Risks: A large risk exists if you gamble all your funds on one option. You're making a side bet on what will happen to the stock. A major risk is that options expire in less than one year. You have to watch them closely.

Liquidity: Options can be bought and sold any business day, through a securities broker. The settlement date is one day after your order is placed. Although conveniently liquid, the value of an option in the immediate future is always in doubt.

❏ Mutual Funds

Scope: Mutual funds are run by managers who pool money from many investors and then invest in a variety of stocks (or bonds), giving you wide diversification. The fund is managed by professionals, so you don't need to keep up to date on what's happening in the stock market.

Mutual funds are available for a wide range of goals. There are growth funds, emphasizing appreciation of capital; income funds, aiming for high dividend yields; tax-free bond funds, investing only in bonds that are not subject to income tax; stock and bond combination funds; and money market funds.

Tax treatment: Dividends are reported monthly and are taxed with the same exclusions explained earlier in this chapter.

Capital gains are produced from profitable sales and are taxed as previously explained.

Yields: Past performance of mutual funds has been impressive. Several funds have had returns of over 100 percent in just a few years. Choose a mutual fund that has done well consistently, in both up and down markets.

Risks: A principal advantage is the wide diversification you get. Spreading risk reduces both the chance of significant loss and the likelihood of astonishing gains.

Liquidity: Mutual funds can be bought through securities brokers or directly from the fund company. To sell shares, you have to complete an authorization form. It may take from one to six weeks to receive funds. Mutual funds should be considered long-term investments.

❏ Money Market Funds

Scope: These are specialized mutual funds that invest shareholders' funds in high-grade, short-term investments like large denomination Treasury Bills, commercial paper (notes issued by businesses), and bank Certificates of Deposit. Most individual investors don't have the large sums required for these types of investments. The fund pools money from many investors to get the advantage of the higher yields that these larger notes usually pay.

Money market funds are available to individuals, partnerships, corporations, and retirement funds. They are especially well-suited for investing cash that will be available for only a few days or weeks. A large deposit, left only a short time, can bring in a lot of interest. Money market funds don't charge for frequent deposits or withdrawals.

Tax treatment: Dividends paid by money market funds are taxed as interest in the year received or credited to your account. There is no deferral or tax advantage unless accounts are opened as part of a qualified retirement account.

Yields: The dividend amount changes but it's often the highest rate available to short-term investors.

Risks: Investments are diversified so that risks are spread. There is no insurance on a money market fund itself, but a fund is as sound as the notes and certificates it buys.

Liquidity: Many money market funds offer free checking account privileges. If you want to withdraw all or part of your money, just write a check. There may be little or no charge for each check. Most funds require that checks be written for $500 or more.

For temporary cash floats, money market funds give you complete liquidity with high interest income.

❏ Bonds

Scope: Bonds are long-term promises to pay, issued by corporations and government agencies. Investors who purchase bonds are loaning money to the issuer.

Tax treatment: Bonds may be purchased at a discount (an amount below the bond's par value). If sold later for more or less than the purchase price, there has been a gain or loss.

Interest on some bonds is tax-free. Tax-free bond issuers include states, cities and counties, the District of Columbia, U.S. possessions, port authorities, utility service authorities, toll road commissions, public improvements districts, reclamation districts and mass transit authorities.

Yields: Rates vary with the maturity periods and the bond rating. Extremely safe bonds pay less interest. Discounts also produce yields that can be amortized over the holding period.

Risks: The issuing entity may default on its obligation to pay you. Select bonds as carefully as you would select stock.

When interest rates are higher than your bond pays, its value goes down. If you sell the bond at that point, you suffer a loss.

Liquidity: Public trading in bonds gives liquidity. They should be considered long-term investments.

❏ Real Estate

Scope: Real estate investments include owning buildings and land, lending on deeds of trust secured by someone else's property, and participation in Real Estate Investment Trusts or partnerships.

Tax treatment: Commercial property can be depreciated over 15 years. This depreciation allowance can shelter considerable income. All related investment expenses are deductible and profits on commercial property are taxed as capital gains.

Interest received from deeds of trust is taxed as received.

Yields: The yield depends on the type and location of property, management practices, length of your holding period, and the market for property. Many subtle and not-so-subtle factors influence the value of real estate.

Risks: Real estate is a relatively safe long-term investment. Tax benefits and income serve to offset investment costs and the burden of mortgage payments. A high vacancy rate in commercial property is a major risk. You may need more capital to overcome unexpected vacancies. Property insurance protects against unexpected losses due to fire, natural disaster, and vandalism.

Deeds of trust (mortgages) are promises to pay, secured by property. If the borrower can't make the payments, your principal is recovered through sale of the security.

Liquidity: Real estate is not a liquid investment. It usually takes time and is relatively expensive to sell property. Plan to invest only for a longer term. If the property has increased in value, you may be able to raise cash by borrowing against that higher value.

Low demand and high interest rates may make sales difficult. You might have to accept a promissory note from the buyer to sell the property.

❏ Precious Metals

Scope: An active market exists for scarce metals (such as gold, silver or platinum). Values change daily. Precious metals can be bought as coins (like Krugerrand), bullion, or certificates for bullion held in storage. All of these are easily traded.

Tax treatment: Precious metals are taxed at capital gains rates when sold.

Yields: The value of gold increased more than 1,000 percent during the 1970s. Don't expect that to be repeated in the near future.

Risks: Values are affected by world events, inflation, and the ever-changing attractiveness of other investments. Industrial demand may decline as it has for silver in recent years. Investment in precious metals is considered a hedge against inflation.

Liquidity: Metals are easily traded. Even certificates for stored bullion can be exchanged in banks at current rates.

❏ Collectibles

Scope: Rare objects, such as stamps, coins, art and antiques, are usually referred to as "collectibles." The demand for rare and beautiful tangible assets is subject to investors' unpredictable moods. Some types of collectibles become fads overnight, and then fade just as quickly. The successful investor has to accurately judge the current market trends.

Tax treatment: Changes in value on collectibles are taxed as capital gains and losses. But objects held primarily for personal enjoyment don't qualify.

Yields: Profits have been high in some years. But a dramatic decline in value may be just as likely.

Risks: Demand changes constantly. Today's market for an item could be gone completely tomorrow. Also, you have to insure against loss from theft, fire and other damage.

Liquidity: There may be no cash market for some collectibles. When sold through auctions, a sale is likely, but the commission or consignment fee may be about 20 percent of the sales price. Values are difficult to establish, and there is no fixed market for most items that fall into this category.

❏ Life Insurance

Scope: Life insurance plans can provide coverage, cash values and policy loans, and a form of investment for retirement plans.

Tax treatment: Dividends from mutual insurers are treated as a non-taxable return of premiums. Accumulating cash values in whole life policies are not taxed as income, even when borrowed.

Yields: Whole life insurance (with cash values) offers an extremely low average yield. It has been estimated at 3 percent by the Federal Trade Commission. The same protection is offered with term insurance (without cash value).

Risks: Risks are low. The possibility of loss of cash values is remote. The hidden risk is that inflation will cancel the return and erode the principal.

Life insurance is understood as risk protection. You buy to protect against economic loss from premature death.

Liquidity: Life insurance contracts are long-term (to a specified age or until death). Cash values can be borrowed and repaid at attractive interest rates. The amount of insurance is reduced by the loans until they are repaid.

Finding Investment Advice

Finding professional investment advice is difficult. Any advisor who doesn't consider your individual goals and needs is doing you a disservice. Beware of any "investment advisor" who counsels you to buy some investment device which he happens to sell. That's a sure prescription for trouble. Don't pay for investment advice through commissions earned on the money you invest.

Avoid schemes that emphasize tax savings almost exclusively. Far too many "investors' have received more than 100 percent write-offs and 0 percent returns from these shams and swindles. For tax purposes, you can do as well giving the same amount to a charity.

Start your investment plan by defining your goals. What do you need the money for? Retirement? College tuition? Accumulation for specific purchases? What are your primary and secondary interests? Preservation of capital, high current income, tax-sheltered income, etc.

Begin your financial planning by training yourself. There's no substitute for an informed, aware, cautious investor. In the end, you are responsible for how your money or your company's money is invested. You can rely on others to keep you informed, but you and only you carry the risk of loss.

No one knows your goals and objectives better than you do. No one will take more care than you in finding the right investment. Research what is available. Write down your goals. Plan a way to meet those goals. A good investment program should be able to survive the unexpected. It should combine the current and long-term needs you define, and protect against loss. Your financial plan should combine the best features of insurance, income production, and capital preservation and growth. Your concerns should include inflation, taxes, and retirement.

When you act as your own financial planner, you direct your own program. Use a broker, accountant, lawyer, banker or insurance agent to offer advice. But they follow your orders to earn their fee.

The more involved you are in making investment decisions, the better your plan is likely to be.

If you want help in developing your financial plan, you'll find no end to the number of people anxious to offer counsel on where your money should go. Some will be helpful, others will be sophisticated swindlers. Be certain the individual is a Registered Investment Advisor.

As a general rule, investments are sold to you by a securities-registered representative licensed by the National Association of Securities Dealers (NASD) who works through a broker/dealer. Be certain that any people offering to sell you interests in investments are so licensed. In comparing investments, study each prospectus and find out how much commission the salesman will receive. A higher commission means less profit for you. Smart investors work with professional and knowledgeable people and avoid high-pressure salesmen with products that have to be pushed.

Insurance agents emphasize whole life insurance and annuities as investments. Neither yields well enough to produce real profits. Securities brokers offer stock and option investments and, in some cases, access to mutual funds and money markets. Some brokers also offer limited partnerships in tax-sheltered programs. But even so, your goals will not always be the primary consideration.

Some financial planners are really insurance agents or mutual fund salesmen. They provide no real financial service.

If you feel you must place trust in someone sophisticated in financial matters, seek out a Certified Financial Planner who is also a Registered Investment Advisor. These professionals are more likely to prepare a financial plan that's tailored to your needs. There's a fee for this, but the service may be worth more to you than it costs.

Finally, be aware that both federal and state laws protect investors. Federal law requires that a prospectus be offered to all prospective investors on many types of investments before any money is accepted. The law is very detailed about what must be in the prospectus. It's usually a fairly fat little booklet with lots of small type and plenty of legal terms. But it has a surprising amount of information that you should know — all the bad points about what's being offered and many details that may be omitted or glossed over in the oral sales presentation. The prospectus may be 50 or more pages long, but read it. Where the prospectus contradicts what you're told by the salesman, trust the prospectus.

But always remember this: there's no law that guarantees return of your money. It's up to you to invest based on informed judgment.

Investment Objectives

Every investor has an investment goal or objective. It isn't necessarily to make as much money as possible in the shortest time possible. You should give some thought to your own goal, and examine how likely your investments are to meet that goal.

Tax reduction or elimination should be an important part of your investment objective. If you reach the 50 percent tax bracket, half of all profits from investments can be lost to state and federal income taxes. Tax planning should be a key element in your investment picture.

Along with reducing taxes, here are some goals that may influence your choice of investments:

1. High current income
2. Long-term growth in income
3. Growth that will exceed inflation
4. High-risk growth
5. Retirement fund

Your goal may be much more specific:

1. College education for children
2. Protection in case of early death or disability
3. Monthly income for a period of time (an annuity)
4. Reduction of living expenses

Earlier in this chapter, we noted the power that compounding interest has in increasing wealth. If you put aside a set amount each month, eventually the monthly interest on the principal will exceed the amount you deposit each month.

The "rule of 76" is understood by most financial officers and investment advisors. It's a quick way to estimate how long it will take a fund, earning a given rate of interest, to double in value. If you know the interest rate, it's an easy calculation. You simply divide 76 by the interest rate. The answer is the number of years you'll have to leave the money on deposit before it will double through accumulation of interest. (This is before taxes and inflation are considered, of course.)

5 Percent Table				
Period	Accumulated Value of 1	Present Value of 1	Accumulated Value of 1 Per Period	Present Value of 1 Per Period
1	1.050000	0.952381	1.000000	0.952381
2	1.102500	0.907029	2.050000	1.859410
3	1.157625	0.863838	3.152500	2.723248
4	1.215506	0.822702	4.310125	3.545950
5	1.276282	0.783526	5.525631	4.329477
6	1.340096	0.746215	6.801913	5.075692
7	1.407100	0.710681	8.142008	5.786373
8	1.477455	0.676839	9.549109	6.463213
9	1.551328	0.644609	11.026564	7.107822
10	1.628895	0.613913	12.577892	7.721735

Figure 12–5

A combination table

Let's go through a sample calculation. If you deposit $5,000 at 7 percent interest, how long must you leave the money on deposit before it grows to $10,000?

Answer: Divide 76 by 7. This will give you the number of years the money must be left on deposit. 76 divided by 7 equals 10.9 years, or 10 years and 11 months.

When money is put on deposit and left to earn interest, the result is called *accumulated value*. Bankers and insurance actuaries use a series of tables to quickly calculate the accumulated value of any amount of money left on deposit over a period of time.

Here's another question: "How much do I need to deposit every month (or year) to have a specific amount at the end of five years?" This is called *present value*. For example, if you want to have $1,300 in five years, how much will you need to put away every year at 8 percent simple interest? A present value table would tell you to invest $205.18 per year at 8 percent simple interest:

Year	Deposit Amount	Interest Earned	Balance of Fund
1	$205.18	$16.41	$ 221.59
2	205.18	34.14	460.91
3	205.18	53.29	719.38
4	205.18	73.96	998.52
5	205.18	96.30	1,300.00

You can see that this type of calculation could be complex. A present value table makes it much easier. For more complex problems, different tables are used. The illustration above used simple interest. You can expect better than that today on nearly all investments. For example, if you want to accumulate $1,300 in one year at 8 percent, compounded quarterly, you can look at a present value table at 2 percent for four "periods." You'll see that 8 percent, compounded quarterly, is the same as 2 percent for four quarters, and will give the right answer:

Quarter	Deposit Amount	Interest Earned	Balance of Fund
1	$309.23	$6.18	$315.41
2	309.23	12.49	637.13
3	309.23	18.93	965.29
4	309.23	25.49	1,300.01

The present value table would tell you to deposit $309.23 per quarter.

The number found in a present value table is usually accurate to six digits or more. You need greater accuracy when using larger figures.

If you look at a 5 percent simple interest table and want to know present value for five years, you'll find the factor 0.783526. Use it to figure how much money has to be left on deposit to have $5,000 at the end of five years. Multiply the factor, 0.783526, by $5,000 and you get $3,917.63.

These calculations become important when you're considering the effects of long-term investments and the accumulations of interest-bearing deposits. Then the tables are extremely useful.

Most books of tables of this type show: the accumulated value of 1, the present value of 1, the accumulated value of 1 per period, and the present value of 1 per period.

These tables can be used for many investment calculations. If you understand how to use the tables, you can calculate your own earnings or payments over a period of years.

Figure 12–5 is an example of a combination table:

Accumulated value of 1— Shows how $1 will increase at 5 percent when left on deposit for a number of periods.

Present value of 1— Shows the discounted value of $1 for a given number of periods at 5 percent.

Accumulated value of 1 per period— Is used to calculate a deposit or payment per period at 5 percent over a number of periods.

Present value of 1 per period— Is used to calculate the discounted value of an amount of money when deposited or paid over a number of periods at 5 percent.

13

Buying and Leasing Equipment

Before adoption of the Economic Recovery Act of 1981, there were tax advantages to leasing rather than buying business equipment. But the accelerated depreciation schedules now in effect usually make purchasing much more attractive.

In the past, write-offs of lease expenses gave the builder immediate benefits. If the equipment was bought, depreciation was deferred. Now equipment can be written off in the same period as a lease. But there may still be other considerations that justify leasing over purchasing.

Advantages of Leasing

Most builders rent equipment occasionally to meet job requirements. It would be foolish to buy equipment that's in use only a few days a month — especially if the same type of equipment is offered by a rental yard for a modest daily charge. But when you need a particular piece of equipment nearly every day, it's time to examine either a long-term lease or a purchase.

The primary reason to lease is that you can't afford to buy. Sometimes maintenance provided by the lessor will also be better and available faster.

The lease payment is fully deductible when paid. On a purchase, only the interest on the loan is fully deductible immediately. The purchase price in excess of $5,000 must be depreciated over a period of years.

Leasing may help you overcome the problem of obsolescence. Any piece of equipment *may* become obsolete or ineffective in a fairly short period of time. In a lease, the lessor runs this risk. Your obligation ends at the end of the lease term. Why invest in an asset that you'll want to replace in a year or two?

If you can't anticipate a permanent need, leasing is the answer. Here's a custom-made situation for a lease. Suppose you get a contract that will take at least two years to complete. It requires specialized equipment that you don't currently have. A two-year lease offers several advantages. You'll have brand new and maintenance-free equipment, with no down payments or loans. When the job is complete, the lease — and your cost — will expire!

The cost of owner maintenance can be substantial, especially as equipment gets older. Leasing can help you avoid maintenance costs entirely. On some equipment, it isn't unusual for maintenance costs to exceed the original purchase price after several years.

Leasing can help create a healthy financial statement. Committing yourself to the repayment of an equipment purchase reduces your working capital and may affect your credit rating. When you buy equipment, depreciation deductions are temporary. By renewing a lease, you have two advantages. You maintain a current deduction while avoiding increasing maintenance costs.

The current ratio (current assets compared to current liabilities) is a common yardstick for measuring a builder's financial health and his ability to manage cash flow. When you buy equipment, several bad things happen to your current ratio.

1. Current assets (cash) are reduced by the amount of the initial deposit you're required to make.
2. The addition of the asset is to long-term assets, which do not help the current ratio.
3. Current liabilities are increased by the amount of one year's payments on the loan.

Figure 13–1 shows how buying equipment changes your current ratio.

	Before Purchase	Change	After Purchase
Current Assets:			
Cash	$23,580	$(16,000)	$7,580
Receivables	36,014		36,014
Inventory	88,600		88,600
Total	$148,194		$132,194
Current Liabilities:			
Payables	$24,551		$24,551
Current Notes	46,000	12,800	58,800
Taxes Payable	4,265		4,265
Total	$74,816		$87,616
Current Ratio	1.98 to 1		1.51 to 1

$80,000 purchase
$16,000 down payment and $64,000 note with a five-year repayment
($12,800 current portion)

Figure 13–1
Current ratio and the effect of equipment purchases

2. The total of the lease payments is much higher than the asset's fair market value.
3. You assume title to the asset after a specified number of payments.
4. You can take title to the asset at the end of the lease by paying a price substantially less than the fair market value.
5. Part of the payment is identified as interest, effectively making the "lease payment" part principal and part interest on a loan within a sales agreement.

The Option to Buy

Including an option to buy in a lease may give the IRS grounds to consider it a conditional sales agreement. If so, deductions for lease payments would be disallowed.

To avoid this, the option to buy must include a "nominal" price. "Nominal" should be a fair and reasonable value. The lease may specify that the option price will be the fair market value at the time it is exercised. This may be estimated by contract or subject to independent appraisal.

If the IRS judges it to be a conditional sales agreement, the burden of proof is on the builder. These factors make a lease agreement look like a sale:

1. Part of the monthly payment is to be applied against the purchase price.

Rental Deductions

Deductions are disallowed in lease agreements between related parties (closely-held corporations or subsidiaries with similar ownership).

For example, related corporations may wish to transfer funds tax-free. If one is healthy and the other operates at a loss and has little cash, an unusually large lease payment will invite question. Any part of the payment that is above the going rate will be disallowed. You'll have to prove that such an arrangement isn't intended to shelter income.

Deductions will also be disallowed when there is a disguised dividend. For example, if the sole stockholder leases equipment for $5,000 per year, and sub-leases it to his corporation for $20,000, the excess could be ruled a disguised dividend and disallowed.

There can also be disguised capital contributions. If a corporation leases equipment to an employee, who is also a stockholder, for an unusually large amount, it will be disallowed as a disguised capital contribution, if not proven otherwise.

Other Tax Aspects of Leasing

The new depreciation rules eliminate salvage values in determining an asset's basis for write-off.

When deciding if you should lease or buy, be sure to compute depreciation on the entire cost. Also consider the real value (salvage) of the equipment at the end of a lease period and the resale value of owned assets.

The lease agreement can involve some costs that get special treatment for tax purposes.

❏ Security Deposits

Generally, security deposits are designed to protect the owners against damage to property. At the end of the lease term, security deposits are returned. If unrepaired damages are found, some or all of the deposit will be kept. The security deposit is not deductible. However, if you don't receive a refund, you can take a deduction in the year of forfeit.

❏ Advance Rentals

Rents paid in advance do not provide any tax benefits. They are deductible only in the years to which they apply. Any advance payment must be deferred, and a deduction claimed in the proper year.

❏ Bonuses

You may pay a bonus to get a lease. This is not deductible all at once. It must be amortized over the period of the lease.

In summary, prepayments in leases and rents offer no benefits. Deductions must be reasonable compared to similar agreements.

Transactions Between Related Parties

Transactions between related individuals and companies usually receive close scrutiny from the IRS. There are a number of special rules that apply to these situations. The IRS has the authority to reallocate income and deductions between taxpayers who have a common interest and have been making transactions that:

- appear to be arbitrary
- result in avoiding taxes
- are not business-related

If you control more than one company, you're going to have inter-company transactions between the two. It's in your interest to record and justify all inter-company dealings.

If you have relatives on your payroll or do business with relatives, the same caution applies.

When transactions between related parties (either individuals or companies) don't appear to be conducted on an "arm's length" basis — and they tend to reduce taxes, IRS can recalculate and adjust the net income of each party. The basis for any adjustment will be what the transaction would have been if done at an "arm's length" between parties that had no common interest.

Here are some examples of transactions between related parties that will draw IRS scrutiny:

1. Unusually high lease payments
2. Shared operating expenses that are assigned for tax benefits instead of being based on a reasonable formula
3. Reimbursement of salaries and wages without proof of actual service by the employee
4. Payments made from one affiliate to another that absorb or eliminate tax liabilities, but which don't serve a business purpose
5. Expenses paid by one company when benefits or services are received by another
6. Transfer of gross income from one associate to another, without proof that it was earned by the receiving company
7. Purchase of a capital asset by one associate, who will benefit from depreciation, when the asset will actually be used by another company in the affiliated group

Many transactions between related parties are perfectly legitimate. But you carry the burden of showing that shifting of income or deductions was not arbitrary. Be extra careful in supporting allocations.

One way to avoid problems is to avoid inter-company transfers and have no business dealings with relatives. But that isn't always practical. Sometimes there are very valid reasons to conduct business with related parties.

For example, if you own two or more companies, you'll probably have them share office space to reduce overhead. The two companies have to allocate many office expenses on some logical basis. The best way is to have one company pay the entire amount of each item and submit an invoice to the other. If possible, don't create situations where a clear division is obscure, such as when an employee works for both companies.

Here's an example of how to document the expenses of companies with common ownership. A general contractor has an affiliated architectural consulting company that occupies the same office building. The general contracting company pays the full amount of all expenses that are to be divided.

Each month, the contracting business documents the expenses and bills the consulting firm as follows:

Receptionist's salary: This is precisely the type of expense that's most difficult to divide. The tax code may include requirements that seem demanding, but it doesn't require the absurd.

In this case, it doesn't make sense to hire two receptionists for the two companies. First, neither firm needs a full-time person. Second, the reception area is central to both operations. Finally, the builder can document the split accurately and completely. Analysis of telephone calls shows that 40 percent of telephone costs are for the consulting firm. As further support, the receptionist's time card shows specific time spent on other than routine business for each company. The split is adjusted quarterly.

Office supplies: This is supported by requisitions. The contractor purchases all office supplies, which simplifies bookkeeping and allows taking advantage of discounts. When the consulting company uses supplies, they put a receipt in the contracting company's cash box. At the end of the month, these receipts are reimbursed with a check from the consulting company.

Photocopy expenses: It isn't practical for each company to lease its own photocopier. To reduce record keeping, the contractor leases a machine with a counter which keeps track of the number of copies run. At the end of each month, the consulting firm is charged 5 cents per copy.

Rent: The building lease is in the contractor's name. The consulting firm occupies 37 percent of the total space and pays that proportion of the monthly rent to the contracting company.

Salaries and wages: Each company hires its own employees and reports its own payroll taxes. The annual payment for workers' compensation is split based on exact totals.

Accounting fees: One accountant serves both companies and itemizes monthly billings. The contractor pays the bill. The consulting firm is billed each month for its share of the accountant's service.

Each item on the inter-company invoice is supported by documentation, a copy of either a worksheet or a billing. Figure 14–1 shows an example of a monthly invoice and attachments.

Other Related Party Transactions

There are several potential problems to avoid when dealing with a related party.

❑ Loans

Loaning money to an affiliate without interest charges may cause the IRS to compute a fair rate of interest, and adjust net profits accordingly.

❑ Free Use of Property

When assets are used by another affiliated company without charge, there may be a readjustment for a fair lease or rental rate.

❑ Free Services

When employees, executives, or consultants provide services to another company in the affiliated group, the IRS can compute the value of those services. The adjustment will be based on the value estimated to have been received by each.

❑ Sale of Assets

Assets sold between affiliates should be at the price that would be charged to an outside buyer.

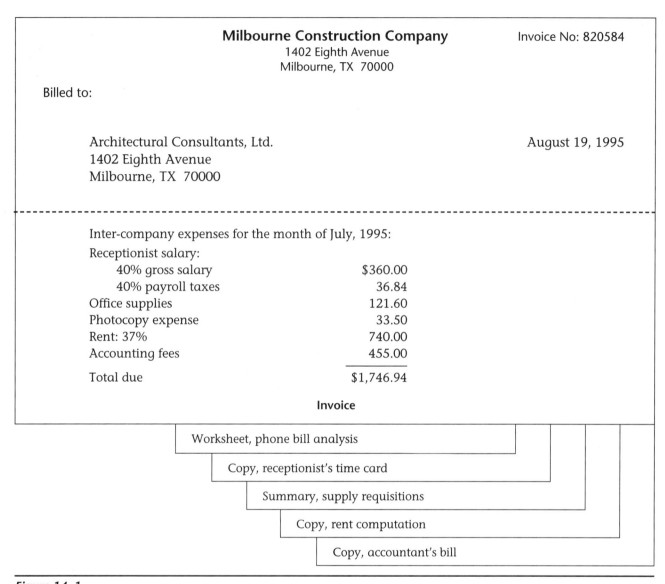

Milbourne Construction Company
1402 Eighth Avenue
Milbourne, TX 70000

Invoice No: 820584

Billed to:

Architectural Consultants, Ltd.
1402 Eighth Avenue
Milbourne, TX 70000

August 19, 1995

Inter-company expenses for the month of July, 1995:

Receptionist salary:	
40% gross salary	$360.00
40% payroll taxes	36.84
Office supplies	121.60
Photocopy expense	33.50
Rent: 37%	740.00
Accounting fees	455.00
Total due	$1,746.94

Invoice

Worksheet, phone bill analysis

Copy, receptionist's time card

Summary, supply requisitions

Copy, rent computation

Copy, accountant's bill

Figure 14–1
Typical inter-company invoice

The IRS will be interested only if there is a difference in the taxes paid. Note that the interest rate established between the parties can have a major impact on the taxes paid by each.

Consequences of Reallocation

An IRS reallocation can have serious consequences:

1. The loss of usable deductions or credits assigned to companies not needing write-offs.

Write-offs could be lost entirely, when the carry-over periods expire.

2. The creation of losses to corporations that have declared and paid dividends. If this happens, it could turn out that the dividend is more than the company's earnings. The directors could be held criminally liable even though the loss was unforeseen.

3. Deductions could be transferred to a company that can't legally recompute taxes due for the year in question. These deductions would be lost entirely.

4. Income may be assigned to a company which is not allowed by state law to receive it. State penalties could be assessed.

5. Allocations could be reassigned for profit-sharing plans. If the time for contributions has expired, a deduction won't be allowed.

6. Income transfers could be treated as dividends, disallowing the corporate deduction and resulting in double taxation (to the recipient as dividend income and to the corporation as distribution of earnings).

7. Net income could be increased for a subsidiary in a state with a higher tax rate. This would cause a higher state tax expense without an offsetting benefit.

8. If an individual's income is reassigned to a corporation he controls, he may be taxed for receipt of a "constructive dividend."

Multiple Corporations

If you own a substantial part of several corporations, the IRS could rule that they should be taxed as a single entity. This is likely under the following conditions:

1. Stockholders of the one corporation own controlling interest in the other companies.

2. The usual operating expenses (salaries and wages, rent of office and facilities, etc.) don't exist in the additional companies. They are paid by the one operating company.

3. Loans taken by the phantom companies are guaranteed by the operating corporation.

Be prepared to justify the use of multiple companies with good business reasons. These can include:

- Establishment of operations in different states, with different licensing, permits and standards
- Distinguishing different qualities of products and services provided
- Isolating conflicting personalities among key executives
- The need for control over an expanded area of operations

Transactions between related parties can be a very complex subject. The IRS has a considerable body of law and a number of rules that they can apply to discourage even the most ingenious tax avoidance schemes in this area. This chapter is intended only to alert you to the problem and suggest how to avoid the most common pitfalls. Talk to your lawyer or accountant if your company engages in transactions between related parties.

15

Corporate Contributions

The contributions your company make can be more than simply giving money to charitable organizations. They can play an important part in the preservation and expansion of your business. This chapter explains how.

A corporation can give away up to 10 percent of net income as qualified contributions each year. If your contributions total more than 10 percent of net income, the excess can be deferred to future years.

Anything over 10 percent can still be deducted in the year made *if* you can establish that the contributions were ordinary and necessary. For example, if you had to make a contribution to a local school so that key employees had a place to educate their children, that contribution would probably be an ordinary and necessary expense. The expense is ordinary because similar deductions would be allowed in the same situation for other businesses. The contribution is necessary because there are sound business reasons for keeping valued employees with the firm.

Reasons for Making Contributions

Contributions can be deducted only when an actual transfer of ownership occurs. You can't keep control over what is donated, and you can't have a plan to recover it at a later date. The organization must receive unrestricted right to the property. The rules are the same as for the sale of property.

There are many reasons for making voluntary contributions. It's unlikely that the IRS will question your motivation. The one requirement is that the contribution goes to a tax-exempt charitable organization for the purpose that organization represents. Here are some acceptable motivations:

Tax avoidance: It's good, legal business practice to avoid income taxes. Tax evasion, which is inaccurately reporting your tax liability, is illegal. Contributions made only to avoid taxes are allowed.

Creating or maintaining goodwill: One of the most important reasons for establishing goodwill is the reputation that is built up over the years for quality products and services. Another is the participation in charitable programs. Making a contribution just to build goodwill is acceptable.

Negative response and pressure: By not making a contribution, you could be the subject of scorn or ridicule. Avoiding criticism is an acceptable motive for contributions.

Keeping assets from heirs: Some business owners don't want their heirs to receive the assets of their corporation. A contribution can be made to disperse net worth over a period of years. This motive is not questioned by the IRS. Their interest is in the qualification of the receiving organization.

Prestige and conscience: Contributions may be made to enhance prestige or to relieve conscience. As with all contributions, the only rules are qualification, use, and proper transfer.

❏ Qualified Recipients

The IRS publishes a list of all qualified organizations. Qualified recipients include:

1. State and federal government (as long as funds will be used for public projects)

2. Tax exempt organizations, formed to pursue activities related to religion, education, science, literary purposes or prevention of cruelty to children or animals

Other Contribution Rules

The deduction won't be allowed if you receive anything in return. If you donate money and receive tickets to an event, only that part of your donation above the value of the tickets is deductible, even if you don't use them. The entire amount is deductible if you refuse the tickets altogether.

The payment must actually occur. There is no provision for accruals. The contribution must be paid in the year the deduction is claimed. The one exception to this rule is when a corporation's Board of Directors approves a contribution before the end of the year, and it's paid by a specified date. If you're on a calendar year, the deadline is March 15. This time can't be extended. You can deduct the accrued contribution in the previous year or in the current year.

Of course you can contribute cash, but other things of value also qualify:

- Transfer of stock in trust

- Assignment of a life insurance policy

- Transfer of title of assets. But allowing a charitable organization to *use* a corporate asset will not qualify. Something must be

given away completely and permanently to be a contribution.

- Forgiving a charity's debt. But it must be a valid and enforceable debt.

No deduction will be allowed for loaning goods or services. Although related travel and transportation costs will be allowed while working for a charitable organization, your time and effort can't be given permanently.

There are situations where a contribution can lower costs and expenses (taxes included) more than the contribution itself. Here are four benefits of making a contribution:

1. Reduction of corporate taxes by as much as 50 percent of the contribution

2. Reduction of state income taxes

3. Reduction of the amount required to be contributed to a profit-sharing plan

4. Elimination of earnings that will cause the IRS to assess an accumulated earnings tax. This is a tax that limits a corporation to keeping $250,000 or less of accumulated earnings in the corporation. It is intended to limit the tax advantages of deferring income to shareholders, particularly of a closely-held corporation.

Contribution Strategies

For a contribution to qualify fully, it must be made without strings. If you receive something of value (such as tickets, refunds, discounts or advertising) in return for your contribution, you can't deduct your contribution completely.

❏ Consider the Tax Consequences

Before you contribute, think through the tax consequences. Corporations can deduct accrued contributions that are made up to 75 days after the end of the tax year. But note that those contributions have to be approved by a resolution of the Board of Directors before the end of the year. Otherwise, they are deductible only in the year paid. This rule applies also to partnerships and sole proprietorships.

Because you're limited by a ceiling each year, be sure to plan your contribution payments. As with any deduction, the maximum benefit gained from contributions is limited. You can never save as much in taxes as the amount of the deduction. Every dollar contributed has a maximum benefit equal to the effective tax rate. For example, a company paying 28 percent in tax will benefit by 28 cents per dollar contributed.

❑ Consider Other Benefits

Carefully planned contributions may have advantages beyond reducing current taxes. Contributions can promote goodwill and reputation, and may even be as profitable as a more direct advertising campaign.

Recognition given to any business is usually beneficial, though there may be no clear way to evaluate whether the money contributed made enough difference to justify the cost. So contributions are a form of promotion that may be difficult to evaluate.

For sole proprietors and partners, a contribution can have three advantages:

1. Reduction of tax on federal returns
2. Reduction of tax on state returns
3. Reduction of the basis of net profits for computation of self-employment tax (Social Security)

❑ Advantages for the Individual

Self-employment tax is calculated on an individual's net earnings from self-employment. So a contribution will reduce this basis. Assume that an individual in the 31 percent tax bracket pays approximately 15 percent self-employment tax and 15 percent state tax. What's the value of a $1,000 contribution (without considering promotional benefits and changes in tax bracket)?

Amount contributed		$1,000
Federal tax savings	$310	
Self-employment savings	150	
State tax savings	150	
Total savings in taxes		$610
Net cost to individual		$390

Then ask yourself:

1. What was the promotional value of the contribution?
2. Is that value worth risking a $390 net expense?
3. What additional benefits were realized by moving into a lower tax bracket?

It's possible that the promotional value and additional benefits could exceed your $390 net cost. There may even be a direct financial "profit" in making the contribution. But this is hard to calculate before the end of a year; you don't know exactly how much tax you'll owe until you close the books. And of course, since the contribution costing you $390 is worth $1,000 to the recipient, there is also a social benefit.

❑ Consider Retirement Plans

One disadvantage of contributions is that they reduce income and thus can reduce the amount of money that individuals can contribute to a retirement plan. You can put 25 percent of income, up to a specified limit, into a retirement plan each year. A $1,000 contribution will reduce by $250 the amount of money that you can invest in a tax-deferred account. But this may not be a consideration under the following circumstances:

1. You weren't planning to deposit the full amount allowed
2. Your earnings exceed the maximum amount against which contributions can be made
3. The contribution is timed to fall into the following year
4. You want to reduce the basis of contributions to be made for yourself and your employees

For corporations with corporate retirement programs, the same considerations apply. If contributions are to be a factor in planning for taxes and cash flow, consider whether retirement programs are tied to net profits or to employee earnings.

❑ Donating Equipment or Inventory

In some cases, a contribution may not really reduce taxes but it may help cash flow. Consider the donation of equipment or inventory. This type of contribution is especially valuable when you don't plan to use an asset and probably couldn't recapture your investment if you sold it for scrap or at a discounted value. But it may still be valuable to a charitable organization.

The donated asset's value is based on your method of inventory valuation, in the case of inventory, or, in the case of equipment, on the net depreciated value. In some cases, an appraisal and documented assigned value may allow you to take a deduction for "fair market value" rather than book value. This depends on the nature of the asset and how you acquired and depreciated it.

Donating inventory or equipment gives these advantages:

1. You still get the tax benefits mentioned previously

2. No cash is taken from your business

3. You dispose of assets that have a market value but are useless or of little value to you

Review inventory and equipment at the end of each tax year to consider whether a well-timed contribution will produce these benefits. In the case of inventory, disposals through contribution also give you more storage space, the reduction of "dead" stock, plus lower insurance premiums and risk. The same advantages apply on equipment donations. You don't have to pay motor vehicle registration on vehicles contributed, and you can reduce overall equipment maintenance costs.

This type of tax planning is especially important in years when profits are high. The greater the profits, the higher the tax bracket. And as your tax liability increases, so does the value of a contribution.

16

Death of Partners or Stockholders

When a partner or a corporate stockholder dies, ownership passes to the decedent's estate and then to his or her heirs. But in the process, the normal flow of business may be disrupted. Substantial taxes may be due on the estate; control and ownership may have to be transferred; it may even be necessary to dissolve the organization.

This chapter explains what happens when a partner or stockholder dies, and offers some alternatives available to the surviving partners or stockholders. It also advises how to prepare company affairs for an unexpected death.

Comparison Between Organizations

Partnerships exist only as long as the individual partners are alive. If the partners retire or sell their interests, the organization must be dissolved and then reformed if desired.

A partner's death presents a special problem. All pending transactions must be assigned or liquidated. So dissolving disrupts business for the remaining partners, employees, creditors and customers.

The corporation, in contrast, is a much better form of organization for a construction company. The sudden loss of a shareholder is less of a problem, and should be less disruptive.

If a partnership is formed for a specified time only, or as a transition to the formation of a corporation, or to handle a specific job only, the problems of an untimely death are less complicated. In this case, the partnership works reasonably well.

❏ Partnership

Death or retirement dissolves a partnership. But it may be possible for the remaining partners to continue in business. This decision should be documented in the partnership agreement. Also include an agreement on how the decedent's estate

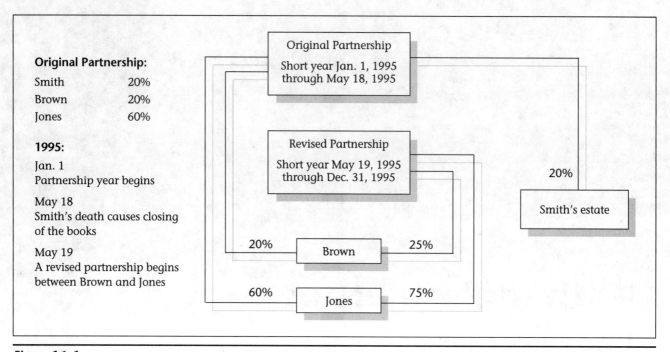

Original Partnership:

Smith	20%
Brown	20%
Jones	60%

1995:

Jan. 1
Partnership year begins

May 18
Smith's death causes closing of the books

May 19
A revised partnership begins between Brown and Jones

Original Partnership
Short year Jan. 1, 1995 through May 18, 1995

Revised Partnership
Short year May 19, 1995 through Dec. 31, 1995

Smith's estate 20%

Brown 20% 25%

Jones 60% 75%

Figure 16–1
Distribution of profits

is to be paid for transfer of the decedent's interest to the other partner or partners. Other provisions to be considered in the partnership contract are:

1. That the company's books will be closed at the death of a partner. This way, the exact value of the decedent's interest in the partnership can be determined. This will help avoid having to go back and reconstruct the books to establish the value.

2. That a specified time will be allowed for the remaining partners to liquidate the partnership and obtain funds to pay the estate.

3. That there is an agreed method for computing interest on funds payable to the estate during liquidation.

It's hard to determine the value of a partner's equity at death. You won't know, for example, if work in progress will be profitable. How much effect did the deceased partner have in producing project-to-date profits? Exactly what percentage of those profits were earned as of the date of death? It could be that some part of the job has lost money and that another phase will make money.

Deciding what value belongs to one partner at a given moment isn't easy. The most accurate way to assign value may be to assign a percentage of future profits to the estate.

The normal procedure upon death of a partner is to close the books and prepare a "short-year" tax return. Then a new partnership is made up of the remaining partners, with its first fiscal year covering the remaining of the current calendar year. A new fiscal year could be chosen, but in most cases, individual partners participate in calendar-year partnerships.

Figure 16–1 shows one way to handle distribution of profits from two partnerships in one year. In this example, the original partnership consisted of Smith and Brown, each with 20 percent and Jones with 60 percent. To compute proportionate interests, consider the surviving partners only. Brown and Jones together represent 80 percent of the original equity. Of this, Brown has 25 percent of the total (20/80ths). Jones owns 75 percent (60/80ths). This may form the basis for the new partnership. See Figure 16–2.

❏ Corporations

The death of a shareholder in a large corporation presents little or no problem. The decreased shareholder may have had little or no influence on the management of day-to-day affairs. But in the case of smaller corporations, the death of a major shareholder-manager can result in one of the following consequences:

	Original Partnership	Revised Partnership
Smith	20%	—
Brown	20%	25%
Jones	60%	75%
Total	100%	100%

Figure 16–2

Proportionate ownership of partnership

Liquidation of the company: When it is necessary to liquidate because of a shareholder's death, no one benefits. The other shareholders lose investment value — a going business is almost always worth more than the sum of its assets. The employees are out of a job. The creditors lose a customer. Work in progress must be finished. This can make the value of the stock very questionable.

The primary advantage of incorporation is that the organization can outlive its shareholders. This is ideal for a building business. Don't liquidate the corporation after the death of a key shareholder if there's any other reasonable alternative.

Beneficiary ownership: If the heirs of a deceased shareholder decide to retain the shares, capital gains taxes can be deferred. The basis of the shares' worth is their value at the time received. A well-run business will increase in value in the time between the death of a stockholder and when taxes are due. Ideally, operations can continue with competent managers and employees. But interference by new co-owners could threaten the business. Even the best intentions can't help if the new co-owners lack the experience needed to operate the company successfully.

Sales of the corporate stock: If a major stockholder dies, selling that owner's stock could have the same effect as liquidation. Employees may be replaced when the new controlling interests take over. Other shareholders could be shuffled to different positions. The change could severely disrupt operations.

Sometimes part of the deceased stockholder's shares can be sold without losing control of the corporation. This makes cash available to meet current expenses, but operations are not disrupted. The overall value of the shares would be maintained.

It's hard to sell the stock of a closely-held corporation because the value is difficult to pin down.

Unlike publicly-traded stock which has an established value, there is no real market for shares in a closely-held corporation. Book values (excess of assets over liabilities) are useful for estimating future income, but don't show what the company is worth to an outsider.

Potential investors may be suspect of any financial report that isn't the result of an audit by an independent certified public accountant.

It isn't easy to decide what to do upon the death of a key stockholder. Each of the three choices outlined above presents problems. The best choice is nearly always to have the corporation continue in business. That's why a little planning before the need arises can go a long way. A buy-out agreement is nearly essential when two or more individuals are running a small contracting company.

Buy-Out Agreements

There are two types of buy-out agreements:

Buy-and-sell agreements: The surviving shareholders will, upon the death of a major shareholder, buy his shares. Figure 16–3 shows how this works.

Use the same method as for partnerships to calculate the amount to be added to each surviving stockholder's shares. For example, Stockholder B owned 15/80ths of the stock held by the survivors, so he's entitled to buy an additional 3.75 percent of the stock left by the deceased (15/80 x 20 = 3.75).

Stock retirement agreements: One or more shareholders and the corporation agree that, upon the death of a major shareholder, they will buy his shares. When a corporation buys back outstanding shares, it effectively retires them. This increases the remaining values proportionately.

Buy-out agreements can be funded by the personal assets of the shareholders. Too often, though, the cash isn't available when it's needed. The death of a stockholder is usually unexpected, and the buy-out must be completed soon after.

Of course, the corporation could borrow money to pay for the shares of a deceased shareholder. But the corporation may not be able to borrow immediately after the death of a key shareholder.

The simplest way to prepare for the unexpected death of a shareholder is to buy life insurance. The

Stockholder A	Stockholder B	Stockholder C	Stockholder D	Stockholder E	Total
		Percentage Owned			
25%	15%	15%	25%	20%	100%
+6.25%	+3.75%	+3.75%	+6.25%	Deceased	
31.25%	18.75%	18.75%	31.25%		100%
		Shares Owned			
2,500	1,500	1,500	2,500	2,000	10,000
+625	+375	+375	+625	-2,000	
3,125	1,875	1,875	3,125	-0-	10,000

Figure 16–3
Buy-and-sell agreement

shareholders buy life policies on one another, with the proceeds to be used to buy the stock of the first to die. Another choice is to have each shareholder carry insurance on his own life, assigning the policy to the other shareholders as a unit.

Upon the death of one shareholder, the value of each remaining shareholder's equity increases because fewer shares are outstanding. There is no tax on the increased value until a distribution is made. When a surviving shareholder sells his shares, the increased value will be taxed at capital gains rates.

Insurance premiums paid by the corporation are not deductible. The expense is not directly related to the ordinary and necessary costs of running the business.

Partners can also insure themselves with other partners as beneficiaries. Or they may insure each others' lives. Again though, life insurance expense is not a deductible business expense. The protection afforded by "key person" insurance, however, is worth it.

Keep in mind the consequences of an unexpected death when choosing a form of organization. There's more at stake than just interruption of the business. Long-range contracts, tax planning, and the life of the business itself can be threatened. Proper planning, a buyout agreement and life insurance can overcome these difficulties.

Consequences of Liquidation

Liquidation of a going business can be more expensive than you might expect. Not only does all income cease immediately, but the accumulated goodwill and business reputation are lost instantly as well. Goodwill is difficult to recapture, and must be rebuilt again in a new business. Goodwill can disappear quickly as it's usually associated with a company name or an individual.

When you sell business assets (as opposed to selling a going business), you'll probably find that their value on the open market is lower than you expected. Equipment and inventory have a higher value while in use in everyday business situations than when sold at auction or to competitors.

If you plan to go back into business again, liquidation and disposal probably won't raise enough cash to repurchase the same equipment or inventory again at a later date.

Here's an example: Suppose Smith Construction has a backhoe that's several years old. It's been modified to meet the needs of Smith Construction exactly. It's been well maintained. The contractor knows exactly what's needed to keep it running smoothly. Over the years, it may have been at least partially rebuilt. Its operating cost is probably much less than the cost of a new backhoe.

But when the business is liquidated and that backhoe is sold, its value will be much less in the hands of the buyer. Replacement later will require a major investment.

If the overall value of your company is more than the net worth shown on your balance sheet, as is often the case, having at least some life insurance coverage is important. This is most obvious in partnerships or closely-held corporations. Insurance proceeds provide a cushion to help settle liabilities and form a new partnership without an urgent search for outside capital. During the transition, operations can continue smoothly. All inventory and equipment can be protected from liquidation.

❏ Goodwill

Goodwill and business reputation are protected if:

1. Insurance helps avoid financial problems and operations don't have to stop.
2. The business name doesn't change, regardless of ownership.
3. Settlement of liabilities occurs while the transition is taking place, and no sale of assets is required.
4. Existing contracts for work in process can be continued, with the beneficiaries assuming the contractual responsibilities of the deceased partner.
5. The same creditors and vendors honor existing commitments taken over by the new partnership, especially if the relationship with the former partnership was good.

The corporate form of organization offers the best protection against the unexpected death of a principal. A successful operation deals with a variety of creditors and has ongoing contracts. In a partnership, the death of one member means that everything has to be reorganized. If any outsider refuses to continue the relationship, the remaining partners may be unable to go on.

Under corporate organization, it's the corporation that does business with outsiders. Legally, the corporation is like an individual, but an individual who never dies. So contracts continue in force even after the death of a sole stockholder. Business of the corporation proceeds uninterrupted. The only change is in ownership of the stock. The owner's estate, and eventually the heirs, become the new shareholders. If the corporation has key person life insurance with the corporation as beneficiary, the proceeds could even be used to buy back the stock owned by the deceased owner.

Taxpayers' Elections

The tax code requires taxpayers to choose between certain alternative courses of action. These choices (called *elections*) apply to income reporting, filing dates, form of business organization, accounting methods, inventory reporting, depreciation methods, and capitalization of assets. Elections allow builders and other business owners to modify the rules, within boundaries, to best suit their own special needs.

Once an election has been made, it usually can't be reversed except by making a subsequent election. This is often subject to a time limit, and may require prior approval by the IRS. Some elections are made by taking a specific action such as filing a notification or request with the IRS, or by the way you report a transaction. Other elections are made by not acting (such as not filing a request to extend the time to file a tax return).

The code may require that you stick with your election once you make it, even if you later change your mind. So it's important to understand what elections are available, how to make or reverse them, and how they affect your tax liability and future choices in reporting and paying taxes.

To change one of these elections, you may have to explain the reasons for your choice. The reasons must have a sound business basis. Making a mistake on a previous election isn't an acceptable reason.

Extending Filing Deadlines

You can elect to extend the date for filing your income tax returns. The first extension is usually automatic, if you file for it before the original due date. Succeeding requests must be based on a good business reason. Being unprepared isn't reason for additional extensions. And delaying your filing several times may also draw IRS attention. Listed below are examples of sound business reasons for an extension:

1. You need more time to complete an outside audit.
2. You are waiting for a tax opinion on treatment of unusual items.
3. The books are being reconstructed following fire, theft, or other loss.
4. A computer conversion is taking longer than expected.
5. Someone important to the completion of the return is ill.
6. You're waiting for copies of previous returns necessary for this year's computation.

It's important to note that an extension doesn't postpone the due date for paying any tax *liability*. You still have to estimate the amount due and pay it on time. If you pay late, or underestimate the amount due, you'll be liable for penalties and interest.

Amending Tax Returns

You can amend a tax return by refiling before the statute of limitations expires. Amended returns can add or revise an original election *if* the deadline hasn't expired. Amended returns can be filed for many other reasons, including:

1. To pick up carry-over losses or credits previously overlooked
2. To average income
3. To report additional income, deductions, or credits
4. To change methods of depreciation or computation of auto mileage
5. To report as capital assets items previously deducted as expenses
6. To change accounting methods

One problem in amending your tax return is that you draw attention to your return. If you're changing the method of computing mileage for business use of a personal car, for example, and you increase the deduction significantly, it could trigger an audit.

Form of Organization

If you qualify, you may choose to report and pay taxes as any of the following forms of organization:

Sole proprietorship: An individual, reporting income and deductions on Schedule C as part of the individual tax return. If a sole proprietorship loses money, the net loss is deducted from other income. Any profit is added. A highly profitable business will raise the tax bracket substantially. This form of organization is simple and is changed easily, but offers few tax advantages and does not limit personal liability.

Partnership: Two or more people, corporations, or other partnerships, formed into a single unit by the partnership agreement for specific business activities. Partnerships don't pay income taxes. The members account for their share of income, deductions and credits. The partnership return reports the whole and divides it among the partners. There is less tax and liability protection than in a corporation, and the partners may be required to pay taxes on profits not taken from the business.

Corporation: An independent entity owned by shareholders. The corporation pays its own taxes and limits the liability of shareholders to the amount contributed by each. The shareholders protect their own incomes from higher tax brackets because only dividends are taxed.

S corporation: A corporate entity taxed as a partnership. Profits and losses are distributed to the shareholders each year in proportion to the ownership by each shareholder. This may have tax advantages in a company's early years, when losses can be used to offset other earnings. A corporation doesn't benefit from losses except as carry-overs into future years.

The organization election can be reversed later. The sole proprietorship is the most easily changed. When you form another type of organization, you simply stop operating as a sole proprietorship.

Partnerships are formed by notifying the IRS when you apply for an employer identification number. The partnership is firmly established when the first return is filed. To reorganize into another partnership, a series of sole proprietorships, or a corporation, the partnership must file a final tax return.

Corporations are chartered by the states, not the federal government. The IRS won't automatically recognize your corporation. If an organization doesn't have economic substance, the IRS might disallow the corporate tax return. The burden of proof is on you to show that the business is real and has substance.

To reverse your election to be taxed as a corporation, you must dissolve the corporation, sell the company or merge it with another, or make the election to be taxed as an S corporation.

To make the election to be an S corporation, there must be 35 or fewer shareholders who all agree to the election. To revert back to regular corporate status, a notice of revocation must be filed with the IRS within one month of the end of the fiscal year. You don't revert until the following year. Once S corporation status is reversed, you may not elect it again for several years. This prevents flipping back and forth to control profit distributions to shareholders or to avoid dividend treatment of profit-taking.

Accounting Methods

You may choose and later change your *accounting* method by election, with IRS approval. You apply for a change in accounting methods by filing Form 3115 within the first six months of the fiscal year. You can assume it will be approved. You don't need permission to change *bookkeeping* methods. For example, you can change from single to double-entry bookkeeping at any time.

You can use cash accounting methods, if you prefer. But cash accounting is not as accurate in reflecting actual income and deductions, and it may result in a higher tax liability. If you want, you can keep books on the accrual method and pay taxes on the cash method. If you have inventory, you must use the accrual accounting method.

The completed-contract method of accrual accounting doesn't show current activity on jobs in progress. Only when a project is 100 percent complete and accepted is the net income brought into the books. With this method, your financial statements won't be accurate because they won't show work in progress. And if you finish several big contracts in one tax year, you'll have a large tax liability.

Under percentage-of-completion accrual accounting, you report the income and costs of a project by estimating the degree of completion. It has the advantage of reporting net income throughout the life of a project.

You can use any of these accounting methods and your choice will most likely be respected by the IRS as long as you use the method consistently.

Fiscal Year

Taxpayers can select the beginning and ending date for their financial year. Most sole proprietorships, partnerships, and S corporations report on a calendar year basis.

Individuals usually follow a calendar year because a non-calendar fiscal year creates a number of inconveniences. A working spouse will have to report income halfway through the year, even though the employer continues to supply wage statements on a calendar year basis. Non-calendar year individuals tend to have processing delays in refunds.

When a corporation goes into business, the fiscal year election is made by filing the first tax return at the end of a chosen month. The fiscal year can be changed later by filing Form 3115. As long as the change is based on a sound business reason, there should be no problem. Taxes are computed on an annualized basis for changes. For example, a 3-month year's results are multiplied by 4; the appropriate rate is applied against annualized results, and divided by 4 to arrive at the short-year liability.

You might select a fiscal year that does not coincide with a calendar year for any of several reasons. It's common to end a year and close the books at the natural end of a business cycle. Builders who are busiest in the summer may want to end their fiscal year in August. Some accountants encourage their clients to select a fiscal year that fits the accountant's schedule.

Depreciation Methods

The Modified Accelerated Cost Recovery System (MACRS) defines four simple categories for all assets and allows one depreciation method. But you still have several elections.

You can elect to use the straight-line method instead of the prescribed 150 percent declining balance method. This would be to your advantage if any equal write-off would be more valuable in later years. You may also elect to write off a limited amount of new fixed assets (as discussed later in this chapter).

You are not limited to asset recovery in the specified categories. These can be extended at straight-line rates. The election to do this must be applied to all assets in those classes. For real estate, the election can be made on an asset-by-asset basis.

Auto Mileage

You can make the auto expense election each year. The two methods are:

Actual expenses: The business use of an auto is computed yearly as business miles over total miles. This percentage is applied to all expenses: gas and oil, tires, repairs and maintenance, interest on an auto loan, insurance, bridge tolls, parking, registration fees, and depreciation.

Mileage rate: An allowance is given per mile of business use, in addition to documented bridge tolls and parking fees. But you can use the mileage rate method only if you use just one car for business. If you have two or more vehicles, you must use the actual expenses method.

You have to decide which method is best for your situation. If an auto is used for business and later sold, the basis used to determine capital gains must be adjusted to allow for the depreciation on business use. If the mileage allowance method was used, you must consider the depreciation that would have been deductible under the itemized method.

Contributions

In most cases, contributions are deductible only in the year they are paid. But an accrual-basis corporation whose Board of Directors authorizes a contribution before the end of a fiscal year can elect to deduct it if it's paid within 75 days after year-end.

The contribution must be supported by a written declaration stating that it was approved by a board resolution. A copy of the resolution must also be attached to the tax return.

The contribution can be taken in the year paid. Based on tax considerations, the election can be made to accrue or to treat it as a current expense.

Deferrals

Many income and expense items can be reported over a period of time, even if cash is received or paid all in one year. Sound accounting policy should be the basis for a deferral. You should be consistent in treating all like transactions in the same way.

For instance, consider the cost of printing a two-year supply of letterhead and envelopes. You may take the deduction when the printer's bill is paid, or amortize the expense over a two-year period. There are two factors to consider: How did you treat previous similar transactions, and how large is the bill?

Prepaid interest and rent are not deductible until the period they cover. Insurance premiums covering a period beyond the current year must be deferred. But for many categories of expense, you can make an election.

Expensing

You can write off, instead of capitalize, a small amount of capital assets (up to $10,000) each year. This is an election, and is limited to property used in business. Knowing the consequences of your elections will help save tax dollars, often for years in the future.

The expensing rules apply only to purchased property, not to gifts or leased assets. For a controlled group of corporations, the limits must be apportioned among the companies in the group. The election can't be reversed once it's made. When expensed property is sold, the recapture allowance is treated as depreciation. A 100 percent expensed asset has an adjusted basis of zero for computing capital gains.

To a very limited degree, you can expense small assets. As long as your policy is constant and fair, purchasing small assets doesn't always require capitalization. Staplers and small tools may be classified as office supplies or operating expenses. As long as the total is small, there should be no problem in expensing such items. The tax code doesn't set a dollar minimum or maximum.

A large number of elections must be made by a controlled group of corporations. Limits on compensation and dividends involve elections. Many accounting questions that affect tax treatment must be addressed, such as accounting methods or S corporation elections. These should be part of a comprehensive tax planning procedure. The election timing is crucial because elections made by the end of a fiscal year could affect taxes drastically in the future. For example, you might like the S corporation election this year, but regret it in more profitable years to come.

Inventory Valuation Methods

If you keep an inventory of construction materials, you must keep books and pay taxes on the accrual method. But you can elect from one of several methods of inventory valuation. The more common methods of inventory valuation include:

1. Lower of cost or market
2. Cost
3. Last-in, first-out (LIFO). Use the latest prices paid for inventory to value all similar items in stock.
4. First-in, first-out (FIFO). Use the actual prices paid to value inventory in stock.

The best method varies by business. You should consult with your accountant before making the final decision. In the first year of business, you can use any method of inventory valuation, as long as it clearly reflects income. You must then continue to use this method unless you make an election to change. Changing methods of inventory valuation is considered an accounting change, which means that you have to file Form 3115.

Retirement Plans

You have several choices in selecting a retirement plan. What you choose will depend on your form of organization, available investment capital, employees on staff, and labor union agreements. There are many types of pension, profit and retirement plans for corporations.

Individuals have the option of opening and funding an Individual Retirement Account (IRA). Anyone with earned income (from salaries, fees, self-employment, etc.) can have an IRA, even if they belong to another retirement plan.

For the self-employed, Keogh plans are another option. They may be defined benefit plans or defined contribution plans.

A *defined benefit plan* establishes a target amount to be paid monthly after you reach a certain age. Contributions are scaled so that the money needed (to meet the target amount) will be available upon retirement.

A *defined contribution plan* puts aside a set amount (percentage of earnings) for each employee each year.

A self-employed individual may have both a Keogh and IRA. But what if the business is sold, a partnership or corporation formed, or, for any reason, the Keogh contributions are stopped? You may make the election to either "freeze" the Keogh or roll it over. When you freeze a retirement account, you may continue to direct various investments within the plan, but you cannot make additional contributions. But you aren't required to leave funds where they are.

You can roll a Keogh plan over into an IRA, if, for example, you incorporate your business, take a job with someone else, or sell out to another builder.

Another election for individuals involves the amount of contribution. Each employee can contribute to the Keogh or IRA fund each year, up to a maximum amount. But it's not required that you contribute the maximum. For example, the maximum IRA contribution you can make for yourself is $2,000 per year ($2,250 if an unemployed spouse also participates). But you don't have to contribute this amount. You can contribute as little as you want, limited only by the minimum a trustee will accept. The same is true for Keogh plans. Contributions made to properly-established plans are deductible if made by the deadline each year.

You may have IRAs and Keogh plans with as many different trustees as you desire. Many people place IRA funds with different trustees each year. This provides diversification of retirement funds, but there are disadvantages, including:

1. A greater need for management of accounts.
2. Eventual need to roll over funds. (Rolling over funds is limited after retirement.)
3. Payment of more trustee fees.
4. The limit on the amount you can invest each year limits your ability to diversify investments.

After several years, it usually makes more sense to combine investments under a single trustee who allows you to diversify within a single plan. This type of election won't affect your tax status if the trustee is qualified under the law and the rollovers are done according to the current rules. Combining retirement accounts into a single trust can provide a higher level of diversification and minimize your cost and the time required for asset management.

Many trustees qualify to hold IRA and Keogh funds. Which trustee you choose depends on the amount of money involved and your level of interest as an investor. Banks and savings and loan associations are popular trustees because they are nearby, easy to find, and inexpensive. You are, however, limited to investing in the interest-bearing products offered by these institutions.

Mutual fund companies offer retirement trustee arrangements and charge low fees, often only five or ten dollars per year. But again, you will be limited in your investment alternatives.

Trust companies offer the greatest flexibility, but their fees are $200 or more per year. Also, transaction charges are assessed whenever you make an investment decision. A trust company may be inconvenient if it isn't located near your home or business.

Another alternative is a stock brokerage company. You can set up a retirement fund and invest in any product handled by that broker. Several of the large brokerage houses offer trust plans with fees of $25 to $50 per year and no extra charges. Some broker-trustees offer plans where "idle" or uncommitted funds are left on deposit in money market accounts. Your money is always working for you. You can place orders by telephone, with no other effort on your part. And as trustees, brokers will be particularly well suited to offer investment advice.

Capital Gains and Losses

When planning the sale of a capital asset, you can time the sale so it gives you the maximum tax advantage. Capital assets include business equipment, investments, your home and other properties, and any other asset into which you invest funds and realize appreciation (or experience a loss).

The election you make is the timing of the sale. Many tax strategies apply. For example, try to sell assets that will produce gains when you have a large long-term capital loss. This is especially important, because there's a limit to the amount you can deduct for a capital loss. The losses will offset the gains and protect the tax benefits.

To help offset taxable income in a highly profitable year, consider selling some assets at a loss. That can move you into a lower tax bracket.

Tax Planning

Tax planning is a year-round process. It begins the day you open your business and never stops.

The tax plan is a key element in the survival of your business. When you choose an accounting method, form of organization, and fiscal year, you've started to plan. These early elections are the most important decisions you'll make. But your overall tax plan includes choosing your methods of depreciation, inventory valuation, bad debt accounting, and internal record-keeping.

Every builder is (or should be) involved with tax planning. Since income tax rules affect every phase of business, tax planning is a necessary tool. Tax planning and profit planning are very much the same, since lower taxes will translate into higher net profits. And many of the business options available provide dual benefits. Qualified retirement plans, for example, give employees attractive and valuable benefits, plus current deductions for you.

If you wait until the year is over, it's too late for effective tax planning. What has already happened can't be changed. So plan ahead as far as possible. Spend a few hours each month anticipating events and thinking about taxes. It can save thousands of dollars in taxes each year. Here are some examples of how to plan for lower taxes:

January. Begin contributions to an employee profit-sharing or pension plan.

February. Defer the gain on the sale of an asset by accepting payment on the installment method.

March. Begin an employee benefit plan, paying deductible health insurance group premiums.

April. Decide whether to depreciate new assets as quickly as allowed by law. Will an extended, straight-line schedule benefit you more in later years?

May. Analyze maintenance costs and idle time. It may be profitable to replace older equipment, gaining new depreciation deductions.

June. Take a physical inventory. Sell obsolete items.

July. Review subscriptions to trade publications.

August. Order and pay for a year's supply of letterhead and envelopes.

September. Extend due dates on balances due in December to January 10 (for cash basis builders).

October. Take early delivery of new assets and place them in service this year. Claim partial deduction for depreciation.

Avoidance	Evasion
Business affairs are arranged to minimize taxes legally.	Transactions are not disclosed: false claims are made.
Elections are made that are to the builder's advantage in minimizing income taxes.	Taxes are reduced or eliminated in ways that aren't allowed by tax laws.
Expenses and capital asset purchases are timed to reduce or defer taxes.	Expenses are claimed falsely.
The form of organization and accounting methods are chosen to produce the lowest taxes possible.	Tax returns are not filed at all.

Figure 18–1

The difference between tax avoidance and tax evasion

November. Declare a contribution, payable by March 15 next year (corporations only, on accrual basis).

December. Prepay known invoices for overhead expenses (for cash basis builders).

Many elections can help you do effective tax planning. (We covered the kinds of elections you can make in the last chapter.) Their special nature makes it possible to tailor them to your situation. Consider the good and bad aspects of:

- Cash and accrual accounting
- Percentage-of-completion versus completed contract accounting
- Different methods of valuing inventory
- Regular class depreciation or extended term methods
- Timing of capital asset acquisitions
- Choosing a fiscal year

Tax Avoidance vs. Tax Evasion

What's the difference between tax avoidance and tax evasion? That's simple. It's completely legal to *avoid* taxes. Arrange your business transactions and affairs to minimize, defer or even eliminate income tax. A carefully constructed plan of tax avoidance will help you minimize taxes legally.

Tax *evasion* is illegal. Failing to report income, claiming false deductions, and willfully not filing a tax return are examples of evasion. The penalties are severe. Figure 18–1 compares tax avoidance to tax evasion.

There are two key points to remember about deductions:

1. Spending money exclusively to get a tax benefit won't help you. You can't save more than you spend. If you pay combined federal and state taxes at the rate of 48 percent, the most you'll save by spending an additional $100 is $48.

2. Your purpose and intention in creating a particular transaction should be the deciding factors. Always ask, "What are the primary motives behind this transaction? Is it for a sound business purpose that is ordinary, necessary, and reasonable? Or is it only for the purpose of tax avoidance?"

Sound Business Purpose

You need a sound business purpose for a transaction. Of course, not every transaction will be put to the test. But in most situations, you must be ready to show a business motive for what you've done. Creating transactions simply to avoid taxes can work against you. Simple tax avoidance is not a good enough business reason to claim a deduction.

Here are three examples of transactions entered into for tax avoidance without a sound business purpose:

1. One builder pays another a consulting fee just before the end of the fiscal year. It has the effect of eliminating a substantial part of the payer's tax liability. For the builder receiving the fee, it serves only to absorb part of a large net loss for the year. A month later, in the new fiscal year, the fee is paid back as

a consulting fee. Each builder argues that they provided consulting services. But the IRS rules the transactions lack substance because the builders are unable to document what business value the services provided. The transactions serve to reduce taxes, are made so near the end of the fiscal year, and are repaid — all of these point to tax avoidance without proper justification.

2. A builder subscribes to several general interest magazines. He claims they are for the benefit of his employees, and that they were business expenses because they were paid for by the company. But they're not necessary to run the business. Most of the publications ended up in the builder's home. Without any direct connection to the business, the transaction doesn't qualify.

3. Assets on the builder's premises are repaired to create a current deduction. The builder argues that it was preventive maintenance. But the repairs weren't necessary when made, and there was no record of previous preventive maintenance on similar machinery.

The best tax avoidance is based on a careful choice of elections and the timing of transactions. The question of motive is all-important. Although an item might be both ordinary and reasonable, is it necessary? Or, is the motive only to avoid taxes? Tax avoidance must have a business motive. Examples of business motives include:

1. Producing profits
2. Keeping internal harmony
3. Keeping large customers
4. Complying with the law
5. Attracting and keeping competent employees
6. Generating future business
7. Improving existing systems

You'll have very few transactions which do not have a business motive. They must meet the specifications and rules that qualify them as deductions. It's perfectly legal to incur these expenses. Examples include:

1. Sale of a capital asset, timed to create a capital loss
2. Contributions to a qualified charitable organization
3. Giving gifts to create a current deduction

Tax Avoidance Plans

Avoidance can take two forms: the complete elimination of a tax liability, or the deferral of taxes. Qualified retirement plans (pension, profit-sharing, Keogh and IRA) are long-term deferrals of income. When you pay into a plan for your employees, you can take a current deduction. When the employee begins withdrawing funds, he or she is taxed as the withdrawals are made.

Retirement plans are an excellent method of tax avoidance. They have a recognized business purpose (a benefit that helps the business attract and keep good employees), and they supply several additional benefits as well:

1. Corporate or employer deductions
2. Providing security at retirement
3. A vesting schedule to reduce employee turnover
4. Higher benefits for those with higher compensation (as long as the plan does not discriminate in favor of the most highly-paid employees)

The timing of fixed asset purchases can have a great impact on tax liabilities. A careful plan will help to either bring deductions and credits into the current year, or delay purchases to move credits and deductions ahead.

If you plan to buy a capital asset near the end of your fiscal year, study your timing. It may be possible to defer a significant liability, or to move the tax benefits to the most favorable year.

The best type of tax planning helps you determine your tax liability in advance. An S corporation may choose any fiscal year it desires. If it closes its books on January 31, all earnings for that year-end are payable by the shareholders in the calendar year beginning January 1. Thus, there is an 11-month deferral of income taxes. You have 11 months to legally avoid or reduce those taxes.

The same type of deferral is available in a partnership. You'll need IRS permission to have a fiscal year that does not coincide with the calendar year. The change must be based on solid business reasons, with the deferral of taxes is a secondary result. While selection of a fiscal year is automatic for corporations, a partnership must establish the reason.

Interim Statements

A basic way to predict your tax liability is to prepare financial statements each month. These interim statements are the best indicators of trends. Of course, if you report under the completed-contract method and expect a profitable contract later in the year, take that into account.

For percentage-of-completion accounting, anticipate each job on the budgeted-completion schedule, computing profits through the end of the year. Add these totals to your interim profit balance.

An interim statement is only as thorough as the record-keeping system you use. If your estimates are inaccurate, it's impossible to effectively plan for taxes within the year. Your method of tracking inventory values, estimating interest expense and depreciation, and totaling receivables and payables will affect the accuracy of the interim statement.

Monthly and quarterly reports show seasonal and year-round trends. They will identify the areas where more control is needed. For example, if the value of your inventory changes drastically from month to month, there may be a problem in requisitioning or purchasing procedures.

Tax planning involves all aspects of your operation. A well-conceived strategy will result in higher after-tax profits. Your accountant should be involved in this strategy. His or her knowledge of current tax law and experience in tax planning can help you avoid taxes legally.

Filing Tax Returns

The type of tax return you file depends on whether your company is a proprietorship, partnership, or corporation. This chapter explains the requirements for each type of company, discusses key parts of the return, and summarizes the form.

Tax returns must be mailed on time to avoid late penalties and interest. If you can't make a deadline, file for an extension. That will avoid a penalty for late filing, but interest will still be charged on any late payment.

By filing for an extension, you extend the deadlines for many elections. If you file late, the election may be refused. The IRS strictly enforces the filing requirements.

You must sign your tax return, or it is *not* a tax return at all. The IRS doesn't waive this requirement, even if it accepts and holds a tax return for several years. The signature must be handwritten; a typed or rubber-stamped one doesn't meet the requirement.

Information on tax returns is supposed to be confidential, yet a number of government agencies can get the information. Information will be also given to state taxation and law enforcement agencies. The President of the United States can also order it made available. Your tax returns are not available to lenders and won't be released in civil proceedings.

Corporate Tax Return

Corporations file their taxes on Form 1120. This is a four-page report which must be signed by an officer of the company. Below is a breakdown of the sections of Form 1120.

Page 1
Business, name, address, identification number, and fiscal year.

Income and expense summary: A profit and loss statement. You will probably need to attach supporting schedules. These are covered later in this chapter.

Total net income, tax liability, credits, and the net liability or overpayment: This section is a summary only. The detailed tax computation is found on page 3.

Page 2
Schedule A, Cost of goods sold: This section shows in detail how the single line entry on page 1 was computed.

Schedule C, Dividend income

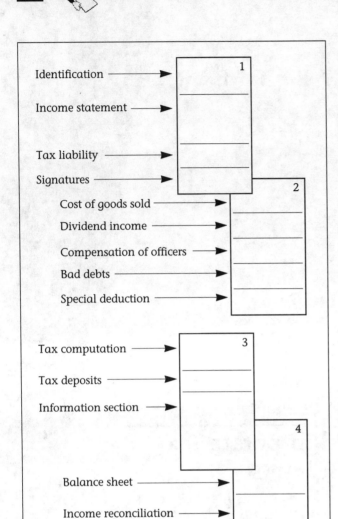

Figure 19–1
Form 1120 — Corporation tax return

Schedule E, Compensation of officers: All pay to officers is listed here, including expense account information.

Schedule F, Bad debts: Complete this section only if you are on the accrual basis, and if you use the reserve method for bad debts.

Schedule I, Special deduction: This section is for corporations receiving dividends only (see Schedule C, above). Portions of some dividends can be excluded.

Page 3

Schedule J, Tax computation: The gross tax is figured, then adjusted by additional taxes, applied credits, carry-overs, etc.

Schedule K, Record of tax deposits: If, during the year, you made estimated prepayments, the dates and amounts are listed here.

Additional information: In this part, you must answer questions about special interest deductions (entertainment facilities, conventions outside of the U.S., etc.), corporate ownership data, the type of business, and whether or not special requirements applied during the year.

Page 4

Schedule L, Balance sheets: Both the end of the previous year and the end of the current year are included here.

Schedule M-1, Reconciliation of income: The total net income on your books may be different from that on the tax return. You account for these differences here:

Income per books
Plus: Federal income tax
Less: Tax-exempt interest earned
Less: Insurance proceeds
Equals: Income per income tax return

Schedule M-2, Retained earnings analysis: This is a summary of changes in your surplus account. Examples of the items on Schedule M-2 are:

Balance at the start of the year
Plus: Net income per books
Plus: Previous year's tax refund
Less: Non-deductible expenses (such as parking tickets or government fines, penalties for filing tax returns late, etc.)
Equals: Retained earnings, end of year.

The sections of Form 1120 are summarized in Figure 19–1.

S Corporation Tax Return

Because the S corporation is taxed like a partnership, the information and schedules are different from those of other corporations. The return must be signed by an officer of the corporation. To qualify, all shareholders must have agreed to this election, and the agreement must have been in effect for the tax year. The form number is 1120-S.

Page 1

Business name, address, identification number, fiscal year

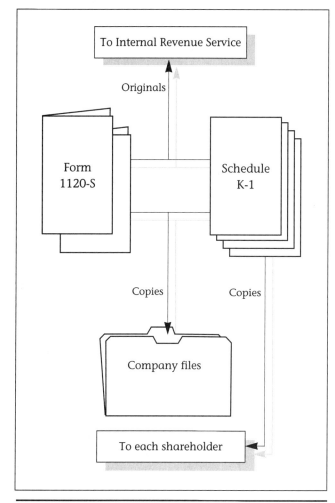

Figure 19–2
Distribution of S corporation forms

Income and expense summary: a profit and loss summary: It is necessary to attach supporting schedules.

Total tax, payments and net liability of the corporation: Note that the only taxes for which an S corporation will be liable are capital gains and the minimum tax on tax preferences.

Page 2

Schedule A, Cost of goods sold

   Schedule E, Compensation of officers

   Schedule F, Bad debts (reserve method only)

   Additional information

Page 3

Additional information (continued from page 2)

Schedule K, Computation of the corporation's undistributed taxable income: This is the overall total of taxable ordinary income, dividends distributed, interest expense, and tax preference items. The total line items on Schedule K are distributed to each shareholder on Schedule K-1.

Page 4

Balance sheets (for the prior and current years)

   Schedule M-1, Reconciliation of income: Per the company's books with the income reported on the tax return.

   Schedule M-2, Retained earnings analysis

   Schedule K-1 (detail of Schedule K)

In addition to the four-page tax return and supporting schedules, S corporations must also supply a Schedule K-1 for each shareholder.

This report shows each shareholder's share of each category in Schedule K. For example, if one shareholder has a 35 percent ownership, he will be credited with 35 percent of the income.

Schedule K-1 also contains a cross-reference to each applicable schedule and line for reporting information on your individual tax return (Form 1040). Figure 19–2 shows the distribution of the S corporation tax return. Figure 19–3 summarizes the section discussed above.

Partnership Tax Return

Form 1065 is the partnership tax return. The partnership reporting process involves showing combined totals for the group, and assigning proportionate shares of income, credits, and capital gains.

Page 1

Business name, address, identification number, and fiscal year

   Income and expense summary and Schedule A, Cost of goods sold

Page 2

Schedule A, Cost of goods sold (continued from page 1)

   Schedule D, Capital gains and losses

   Schedule H, Income from rents

   Schedule I, Bad debts

   Schedule J, Depreciation

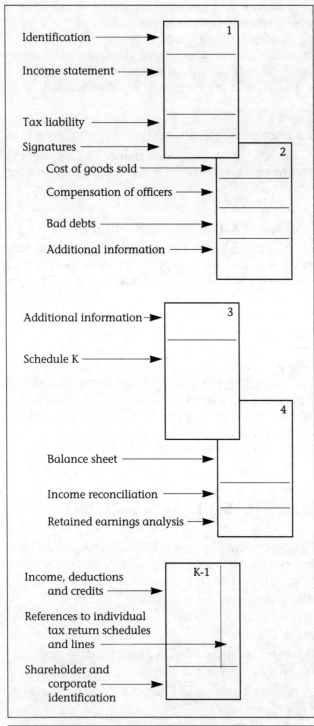

Figure 19–3
Form 1120-S — S corporation tax return

Page 3
Schedule K, Partners' share of income, credits and deductions: The totals are listed for all items transferred to the partners for tax reporting. Each

line item is assigned to the individual partners on Schedule K-1.

Page 4
Schedule L, Balance sheets (previous and current year-end balance sheets).

Schedule M, Reconciliation of partners' capital accounts: This section shows the overall change in capital accounts. Distributions to individuals in the partnership are detailed on Schedule K-1. An example is shown in Figure 19–4.

Schedule N, Computation of net earnings from self-employment: This is a summary of the previous sources of net income for the partnership. Totals are broken down by partner on Schedule K-1 (with the total transferred to Schedule K) for net income reporting on individual tax returns and computation of self-employment tax. The partners are individually self-employed (unless a corporation is a partnership member), and must file Schedule SE with their personal tax return and pay self-employment tax.

Additional information

Schedule K-1 (detail of Schedule K) The partners' individual shares of income, credits, and deductions are listed on a Schedule K-1 for each partner. The sections are:

Partner and partnership identification: Name, address, Social Security or tax identification number, and percentage of ownership.

Additional information: Questions on partner status, ownership, and profit percentages.

Reconciliation of partners' capital accounts

Income, deductions, and credits

Figure 19–5 summarizes the partnership return.

Individual Taxation and Schedule C

Individuals report business income on their personal tax returns. Individuals must pay a self employment tax on net business income. This is a Social Security tax on earnings, and is in addition to the regular income tax.

You report business income from sole proprietorships on *Schedule C, Profit (or loss) from business or profession.* It's a special schedule for the sole owner of a business. Schedule C is a detailed profit and

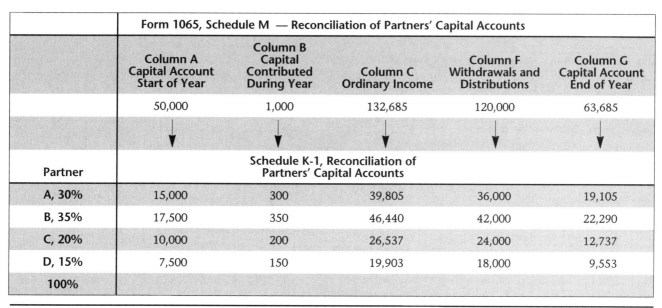

	Form 1065, Schedule M — Reconciliation of Partners' Capital Accounts				
	Column A Capital Account Start of Year	Column B Capital Contributed During Year	Column C Ordinary Income	Column F Withdrawals and Distributions	Column G Capital Account End of Year
	50,000	1,000	132,685	120,000	63,685
	↓	↓	↓	↓	↓
Partner	Schedule K-1, Reconciliation of Partners' Capital Accounts				
A, 30%	15,000	300	39,805	36,000	19,105
B, 35%	17,500	350	46,440	42,000	22,290
C, 20%	10,000	200	26,537	24,000	12,737
D, 15%	7,500	150	19,903	18,000	9,553
100%					

Figure 19–4
Summary of partnership capital accounts

loss summary. There is no requirement for reporting balance sheets or surplus accounts. Below is a summary of the two pages of Schedule C.

Page 1

Name and Social Security number

Business name, address, employer number

Questions: Accounting method used, inventory valuation, home office expenses, etc.

Part 1: Income: This includes the gross income from self-employment, a one-line item for the cost of goods sold, and the gross profit.

Part II: Deductions: A summary of business expenses. Additional schedules may be required. There's room for listing a large number of self-employment business expenses.

Net income

Page 2

Schedule C-1: Cost of goods sold: This is a supporting schedule for the line items in Part I.

Schedule C-2: Depreciation: This is the schedule listing business assets and depreciation.

Schedule C-3: Expense account information

Figure 19–6 shows how a sole proprietorship would report income on the applicable schedules.

Self-employment tax is reported on a separate Schedule SE. Net earnings from Schedule C are transferred and used to compute the self-employment tax. You may be able to lower the basis, if you have other net losses subject to Social Security taxes.

Supporting Schedules

Most corporate and partnership tax returns require supplemental information. Many of the individual line items include the notation "Attach schedule." On that line of the tax return, include a notation referring to the schedule by title, page and line number. See Figure 19–7.

It's a good idea to attach documentation for unusual items. If you have a large deduction, such as a major casualty loss or theft, attach complete documentation. This would include a letter explaining the circumstances of the loss, and documentation to support the claim: invoices, police reports, newspaper stories, insurance appraisals, witness statements, etc.

This documentation is intended to answer questions before they come up. Certainly, providing information is better than attaching nothing at all. Figure 19–8 is a sample documentation letter.

Other Considerations

There are some expenses that are of special concern to the builder. The deduction for a home office has been abused, so the IRS often audits this.

A question on Schedule C asks whether deductions have been claimed for a home office. You should attach a note that covers the following points:

- The deduction is based on a part (square feet or number of rooms) of the home used for the business.
- Show the total cost and the percentage deducted for business.
- The reasons a home office is necessary.

Travel and entertainment expenses must also be thoroughly documented. These expenses are often disallowed. The documentation should include logs or diaries which explain the business need.

Bear in mind that the expense must be ordinary and necessary to be deducted. Be prepared to justify an unusually large deduction. If other builders don't claim such expenses, it makes your case harder to prove.

Every builder should be aware of some special elections. Averaging income can lower your taxes in the current tax year, if you earned substantially more than the average of the last four years. This election is worth checking every year. To qualify for income averaging, you must meet three qualifications:

1. You must have been a citizen of the United States for the last four years.
2. You must have provided at least half your own support for all years involved.
3. The qualifying income must be 30 percent higher than the total base-period income.

You compute income averaging on Schedule G. You can average income every year you qualify. There is no waiting period. If you had two extremely low-income years, following by larger-income years, you could qualify for income averaging three years in a row.

Schedule E

Partners and shareholders in S corporations report their net income or losses on Schedule E, Supplemental Income Schedule. This schedule includes:

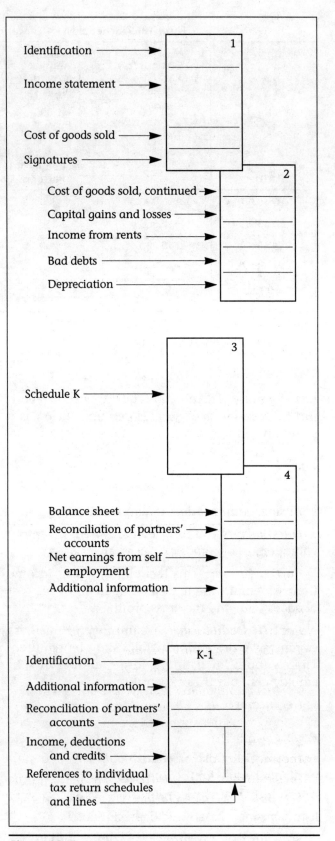

Figure 19–5

Form 1065 — Partnership tax return

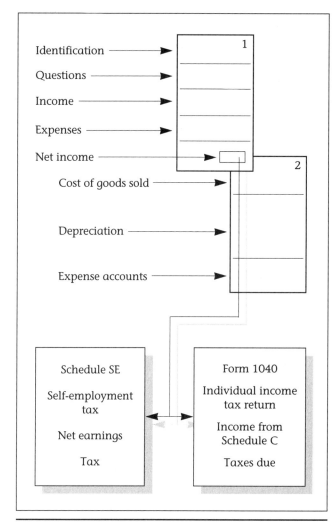

Figure 19–6
Schedule C — Profit (or loss) from business or profession

Larsen Construction Supplementary Schedules I.D. Number 94-1234567 For the Year 1994	
Other Deductions:	
Office supplies	$1,406.23
Advertising	352.00
Telephone	3,166.05
Utilities	1,659.06
Union welfare	26,384.80
Payroll taxes	16,436.77
Travel	2,443.69
Entertainment	1,004.34
Printing	2,310.18
Total, to Page 1, Line 26	$55,163.12
Other Current Assets:	
Refundable deposits	$ 650.00
Certificates of deposit	5,000.00
Total, to Schedule L, Line 5	$5,650.00
Other Current Liabilities:	
Payroll taxes payable	$2,132.60
Sales taxes payable	4,066.81
Total, to Schedule L, Line 17	$6,199.41

Figure 19–7
Supporting schedules

Page 1

Name and social security number

   Pension and annuity income

   Rent and royalty income or loss

   Partnership income: Identify the partnership by name, address, and employer identification number. Show your net share of income as reported on your Schedule K-1.

   Income from estates or trusts

   Income from S corporations: Show the name and address of the corporation, its identifying number, and your share of income or loss from Schedule K-1.

   Total income or loss: The combined total of the above sections.

Page 2

Supplementary schedules: For rental or royalty properties: property descriptions, depreciation and general expenses.

   Schedule E is part of your individual income tax return. For net income from partnerships and S corporations, you must file Schedule SE and pay self-employment tax.

March 15, 1995
Internal Revenue Service Center
Fresno, CA

Re: Smith Construction Company, Inc.
       Employer Identification Number 94-1234567

Gentlemen:

This letter is in reference to an extraordinary deduction claimed on the enclosed corporate income tax return for the year 1994, a casualty loss in the amount of $17,663.

On November 19 and 20, 1994, an unusually severe storm destroyed sections of our warehouse roof, siding and windows. The damage included extensive water damage to a considerable part of our inventory. Such violent storms are unusual and unexpected in this part of the country. The corporation's insurance coverage does not extend to losses from natural causes.

Following the damage, we had a burglary. Access was through one of the broken windows. Part of our remaining inventory was stolen during this entry. Our insurance carrier has reported that coverage extends to losses of inventory from theft.

Enclosed for your review are the following supporting documents:

1.   List of stolen inventory
2.   List of inventory destroyed by water
3.   Photographs of inventory destroyed by water
4.   Newspaper clippings reporting the storm and our theft
5.   Copy of the police report
6.   Copy of an independent appraiser's estimate of structural repairs
7.   Copy of our insurer's claim response

Our total damages are summarized below

Total replacement cost of roof, siding, and windows	$4,750
Total inventory losses (at cost):	
Due to water damage	12,863
Due to theft	4,600
Total losses	$22,213
Less: Insurance payment after $500 deductible	4,550
Amount of casualty loss	$17,663

If additional documentation is required to support this loss, please contact us and we will respond as quickly as possible.

Sincerely,

Figure 19–8
Documenting a casualty loss

Getting Professional Advice

No builder has the time to become a tax expert. It would take months of study to master the complex tax laws and regulations that apply to your business. Instead, rely on trained experts who deal with the tax laws every day. Your cost for hiring this expert advice will be far less than the cost of mastering the law yourself. And, almost certainly, the cost of the advice will be less than what you stand to lose by struggling through without good tax counsel.

This chapter is your introduction to the tax services available. Year-round tax planning and setting long-term goals are essential tools of every growing and prosperous construction company.

Many construction contractors rely on one of the large tax preparation firms. There are many disadvantages to using these services:

1. They are usually trained in individual taxes, and don't have the background to handle the complexities of an incorporated construction company. Questions of fiscal year, inventory valuation, and bad debts are usually outside of the expertise of these specialty services.

2. They are of no value to you unless your fiscal year ends near December. Generally, these tax businesses are not available year-round.

3. The individual who prepares your return probably isn't licensed to represent you in Tax Court in case of a dispute. You would have to hire other counsel.

4. If the IRS disagrees with the results on your tax return, you may have difficulty locating the preparer after April 15. Make sure your tax preparer is going to be around throughout the year.

5. Don't underestimate the importance of year-round assistance. A service that does no more than prepare your return is only taking the final step in the tax-paying process.

6. The same person won't work on your return each year. Familiarity with your specific situation is an important benefit of a dependable tax preparer.

7. The employees are generally paid by the number of returns they prepare, so your work may not receive careful attention.

The best tax planning will be done by a professional who understands your business, your tax problems and your concerns — and is available 12 months of every year. The tax advisor you select should have years of training and should stay

Sales tax payable	**$2,841.15**
Payroll taxes payable:	
Withheld taxes	
State disability insurance	133.09
FICA	1,406.60
Federal withholding	2,638.70
State withholding	674.55
	$4,852.94
Employer taxes	
State unemployment tax	451.00
FICA	1,406.60
Federal unemployment tax	103.40
	$1,961.00
Total payroll taxes	6,813.94
Total taxes payable	**$9,655.09**

Figure 20–1
Taxes payable

abreast of new developments in tax law. Your tax advisor should work full time with tax issues and related financial matters.

The tax-planning process should anticipate your needs. This includes regular reviews of your tax status, the planning of company elections, the timing of capital asset purchases and sales, and the planning of deductions.

Preparing for the Tax Return

Your income tax return is only a report required by law. It simply reports the results of the planning you've done all year. The real work is in the planning, which should be a continual process. That's why I feel it's a mistake to hire a tax expert simply to fill out the return. You need tax-planning advice as much as or more than you need help filling out the form.

The cost of having a tax return prepared varies with the experience and skill of the tax preparer, rates in your community, and how well prepared you are to supply the information needed.

Generally, the more time your preparer wastes hunting for documents and correcting your errors, the more you'll have to pay. Here are some suggestions that may help lower the cost of preparing your tax return.

1. Keep your books accurate and up-to-date. Don't send your preparer records that are incomplete or obviously wrong.
2. Provide good documentation for all unusual and significant items.
3. Have all bank reconciliations completed.
4. Update and balance all subsidiary records. Ask what records will be required before you make your appointment.
5. Prepare a list of accounts receivable. Also prepare a worksheet for all bad debts written off during the year (accrual method), or computed bad debt entries (reserve method).
6. List all taxes payable at the close of your tax year. See Figure 20–1.
7. Provide a copy of inventory sheets, fully extended, added and totaled.
8. List all property abandoned, lost, destroyed, or stolen. Include documentation of the loss. This helps the preparer compare sales and costs to those of previous years.
9. Provide a complete list of accounts payable as of the year-end, by general ledger category. Include photocopies of payable invoices showing receipt or shipping dates and due or payment dates. A classified accounts payable list is shown in Figure 20–2.
10. If your preparer doesn't already have the following documents, provide either originals or copies:
    - Property tax bills
    - Life insurance and casualty insurance payment records
    - Your state and federal quarterly payroll tax returns
    - Your federal unemployment tax returns (Form 940)
    - Estimated tax prepayments made during the year
    - Invoices for major pieces of equipment or property bought during the year

Here are other helpful considerations:

1. Make an appointment to meet as soon as possible after the close of the fiscal year. Every tax preparer prefers to have a little extra time.

| Payable to | Accounts Payable — Year Ending 12/31/94 | | | | | |
	Total	Material	Repairs and Parts	Oil and Gas	Other Amount	Other Description
Abbot Lumber	1,016.35	1,016.35				
Beeman Diesel	362.80			362.80		
Caldron Services	155.00		155.00			
Colling Auto	300.00		300.00			
Dalman Materials	385.00	385.00				
Eagle Quarry	440.86	440.86				
Fenman Lumber	3,208.84	3,208.84				
G. H. Auto Supply	180.65		180.65			
Harris Materials	608.00	608.00				
Jacks & Haines	158.35	158.35				
Kelly Lumber	330.00	330.00				
Layton Hardware	1,608.85	1,608.85				
Macmee Supply	86.80				86.80	Janitorial
Main Lumber	304.18	304.18				
Monty Auto Supply	82.00		82.00			
National Diesel	804.50			804.50		
Perry Distributors	301.30		301.30			
Rasmussen Lumber	223.05	223.05				
Reston & Tilly	90.00	90.00				
Rudolph Cleaners	47.00				47.00	Uniforms
San Antonio Parts	235.00		235.00			
Smith Repairs	40.00		40.00			
Southern Lumber	376.00	376.00				
Tander Hardware	200.00	200.00				
Tesch Oil & Gas	341.75			341.75		
Tom's Electrical	175.00	175.00				
Underman Uniforms	106.35				106.35	Uniforms
Village Lumber	1,007.88	1,007.88				
Wadman Diesel	188.33		188.33			
West Lumber	704.36	704.36				
Total	14,068.20	10,836.72	1,293.95	1,697.38	240.15	

Figure 20–2
Accounts payable

2. Consider a fiscal year change that will coincide with a relatively quiet time in your advisor's schedule. He will be able to devote more attention to your business.

3. Well before the end of the year, review with your advisor any changes in your record-keeping system. Try to anticipate problems before books are closed for the year.

4. If your advisor can't complete a return by the due date, file for the automatic extension before the deadline passes. Of course, you have to estimate the tax due and pay that amount when filing for the extension.

Tax Professionals

Tax professionals have different specialties and backgrounds. You may need to work with several.

❏ Tax Attorney

The tax attorney is a specialist in tax law. He or she is licensed to practice law by your state and can represent you in court, if necessary. He or she can help settle disputes with the IRS or request a private ruling (a letter giving an opinion of a specific tax question or problem). A tax attorney may also be needed to design and install a qualified profit-sharing or pension plan. Good legal advice can help you establish policies that minimize taxes year after year.

Here's an example of how a tax attorney can help. A closely-held corporation wanted to start a program of executive bonus payments at the end of each year. The bonus payments were to be based on profits. The tax attorney offered the opinion that the payments would look like dividends (unreasonable compensation), and might be challenged by the IRS. An alternative was designed to avoid this problem.

❏ Tax Accountant

This individual has an accounting background with an emphasis on taxes. No license is needed to work as a tax accountant. He or she can prepare your tax return and should be able to assist with both short- and long-term planning.

❏ Certified Public Accountant

This professional is licensed by the state and is qualified to perform independent audits of company records. A CPA may also be a tax accountant, and can provide a range of services from bookkeeping to the most advanced tax-planning and business services. A larger construction company may have a CPA serving as a financial officer, accounting manager, or controller.

❏ Unlicensed Accountant

Many competent and talented financial professionals don't hold any particular degree or license. But if you have a dispute with the IRS, an unlicensed professional can't represent you before the IRS or in Tax Court.

❏ Tax Planner and Business Consultant

Anyone can use the title *tax planner*. Many who are in business to prepare and sign tax returns claim that title. Generally, tax planning is worth no more than you pay for it. Beware of tax planning advice offered at no charge by savings and loan institutions, insurance agencies, or real estate offices. It's unlikely that they can offer the level of professional service you need.

Securities salesmen often call themselves tax planners. Some may be fully qualified. But others have little interest beyond selling an investment program that earns them a generous commission. Check their licensing and background. Make sure the services they offer go beyond just selling investment products. Your tax planning needs can't be met by tax shelters alone.

Some large builders need advice from all three categories of tax professional: a tax attorney, a tax accountant and a CPA. But most builders don't need that much advice. It's usually easier and cheaper to work with a tax accountant until you need more specialized help. Then decide exactly what additional services you need and how much you can afford to pay for that help.

Special Situations

The tax professional is indispensable in these situations:

1. IRS audit representation
2. Disputes that go to the Tax Court

3. Major changes in your business (incorporation, formation or dissolution of a partnership, accounting elections)

4. Yearly tax-planning sessions

5. Long-range tax strategy

6. Design of internal systems, procedures and controls

7. Establishing policies for tax records

8. Setting up a subsidiary company

9. Buying or selling a business

10. Getting outside financing

11. Establishing an employee retirement plan

12. Putting together an employee stock option program

Good accounting, budgeting, and business planning require occasional advice from a tax professional. Advance preparation will make the professional's time more productive. Use this service wisely and you'll save more in taxes than you pay in professional fees.

Periodic Meetings

It's a good idea to meet occasionally with your tax advisor. Before meeting, establish an agenda for the discussion. Subjects to cover may include:

1. Designing an executive compensation program

2. Finding outside financing or a line of credit

3. Screening applicants for bookkeeping or accounting positions with your company

4. Declaring a corporate dividend

5. Updating corporate minutes

6. Designing a partnership agreement

7. Finding a data processing system

8. Negotiating or revising a lease contract

9. Reviewing internal systems

10. Revising record retention procedures

Many elections and planning decisions have to be made when setting up a new business. Get off on the right foot by setting up a good accounting system. Help from an accountant or CPA is very important during the first phases of the business. After that, it may be possible to operate without regular tax help for several years. As the business grows and starts to pay significant taxes, tax counsel will again become important.

The Tax Records You Need

Every builder needs a practical, simple, and efficient record-keeping system. This chapter explains how to set up a bookkeeping system that meets your needs *and* IRS requirements.

The best records are not necessarily the most complete records. Saving everything isn't necessary. In fact, the more documents you keep, the more trouble you're likely to have:

1. Finding what you need quickly
2. Using available space efficiently
3. Maintaining files
4. Storing records
5. Distinguishing what's important from what isn't
6. Knowing what constitutes valid documentation

Good record keeping is practical. An elaborate and expensive system isn't worth the effort if it doesn't produce workable and practical records.

Start with the premise that you're going to keep as few records as possible. Do you create file duplicates? Are they really necessary? If you don't need all the reports you're getting now, save only those you must have.

Cash Controls

Records of cash accounts and tax records were discussed in Chapter 11. Every time money comes into your business or leaves your business, some written document should be created and recorded. Organizing and summarizing these documents helps you:

1. Ensure that money is available to pay bills and taxes
2. Safeguard against theft or loss
3. Use excess cash for investments
4. Fully account for cash, both before a deposit and once funds are in the bank

Being able to forecast your cash flow will help you meet tax liabilities and business debts. A good cash forecast can help you:

1. Identify seasonal changes in business volume so you can select a more logical fiscal year.
2. Determine the cash needed to meet tax liabilities
3. Identify the need for more working capital and investment
4. Anticipate the need for outside financing

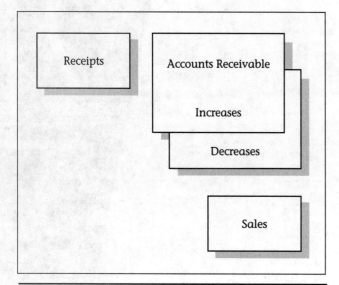

Figure 21–1
Receivable reconciliation

5. Take advantage of discounts
6. Time purchases and sales of capital assets

❏ Receipt Controls

Controls for the receipt of cash should be efficient and consistent, and should create additional documentation for taxes. Good cost controls include:

- Recording the total amount of cash received by mail before payments are applied against accounts receivable. Compare the total received with the total deposited to make sure funds are not being misplaced or delayed.
- Making sure the person who actually handles receivables doesn't also write checks. If possible, have different employees handle cash and keep the books.
- Depositing funds regularly, at least several times a week.
- Separating cash handling and bank reconciliation responsibilities.
- Establishing better records by reducing paper flow.

❏ Disbursement Controls

Your cash account will be a key issue if the IRS audits your return. All cash transactions have to be summarized somewhere on your tax return. The procedures you follow can be both effective and simple. Here are some recommendations that most tax accountants would approve:

1. Use checks whenever possible. Use petty cash as little as possible. Checks make excellent documentation.
2. Require two signatures on checks above a specified amount. This protects you against unexpected or unauthorized payments.
3. Have all checks signed by hand. An imprint of your signature takes away one of your most valuable controls.
4. Keep all voided and returned checks in numerical order.
5. Have documentation for all payments. Keep invoices, vouchers, check requests, and authorizations for payment.
6. Avoid duplication. Don't save copies of hand-written check requests if the company has a file of checks written kept alphabetically by payee.

Accounts Receivable Controls

For cash-basis builders, these controls don't apply for the general ledger or tax record. But good, sensible subsidiary account controls should still be practiced.

On the accrual basis, receipts (increases to the cash account) should be reconciled with reductions in accounts receivable. Sales are reconciled with increases in accounts receivable. See Figure 21–1.

Do an aging list of outstanding receivables every month. This is a good supporting document for write-offs. Records of the computations of bad debts should be kept in a special subsidiary ledger. This would include the computations (reserve method), aging lists, and actual amounts written off. Also include supporting documents of efforts to collect money, such as correspondence with customers owning you money, collection agency reports, records of phone calls, and court proceedings.

Also include any trend analysis which would help to control fluctuations in bad debts.

Keep accounts receivable subsidiary records in balance at all times. An out-of-balance situation throws doubt on *all* your records, and leads to missed deductions.

Inventory Controls

Avoid accumulating stock you don't need or can't return. Every builder has an inventory of materials left over from previous jobs or materials that may be needed on the next job. But keep inventory levels reasonable. Take a physical count occasionally to identify overstock.

Inventory represents money sitting idle. The greater your inventory, the more difficult the task of control, the risk of loss, and the chance for error. Usually it's better to return unneeded items and pay a restocking charge than to let inventory grow stale.

Capital Asset Controls

All capital assets (like heavy equipment or office machines) have to be depreciated over time. You have to identify the purchase price, depreciation and sale price when something is finally sold (or junked). With many purchases and sales occurring over several years, it's easy to lose track of the original purchase price, depreciation claimed, and even what was bought. When the asset is later sold, an excess or incorrect amount of depreciation might be claimed.

Depreciation was greatly simplified by the Economic Recovery Act of 1981. But you still have several classes of recovery property and extended life elections. For the 3, 5, and 10-year classes, all assets bought during the year must be depreciated on the same basis (regular 150 percent declining balance or straight-line on an extended-life basis). The election is made yearly. Precise and complete records are needed. Some suggested controls for capital assets and depreciation are:

1. Estimate your return on investment in capital assets. Estimate the tax benefits of annual depreciation and expensing.

2. Study maintenance costs for each asset. Determine at what point replacement is justified.

3. Keep complete purchase records. These will determine capital gains when you sell the asset.

4. Compute depreciation separately for each asset. Figure 21–2 shows a typical depreciation record.

5. Plan carefully the timing of your purchases.

6. Compute the capital gain or loss before you sell an asset.

7. Decide if new assets could become obsolete.

8. Establish a regular program of preventive maintenance to take proper physical care of an asset.

Accounts Payable Controls

It's as important to control payables as receivables. If your record of accounts payable isn't accurate, there's no way to compute the correct tax liability.

Accounts payable control includes:

1. Computing an accurate total of payables every month. This will ensure accurate financial projections and tax liability tracking.

2. Timing payments to minimize your true cost, and to keep your credit rating and reputation high.

3. Keeping complete documentation that's easily retrieved in an alphabetical file, cross-referenced to the payables and disbursements system.

4. Providing a reconciliation between disbursements and your reported profit and loss. Expenses provide increases to the accounts payable balance as they are incurred; disbursements reduce the balance. This concept is summarized in Figure 21–3.

Notes Payable Controls

Whenever you have an outstanding debt on your books, you must distinguish between the current and long-term portions. These are classified in different accounts in your general ledger, on financial statements, and on the tax return.

The current portion of a debt is the part payable within one year. So a three-year note is originally classified as one-third current and two-thirds long-term. As you pay off the note, the long-term amount is reduced first. Only when it has been entirely reduced will the current part begin to decrease.

Depreciation

Asset No. _____

Page _____ of _____

Asset Description _____

General Ledger Classification _____

Years of Cost Recovery _____ Depreciation Method _____

Purchase Price _____ Purchase Date _____

Year/Month	Amount		Year/Month	Amount		Year/Month	Amount

Year/Month	Amount		Year/Month	Amount		Year/Month	Amount

Figure 21–2

Depreciation record for individual assets

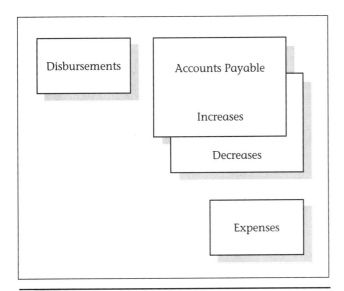

Figure 21-3
Payable reconciliation

This distinction is an important one. It's part of the computation of working capital, current ratios, and inter-account relationships on your tax return. Review current liabilities and current assets to see how well you are controlling working capital from month to month.

Interest is part of each month's payment. The following is a common distribution of an installment:

	Debit	Credit
Current notes payable	$150.00	
Interest expense	13.50	
Cash		$163.50

If interest is applied in equal amounts, your monthly coding will be the same. But if your loan interest is amortized, the amount of interest payment decreases each month as the amount of principal payment increases. If this breakdown is not automatically supplied by your bank or loan company, ask for it.

Other Controls

Know your balance sheet and profit and loss accounts. A monthly reconciliation of all balance sheet (asset and liability) accounts is important. Some of these will already exist (cash account reconciliations, inventory counts), while others are balanced in subsidiary systems (accounts receivable and accounts payable). But the less active accounts should be kept reconciled as well.

An example of an account analysis is shown in Figure 21-4. Note that the details are reconciled each month to the general ledger balance. This is adequate for the fixed asset account. Design each procedure to suit the account and the amount of activity within it.

The longer a balance remains unreconciled, the harder it will be to resolve. Avoid the problem of having to look back many months to find reasons for the problems. Resolve them every month. Unexplained balances indicate poor systems and a lack of controls. This casts doubt on all your records. Don't misuse accounts. Those labeled "suspense" or "items in transit" (and intended to take care of timing differences or deferred items) shouldn't become catchalls for accumulated errors.

Out-of-balance conditions are often due to:

1. Improper code definitions
2. The bookkeeper's failure to understand the system
3. Not following procedures exactly
4. Failure to reverse temporary entries

Inaccurate records lead to undependable estimates of profit and loss. Effective tax planning isn't possible under those conditions.

To clean up the books, look back as far as necessary. Find the original entries that placed the amounts into the balance sheet accounts. Take the following steps:

1. Decide what the proper treatment should have been.
2. Remove items that shouldn't be there. Make sure you catch both sides of a double-entry posting.
3. Eliminate the balance sheet account or install procedures to keep the account current. Make certain these procedures are followed every month. If you keep it active, be sure you use it properly by reversing entries each month.
4. Have your accountant recommend better procedures for monthly coding and analysis.

There are often reasons to analyze or reconcile general expense accounts as well. You may categorize several similar items in one account. But they must be separated on your income tax return. Taxes, for example, may require a supplementary schedule.

Long-Term Asset Analysis — Year: 1994						
	Furniture and Fixtures	Machinery/ Equipment	Autos and Trucks	Small Tools	Total Assets	General Ledger
Balance Forward	4,585.60	124,600.00	63,841.92	3,120.00	196,147.52	
Jan						196,147.52
Feb	600.00		8,130.45		8,730.45	204,877.97
Mar						204,877.97
Apr	455.00		(7,000.00)		(6,545.00)	198,332.97
May						198,332.97
Jun						198,332.97
Jul			11,450.00	800.00	12,250.00	210,582.97
Aug						210,582.97
Sep						210,582.97
Oct		35,000.00			35,000.00	245,582.97
Nov	1,113.04			186.00	1,299.04	246,882.01
Dec						246,882.01
Total	6,753.64	159,600.00	76,422.37	4,106.00	246,882.01	

Figure 21–4

Typical account analysis

You might code expenses in one account which, for tax purposes, would be better if broken into several parts. The account "repairs and maintenance" for example, may include the following expenses, and each may deserve its own line as a deduction:

- Repairs to trucks
- Truck maintenance
- Parts
- Tires
- Equipment repairs
- Equipment maintenance
- Small tools

It's better to show too many details than too few. Showing one extremely large balance invites questions. To overcome this, perform a monthly account summary. Or consider creating new accounts. Be certain that whoever writes checks understands how to code each account you create. This will maintain consistency.

Be sure expense coding is both accurate and consistent. The best system begins with writing an account number on your accounting copy of each check. Someone with the authority to change these numbers (a financial officer) should still review these account numbers to be sure they're accurate before they're posted to your check register.

You may also need to set up some coded expenses as prepaid assets. For example, your bookkeeper might make a three-year insurance premium payment. You are allowed to deduct only this year's portion. The balance is established as a prepaid asset.

The more accurate your coding is, the more accurate your tax return will be. Consistent coding procedures and monthly reviews will give the best possible results.

22

Changing a Tax Year

Most businesses have busy seasons and slow seasons. That's certainly true of most construction companies. If it's true of your company, you can use seasonal changes in business volume to lengthen the period between when profits are earned and when tax is due on those profits. That's like getting an interest-free loan from the IRS. Of course, the fiscal year you select has to be based on sound business considerations. Changing your reporting calendar just to lower taxes isn't allowed.

This chapter explains how to determine your natural business year, the strategies and methods for changing fiscal years, the short years resulting from a change, and the different accounting methods to use throughout the tax period.

You are concerned with three types of years: the calendar year, the tax or fiscal year, and the natural business year.

Many business considerations are tied to the calendar year. Payroll taxes are reported on a calendar-year basis. In most cases, individuals also report and pay taxes on the calendar year.

The fiscal year is the period on which you base your reports to the government and stockholders (if your company is a corporation). You can choose any fiscal year you want, as long as there's a sound business reason for your choice. Some restrictions apply, especially for non-corporate entities. These are discussed later in this chapter.

The Natural Business Year

The natural business year corresponds to a normal activity cycle. Following the end of the cycle, there will usually be a decrease in sales levels, inventory on hand, receivables, and payables. Transactions and business expenses will naturally be at a low.

Ending your fiscal year at a different time in the cycle will have an effect on your income tax. Figure 22–1 shows the relative volumes in key areas of a natural business cycle.

❏ Advantages

There are several advantages to reporting income taxes at the end of the natural cycle, rather than at the end of a calendar year.

Inventory counting: Physically counting inventory on hand is easier when levels are low. Also, you won't interrupt daily business as much. There

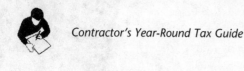

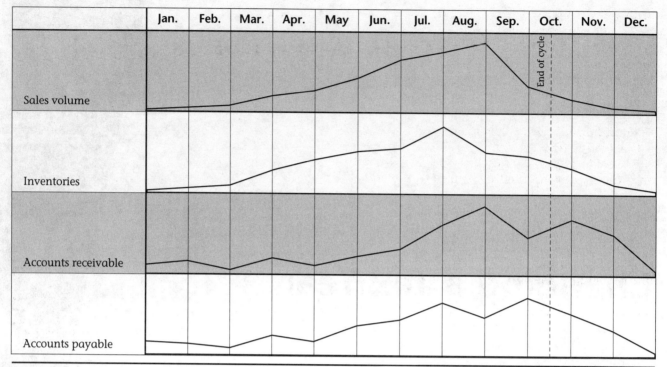

Figure 22–1
The natural business cycle

---

will be fewer counting errors. Employees will have more time.

Outside financing: Banks and loan companies will have a better grasp of your strength and history. A financial statement that interrupts the cycle may give a false picture of how the business is doing. You should establish a year that permits a complete cycle. Of course, this doesn't apply to completed-contract-basis statements.

Annual audits: Audits by independent outside accountants are more easily done if they coincide with your natural business cycle. Income tax return preparation is best performed during an off-time of the year. Accountants do about 80 percent of their business between January and April. This includes:

- annual audits
- annual calendar-year tax returns
- annual payroll reporting (W-2s and unemployment tax returns)
- year-end income reporting (1099 forms)
- on-going responsibilities (bookkeeping, accounting consultation, and financial statements)

- the quarterly or annual taxes (excise taxes, sales taxes, pension and profit-sharing reports, etc.)

Make your fiscal year something other than a calendar year, if that's possible and practical. Your accountant will have more time to devote to your figures. The best time for most builders and most accountants will probably be in early summer or fall.

New procedures: Installing new procedures is easiest at the beginning of your business cycle. This is a natural time to review and modify. Because this is a relatively quiet time in your business cycle, you'll be able to concentrate on these new procedures.

Financial statements: With less volume, your financial statements are easier to prepare and compare. Opinions and estimates are minimized. The accuracy of your closing financial statements is increased.

Year-end tax planning: Tax planners are swamped in November and December. Unfortunately, most tax planning occurs at the last minute. The help that's available is better for a builder that's on a non-calendar fiscal year.

With less activity but a better-than-average cash flow, you can plan with greater flexibility. You also have more time to spend preparing your plan. Corporations can time bonus payments, dividends, and reimbursement of expenses to be beneficial to both the company and the individual employees, officers, and stockholders.

Coordination with other taxes: When selecting a fiscal year, remember to coordinate with other tax considerations. If, for example, you want to end your fiscal year in either August or September, choose September. This way your fiscal year coincides with the end of a calendar quarter.

Fiscal years that end in March, June, September, and December best coordinate with payroll tax returns and workers' compensation annual audits. The quarterly cut-off point makes the preparation of forms like the 1099 and W-2 much more convenient. Figure 22–2 illustrates the coordination between the fiscal year and payroll-related reports.

Comparative analysis: Comparative statements for the middle of a cycle will vary widely each year. Cash flow, inventory levels, accounts receivable, bad debts, and payables all contribute to distortions in the *middle* of the cycle.

When you change a fiscal year, you must go back to the previous periods and identify the end of the cycle. Then, to prepare comparative statements that contain valid and accurate data, you must reconstruct data on the new basis. Trends are only meaningful when comparing one natural cycle to another.

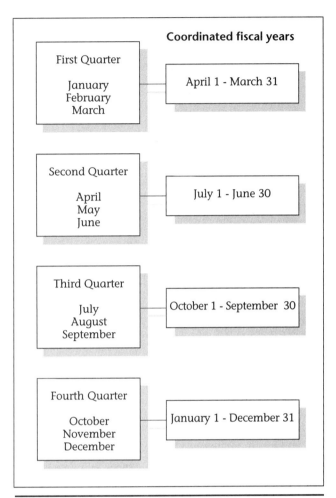

Figure 22–2
Fiscal years and payroll taxes

Changing Tax Years

When a corporation is formed, the fiscal year can be identified in the corporate by-laws. So the first actual year may be anywhere from one to 12 months long.

If a corporation goes a full 12 months without selecting a fiscal year, the election is missed. It's forced to end its year in the twelfth month. It's good tax-planning strategy to review profits and losses from month to month. Then end the year based on those results. Year-to-date losses may be absorbed by upcoming profits. Or quick profits may be absorbed by a following slow period.

To change the fiscal year, you must file for approval with the IRS. Approval by state authorities is usually automatic once you have IRS

recognition. The IRS will approve your request if you present a sound business reason.

Partnerships must get permission for fiscal years other than a calendar year, even when starting out. There must be a good business reason for wanting a different fiscal year. A partnership that can end its fiscal year on January 31, for example, allows its calendar-year partners a full 11 months before they must file their returns. It is a tremendous advantage to know far in advance what taxable income you have. The partners can use exact data for planning. But this is not, by itself, reason enough to justify the new fiscal year requested.

Individuals can apply for a fiscal year other than December 31. But almost all tax matters are geared to December 31:

- annual W-2s and 1099s
- interest and dividend summaries

Net operating income, January through May				$4,318.60
(1) **Annualize the profit**				
$\frac{\text{days in the full year}}{\text{days in the short year}}$	×	short year profits	=	annualized profit
365 ÷ 151	×	$4,318.60	=	$10,439.00
(2) **Compute the tax**				
net profit	×	tax rate	=	annualized tax
$10,439.00	×	19%	=	$1,983.41
(3) **De-annualize the tax**				
$\frac{\text{days in the short year}}{\text{days in the full year}}$	×	annualized tax	=	short year tax
151 ÷ 365	×	$1,983.41	=	$820.53

Figure 22–3

Annualizing in a short year

- pension income summaries
- pension income reports
- interest and taxes on home mortgages
- real estate taxes on your home or personal property

Using an odd fiscal year for your individual income tax return will require much more work. It's harder to get documentation from banks and loan companies on other than a calendar-year basis. You may have to estimate many items. The IRS may be slower in processing your refund.

Taxes in a Short Year

When you change an accounting year, you will have a *short year*. Assume, for example, that a calendar-year builder is granted a change to a year ending May 31. To pay taxes for the January-to-May period, or short year, income is annualized. This process is shown in Figure 22–3.

Application for a change in fiscal year is made on Form 1128. You request permission to change, and give the reason. You don't need permission under the following circumstances:

1. Your tax year hasn't been changed during the last ten years.

2. Taxable income in the short year is at least 80 percent of the year before.

3. The short year doesn't reflect a net loss.

Ending-Day Methods

You must also decide when to end the accounting months. There are several alternatives. You must end your accounting month consistently for several reasons:

1. To get comparable monthly results for analysis

2. For uniformity in accounting and control procedures

3. For ease in closing books and calculating accruals

4. For effective tax planning through dependable data

You may assume that you'll close on the last calendar day, but there may be good reasons to close before or later. You might wish to close two or three business days before the last calendar day, to allow for the input of all transactions. Or it might be necessary to close two or three days after, so that key transactions can be recorded.

The advantages of mid-month fiscal year-ends are often minor when compared to the problems they cause. Here are the reasons to have fiscal months and calendar months coincide:

1. Most builders use the calendar month as their main reference points and cut-off cycles.

2. Customers and vendors almost always operate on a calendar month.

3. Billings between businesses are tied to calendar month-ends.

4. Salaries are usually paid on a per-month basis, coordinated to the calendar year for payroll tax-reporting purposes.

5. Bank statements for corporations are normally created at month end.

The disadvantages of calendar-month reporting are:

■ Months vary in the number of working days. Month-to-month comparisons can be inaccurate.

■ Distortions are caused by weekends and holidays that reduce the number of working days in a month.

The strongest argument favoring the calendar-month reporting method is that it's consistent with common practice.

Monthly Accounting Alternatives

There are some alternatives to the calendar-month system:

13-month year: Each month is 28 days long. That makes a 364-day year. The extra day (or two) each year is used for taking a physical inventory. Each month ends on the same day of the week. This works well for internal controls and closing procedures.

Equal working-day months: Twelve months, each containing 21 working days, conform to the traditional periods in a fiscal year, but allow equal comparisons from month to month. The beginning and ending of each month is established at the start of the year, allowing for holidays (and not counting weekends). You will rarely end a month on the actual last day of the calendar period. The cycles are of the same effective length,

and they are close to those used by customers and creditors. Careful timing is needed for the scheduling of receivables, payables, and payroll.

For reporting to shareholders, you may have to conform to the traditional calendar year. There would be no problem with alternate methods at year-end, since both are 12 months. But interim reports may require adjustment.

Fiscal Years and Personal Cash Flow

For the owner of a closely-held corporation, the selection of a fiscal year will affect both business and personal cash flow. Consider this before choosing your fiscal year. A builder who makes personal tax estimates for both state and federal returns may want to arrange his business year so that liabilities are prepaid in different months.

The selection of the best possible fiscal year isn't a simple matter. The decision will affect all phases of business and tax liability, as well as personal tax planning.

Tax-Year Selection Strategies

Don't forget to consider tax strategy when selecting the tax year for a new corporation.

A calendar fiscal year has the advantage of coordinating with other tax periods, such as payroll and excise tax periods. But it's unlikely that your natural business cycle will correspond with a calendar year.

If, for example, it's management's intention to pay major bonuses to key employees at the end of the tax year, consider ending the tax year early in the calendar year. If the bonuses are paid in March or April, the recipient won't be taxed until April of the following year. If the bonuses are paid at calendar year-end, the recipient will be taxed four months after receipt of the bonus.

If a bonus is paid in December, the recipient doesn't have much time to prepare for the tax consequences of the bonus. But if that bonus is based on corporate profits, it can't be paid until the results of a year are visible. So a fiscal year which ends in March is more convenient for employees who participate in the bonus program.

They have the best part of the calendar year to shelter the extra income or to arrange for estimated tax payments. Also, if those individuals haven't withheld enough during the current year, the delayed extra income may help prevent a sudden financial burden.

If your books are closed and taxes prepared by an outside accountant or tax specialist, consider his schedule as well. An accountant's busiest time of year is the first quarter, from January through March. If your tax year ends in December, you will be one of many clients needing service between January and March each year. But if your tax year ends during your accountant's quiet months, your organization will get more attention.

If your tax year ends in December, many of the tax-planning strategies available may not work as well as when applied to a non-calendar tax year. In December, everyone gets interested in cutting their taxes. Consider the following examples:

1. It may be harder to sell stock at a loss or take profits. December is recognized as a high-volume month for investment decisions affected by tax planning.

2. There's always a last-minute rush in December to establish Keogh plans, and another rush near April 15 to set up IRA trusts.

3. December is a poor time to ask employees to stay late and count inventory for year-end reports.

4. To increase depreciation deductions, many contractors buy new equipment in December. This reduces the number of equipment models that dealers have available, and also delays deliveries. This year-end rush can delay the placement date, resulting in a lost deduction for the current year.

It's always better to plan ahead. But we don't always have the time or foresight to do that. A non-calendar fiscal year can reduce the problems of last-minute planning.

If your tax year doesn't correspond to the calendar year, be prepared to restate payroll tax periods to conform to the required calendar-year reporting. Also be prepared for some inconvenience in responding to worker's compensation audits and union requirements.

Minimize this inconvenience by having your fiscal year end on one of the calendar quarter cycles (other than December): March, June, or September. This way, you isolate an entire quarter, without needing to restate part of one quarter for another purpose.

The Profit Motive

I f your business isn't run to make money — if you don't have a profit motive — you can't deduct business expenses. This chapter explains the basic rules of production of income as the basis for deductions. It discusses the motive to produce profits, and your responsibility to establish that purpose and intent. Chapter 24 will examine deductions in detail.

The Business Purpose

All deductions must have a business purpose. A deduction must somehow produce income. This can be very indirect. For example, expenses incurred to stay in business, maintain goodwill, keep employees happy, or upgrade working conditions do not directly produce profits. But they are necessary to make the business environment suitable for producing profits.

Charitable contributions, membership in civic groups, group health insurance, coffee machine costs, and pension or profit-sharing plans are examples of expenses with a business purpose.

But even if a business purpose is established, you still have to show that it was the motivation for the transaction. Otherwise, the validity of a deduction can be still questioned by the IRS. You may have to prove that tax avoidance was not the primary reason for incurring the expense.

You have the burden of establishing this intent. It's conceivable that the IRS could challenge any deduction you claim. In most cases, the business purpose will be easy to establish. Rent, office supplies, union welfare, and postage are recognized as necessary for all businesses. But an unusual expense could raise the question of intent. You must show how profits can be increased by this deduction.

It's your state of mind at the time of the transaction that establishes true intent. Intent is usually established under the theory that "actions speak louder than words." Most of what you do in business has several possible motives:

1. Buying anything that will increase income (subscriptions, reference books, labor-saving equipment)
2. Actual direct production of profits (entertainment and travel, advertising, telephone)
3. Necessary expenses to stay in business (repairs and maintenance, interest, equipment leases, rent)

4. Tax avoidance (contributions)

5. Employee goodwill (benefit and retirement plans, coffee facilities)

6. Community goodwill (memberships, contributions, donated labor)

A transaction may accomplish two goals at once: one with an established business purpose and intent, and the other for actual tax avoidance. It's the *primary* intent that must be established. As long as tax avoidance isn't primary, the deduction is allowed.

Examples of Intent

Legitimate intent is based on the profit motive. The IRS or Tax Court may consider the following questions:

1. How have profits benefited from the transaction? Have they increased? They don't have to. It's enough to establish the intent to apply new knowledge, facilities, or techniques.

2. How frequently does this type of transaction occur? For example, membership in a local Chamber of Commerce may provide no direct benefit. But you may have felt a pressure to join, because several other well-known builders in your community had done so. This will establish two things: a common practice in the industry, and the desire to avoid pressure or "bad will" for not joining.

3. How is the expense related to the primary purpose of the business? For example, in acquiring a capital asset, what was the purpose of buying it in the first place? Was it to resell to your customers (thus, an inventory item), or for use in your facilities (a capital asset subject to depreciation)?

There are two primary reasons for buying property: either for investment or for resale. If the primary purpose is to resell at a profit, you may not qualify for capital gains treatment. It could be deemed an inventory item based on your primary intent at the time of purchase. If you held the property for several years, as a rental investment, it would be a capital asset, not an inventory item.

Your intent when you borrow money may be very important. Suppose your company borrows money, but you use the borrowed funds personally. The company had no direct business motive, and may not be able to deduct the interest expense. The benefit of these interest deductions may be lost altogether. You must pay self-employment tax on the net profits of a sole proprietorship. A reassignment of the borrowed funds to personal expense will increase net business income and the self-employment tax due.

The MACRS (Modified Accelerated Cost Recovery System) simplifies the issue of intent. The old rules disallowed any depreciation claimed in the year an asset was sold. Now, depreciation periods are dictated by class lives. The concept of salvage values and useful life have been abandoned entirely.

❏ Awareness of Tax Consequences

Awareness of the tax consequences and benefits of deductions can lead the IRS to assume that avoidance is a primary motive. In cases where business decisions were made after consulting with a tax planner, the IRS and the Tax Court have ruled that avoidance was a primary motive.

This doesn't mean that deductions will be challenged just because you seek tax counsel. A qualified tax planner will be aware of the intent and purpose rules, and help you establish legitimate support for deductions.

The IRS takes the position that you must *know* the business purpose in advance of the transaction. Gaining awareness after the fact doesn't qualify the transaction for deduction status.

❏ Business Intent

Below are some examples of business intent for transactions:

Advertising: To pursue an economic advantage, to generate sales, or seek employees. If the ad is political or for lobbying purposes, it won't be allowed.

Automotive expenses: For business use of trucks and equipment. Personal expenses (your family car) are not related to business.

Consulting fees: These are paid to develop efficient or cost-saving systems, to provide business advice in accounting, data processing, or employee benefit programs.

Dues and subscriptions: For trade journals or magazines potentially useful in producing profits or keeping you up to date on legislation or industry trends. Unrelated subscriptions aren't allowed.

Insurance: For business properties and business risks. Personal coverage is not deductible, even if paid through the business. If your home coverage is increased because of business property kept there, the extra amount is a deductible business expense.

Salaries and wages: For labor and office help. It can't be used to compensate shareholders without offsetting services (dividends) or to spread income among family members without a business purpose.

Telephone: For business use. Home phone expenses aren't deductible except for specifically-identified calls.

Here's an example of the distinction between transactions designed to avoid taxes and those with a good business motive:

A builder visited a tax planner who reviewed his situation. The builder revealed he was planning to sell a piece of equipment at a loss, since it had become useless. The equipment had been purchased the previous February. The builder was planning to sell it in March or April of the following year.

The planner pointed out that selling the equipment in November or December would allow a deduction for a short-term capital loss this year, rather than a long-term capital loss the following year. This offered several advantages:

1. The timing could be motivated strictly by tax avoidance. Timing of the sale of assets is a common tax consideration, and does not need to be primarily motivated by other business causes.

2. A short-term loss is 100 percent deductible. A long-term loss saves less tax.

3. A write-off would be especially valuable in the current year, because unusually large profits were expected.

In this case, a sensible and farsighted plan was developed which conformed to IRS guidelines and still reduced taxes substantially.

Here's another example:

A builder in a high tax bracket was advised to incorporate. The tax planner pointed out the many benefits of incorporation:

1. Personal income would not be affected by high profits from operations.

2. Expanded benefit programs (medical reimbursement plan, group health insurance, pension plan) could be provided without increasing taxable income.

3. The builder is protected against civil suits.

4. The option to be taxed under S corporation provisions gives flexibility to the planning process.

The builder opted for incorporation. His primary interest was in continuing his business in the most professional environment possible. He also wanted to pass ownership on to his sons in a few years. The corporate form of organization seemed a sensible way to achieve this goal. The change was made. There were many motives for this change. But a good case can be made to support the business reasons (continuation of the business, benefit plans for the employees, protection against lawsuits). The obvious tax advantages were truly secondary, and the builder had knowledge of the range of advantages before making the change.

Personal deductions are treated very differently from business deductions. In business, the motive is of great importance. But for personal deductions, the validity of the expense is the main concern. Itemized deductions and tax credits of a personal nature are more limited. The motive can be purely tax avoidance. For example, if you purchase a large amount of medical insurance, the premiums you pay are deductible even if you carry more insurance than you need and even if you are motivated only by tax avoidance.

Here are the particularly sensitive areas: home office expenses, travel and entertainment, and advertising. Be ready to support the motive, the amount of the expense, the industry standard, and the timing.

24

Deductions

Y our business expenses fall into two broad categories: deductible and nondeductible expenses. This chapter discusses the most common deductible expenses. Chapter 27 covers nondeductible expenses.

Deductible expenses have to be summarized by category and listed on your tax return. Nondeductible expenses reduce your retained earnings.

Taxable income is reported on your tax return; nontaxable income increases net worth without the loss due to taxes. Taxable and nontaxable income are explained in detail in Chapters 25 and 26. Figure 24-1 summarizes the reporting of taxable and nontaxable income.

The deductions covered here are limited to the common business expenses. Deductions on your personal tax return are far greater in scope. They include medical expenses, some interest expenses, taxes, contributions, and miscellaneous deductions, as well as employee business expenses. None of these personal deductions are discussed in this chapter.

Deductible expenses are listed on these forms:

- for a sole proprietor, Form 1040, Schedule C
- for a partnership, Form 1065
- for a regular corporation, Form 1120
- for an S corporation, Form 1120-S

Here is an alphabetical checklist of typical deductible business expenses for a construction contractor:

Abandonment of property: Some assets become obsolete or lose economic value. You may deduct the lost value of that asset. This can include research and development expenses that are amortized over several years for a project that is later abandoned. When the project is discontinued, the balance of R&D expenses can be written off.

Accelerated cost recovery: The Economic Recovery Act of 1981 provides four broad class lives for all assets, and the election to depreciate over extended periods.

Accounting expenses: Deductible for the preparation of income tax returns, keeping the books, design of internal systems, consulting, and other ordinary and necessary accounting functions.

Accounting texts: Reference books purchased to gain knowledge in bookkeeping, accounting systems, or design and procedures applicable to your specific operation.

Advertising expenses: Connected with generating business or locating new employees. It isn't

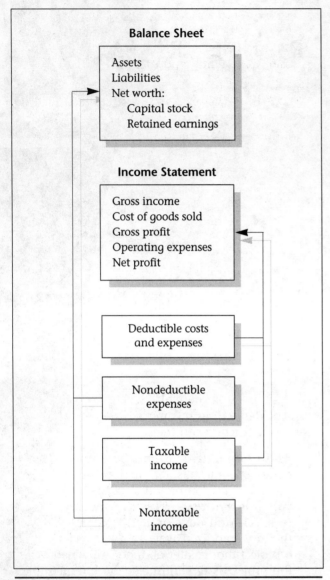

Figure 24–1
Reporting classifications

deductible when intended for lobbying or political endorsements.

Alcoholism treatment: Builders may pay the cost of treatment and rehabilitation as a medical benefit for employees.

Amortization: Improvements, intangible assets, research and development, organizational costs, and prepaid rent or insurance can be amortized.

Answering service: If it's necessary to receive business calls while away from the phone.

Apartment rent: If you travel frequently to a remote job site, the business part of a rented apartment is deductible as a travel expense.

Arbitration fees: Paid to negotiate business disputes.

Architectural fees: May be deducted only if the planned project never advances beyond the planning stages.

Automobile expenses: For autos used for business, even part-time. You can deduct either a standard rate per mile plus parking and tolls, or actual expenses including depreciation.

Bad debts: Deduct business debts that are legal and enforceable. Cash-basis builders can't write off items not previously included as income. Bad debts can be claimed on a case-by-case basis or by using the reserve method. See Chapter 8.

Bank charges: Deduct charges on business accounts, including: monthly service charges, debits for returned items or special services, and charges for having business checks printed.

Bonding fees: Deduct anything paid to protect against unforeseen losses.

Bonuses to employees: Deductible if paid because of outstanding contribution to profits, job performance, or safety achievement. Achievement or length of service awards are deductible if valued at $100 or less, in cash or property.

Books: Deductible when bought to improve or maintain your business.

Breach of contract: Awards and settlements are deductible when paid.

Bribes: Must be legal where they occur, and proven necessary to conduct business. Bribes to government officials are not deductible.

Business gifts: Of $25 or less, or worth $4 or less per unit, can be deducted if they include your business name and are intended for display.

Canceled leases: Deduct payments made to escape or terminate leases before the agreed term has expired.

Capital improvements: Deductible if they increase the value of assets, and are capitalized and depreciated or amortized over the class life of the asset.

Capital losses: If held less than one year, the loss is deductible in full (subject to an annual ceiling of $3,000 per year). If held more than one year, losses are deductible at long-term rates.

Carry-over losses: Net operating losses and tax credits can be carried back or forward.

Cash discounts: Deduct discounts allowed to customers.

Cash shortages: You can deduct losses discovered in general or petty cash fund accounts even if due to theft, loss, or unknown causes.

Casualty losses: Sudden and unexpected losses from natural disasters, accidents, theft, or vandalism. They're deductible to the extent not covered by insurance. This is explained more fully in Chapter 8.

Class action expenses: Expenses involved in filing a class action suit.

Cleaning expenses: For windows, carpets, drapes, and furniture cleaned on your business premises.

Cleaning of uniforms: Cleaning of work clothing that must be worn on the job.

Club dues: Deductible if a sound business benefit can be established.

Collection costs: Deductible when incurred to collect business debts. They can be paid to agencies, individuals, or government agencies (small claims court fees, the serving of a summons, etc.).

Commuting costs: Deductible when associated with moving tools or equipment to the job site. The basic commute from home to work is not deductible.

Compensation: This is the reasonable payment for services provided. It includes salaries and wages, bonuses, incentives, loans that are later forgiven, merchandise given to employees, consulting fees, amounts paid to members of the board of directors (corporations), and fringe benefits. It does not include withdrawals of capital by partners and sole proprietors.

Condemnation: Cost of appraisals, legal work, and engineering fees in a condemnation action.

Contracts: Penalties for nonperformance are deductible. Litigation to form or escape agreements may be deductible or capitalized, depending on the circumstances.

Contributions: Made to the U.S. government or a political subdivision, or to a domestic corporation formed for qualified exempt purposes. They must be cash or property, as explained in Chapter 15.

Conventions: Attendance at conventions for business purposes is deductible. A limited deduction applies to conventions outside the U.S.

Covenants not to compete: Must be amortized over the period of the agreement. A deduction may only be claimed if a payment was made for the covenant.

Credit bureau reports: These are used to check the credit rating of potential or existing customers, vendors or suppliers, or potential business or joint venture partners.

Credit cards: Expenses are deductible when charged, not when the bills are paid (for both cash and accrual-basis builders).

Damage awards: Deductible if paid because of legal disputes. They are deducted when payable or when paid, depending on the accounting method used.

Data processing expenses: Monthly leases of hardware or software, outside systems or programming consulting, other current expenses (supplies, etc.). If you buy the hardware or software, the cost must be capitalized and depreciated.

Delivery and freight: Shipping charges in and out may be costs or expenses, depending upon the nature of the items transferred. (Costs relate to specific projects, while expenses cannot be assigned directly.)

Demolition losses: Deductible as long as the building wasn't purchased with demolition in mind.

Depletion: Applies primarily to mines, oil and gas wells, natural deposits, and timber held to produce income.

Depreciation: As defined in the MACRS rules, you can deduct the depreciation on capital assets.

Director's expenses: Expenses of directors attending board meetings, conventions or seminars, or other company functions are deductible for corporations.

Discounts: Allowed to customers for paying cash.

Dues: Paid to unions, professional societies, trade or community associations.

Educational expenses: Reimbursements to employees as a benefit for courses related to the job. You can also deduct the costs of meeting the requirements of an agency or customer in the performance of a project.

Efficiency awards: Paid to employees as compensation for increasing efficiency on the job.

Efficiency expert: Deduct payments to a consultant paid to analyze and suggest improvements in your business.

Embezzlement: Deductible in the year of discovery. Recoveries are reported as income.

Employee awards: Given for safety achievement or length of service. Amount: $100 or less, in cash or property.

Employee benefits: Qualify if they are reasonable and nondiscriminatory, as explained in Chapter 4.

Employee loans: Deductible as bad debts when not repaid after reasonable efforts to collect.

Employment fees: For placing newspaper or magazine ads, or payment to temporary help or placement agencies.

Entertainment: Must be business-related, supported by full documentation, and reasonable. See Chapter 10.

Estimating expenses: Funds paid for the accumulation of data and preparation of estimates.

Finder's fees: Payments to obtain business or something of value to the business, such as new employees.

Group health insurance: Premiums paid for employees.

Home office: The part of your home used exclusively for business (including rent, depreciation, interest, real estate taxes, fire insurance premiums).

Home telephone: That share identified as business-related.

Improvements: Must be amortized in the same class life as the improved asset.

Individual Retirement Account (IRA): Qualified payments can be deducted. See Chapter 5.

Initiation fees: Such as fees paid for admission to a labor union.

Insurance: Insurance premiums must be deducted over the period of coverage, even if on a cash basis. Coverages which are deductible include:

- automobile
- bonds
- business furniture and equipment
- business interruption
- business papers
- construction or improvement
- credit (losses from business debts not repaid)
- errors and omissions
- fire and casualty
- glass
- group medical and health

- indemnification (against wrongful acts of company executives)
- inventory
- overhead insurance
- public liability
- use and occupancy
- workers' compensation

Interest: Deductible only for business debts in the year it is paid and accrued.

Interview expenses: For screening prospective employees.

Inventory adjustments: Write-downs to cost or market; whichever is lower, is deductible. This includes booking abandonment or loss, disposal due to spoilage, theft or obsolescence.

Investment expenses: If business funds are invested, deduct related investment expenses (broker fees, research publications and books, travel, telephone, bookkeeping, etc.)

Janitorial services: Can be deducted for services on business premises.

Keogh plans: For self-employed builders (sole proprietors and partners), deduct contributions to a qualified plan. See Chapter 5.

Laundry expenses: For maintaining and cleaning uniforms necessary for the job.

Lease payments: For business equipment. See Chapter 13.

Legal fees: Deductible when related to business. They may have to be amortized if the term negotiated exceeds one year (such as fees to negotiate or write a lease, which must be written off over the lease period).

License fees: For permits granted by state and local agencies.

Loan fees (points): Can be deducted if paid solely for the use of money. They are deductible as interest in the year paid.

Maintenance: Deduct anything paid to maintain the life, operating condition, and performance of assets.

Management fees: Paid to individuals or companies managing properties, projects, or subsidiary companies.

Materials: Deducted as a cost of doing business to the extent they are used on projects. Materials in inventory must be reported as assets and are not deducted.

Memberships: In professional or community organizations, when related to business.

Messenger services: To deliver papers or supplies between customers, job sites, or affiliated offices.

Moving expenses: Anything paid for employees to relocate to new premises, or to move the company's business equipment. Also included is the cost to relocate offices, and related expenses such as telephones, new stationery, and public announcements.

Net losses: Must be carried to profitable years, and then can be deducted.

Obsolescence: Deduct losses for abnormal obsolescence on assets abandoned as useless.

Office maintenance: Stationery, drafting equipment, papers, pens, pencils, pads, other office supplies.

Outside services: Accountants, tax advisors and planners, attorneys, and other specialists.

Pension plans: Contributions for employees to qualified plans are deductible as explained in Chapter 5.

Photographs: When used for appraisal, or to document casualty losses.

Physical exams: For employees, if required by a group insurance carrier or as part of their job.

Postage: Stamps, postage machines, special delivery, registered mail, certified mail, and special postage charges related to operations.

Premature withdrawals: Penalties imposed by the terms of Certificates of Deposit for withdrawing funds before the maturity date.

Prepaid interest: Must be amortized over the prepayment period.

Prepaid rent: Cannot be deducted until the due date.

Preparation of tax returns: Deductible for business tax returns.

Profit-sharing plans: Contributions for employees to a qualified plan are deductible as explained in Chapter 5.

Promotions: Deductible if they produce income. (Promotions are a form of advertising intended to draw interest and increase income.)

Ransom: Money paid for the release of a kidnapped company executive or key employee.

Rebates: Payments made to and agreed upon by the customer at the time of the sale.

Referral fees: Paid to get business or locate new employees. These may be paid to employees, but must be included as compensation, and reported to the IRS.

Rent: For business property or equipment. It's deductible only in the year due.

Repairs: On business equipment, if not improved beyond its original use or converted to a new use.

Replacement expenses: For property damaged by negligence.

Reputation expenses: To maintain goodwill or defend against negative impact on your business.

Restitution: Money repaid to customers.

Rewards: Given for the return of stolen business property, for example.

Safe deposit box rental: Deductible if used for keeping business documents.

Salaries: Deduct reasonable compensation paid to employees for services performed. See Chapter 4. Salaries are paid on a monthly or annual basis as opposed to wages, which are normally paid on an hourly basis.

State disability insurance: Deductible if paid for your employees.

State unemployment insurance: Deductible as a payroll tax.

Storage charges: Deductible as rent of facilities or as the cost of transporting storage materials.

Subscriptions: Magazines, periodicals or services providing a benefit to operations.

System costs: To maintain, improve, or develop business systems.

Taxes: On business activity or products. They include: real estate taxes, real property taxes, personal property taxes, state and local income taxes, foreign income taxes, general sales or use tax, excise taxes (on diesel fuel), gasoline taxes, but not federal income tax.

Telegrams: To communicate with business associates, vendors, employees, or customers.

Telephone: Business phone expenses, including automatic message devices and pay phone expenses.

Tenant costs: Real estate taxes and interest paid to a landlord are deductible as rent.

Tips: Deductible while engaged in business activities qualifying for travel, entertainment, or transportation deductions.

Tools: These must be capitalized and depreciated if they have value beyond one year.

Transportation: Expenses qualifying as local transportation are deductible as explained in Chapter 10.

Travel expenses: Must be thoroughly documented. See Chapter 10.

Uniforms: Purchase and maintenance of clothing required on the job.

Union welfare: Payments for the benefit of union-member employees. These are paid to a union for pension benefits, insurance premiums, training programs, strike funds, and assessment. They are deductible as compensation.

Utilities: Gas, electric and water bills on business premises.

Vandalism: Deductible for business property as a casualty loss.

One of your key decisions is deciding how to classify expenses. You need to establish categories under which each expense will be listed. There are a great number of choices. Chapter 29 discusses the classification of costs and expenses.

25

Taxable Income

The income you receive may or may not be taxable income. Classification depends on whether a previous deduction has been taken, whether proceeds of a property sale are reinvested, or the purpose for the payment. This chapter lists the common types of income and discusses the important issue of lawsuit damages.

Taxable Income

Advances: Any advance payment of income without restriction on use (such as the advance receipt of rent) is taxable as income. This does not include security deposits which have to be returned.

Bad debt recoveries: Money recovered on debts that were previously written off as uncollectible.

Business overhead insurance: The proceeds of business insurance received while your company can't do work are taxable because they cover expenses that are generally deductible.

Canceled debts: When someone forgives and cancels a debt, the debtor has received income.

Cancellation proceeds: Money paid when someone wants to escape the terms of a lease. It's taxable income to the recipient.

Capital gains: From the sale of business assets, real property held for investment, or other investments. If assets were held for less than one year, the gain is fully taxed as a short-term capital gain. If assets were held for a year or more, they're taxed at favorable long-term rates.

Commissions: Are taxed when earned, received, or made available.

Compensation: Includes: salaries or wages, consulting fees, contract or project fees, dividends, bonuses, and any other form of pay for services rendered. It's taxed when earned (accrual basis) or when received (cash basis). It's considered to be "received" when funds become available for withdrawal.

Condemnation awards: The gain from conversion of condemned property is taxed as a capital gain. The gain may be deferred by reinvesting in similar property.

Covenant receipts: Funds received under a covenant not to compete are taxed as received.

Damages: Received as settlement in a lawsuit may or may not be taxable income as explained later in this chapter.

Director's fees: Paid to a member of a corporation's board of directors, and considered income for that director.

Discounts on advance payments: Are usually recorded as miscellaneous income.

Discounts received: May be recorded as a reduction of your cost of goods sold or as miscellaneous income.

Expense allowances: Cover necessary business expenses. They are usually recorded as income to the recipient, but are offset on the personal return by actual, supported expenses.

Illegal activities: Profits are taxable even if from an illegal activity.

Independent contracting receipts: Received for outside work.

Individual Retirement Account (IRA) proceeds: Are income when withdrawn. An early withdrawal without penalty is permitted when there is permanent disability or death.

Insurance proceeds for lost rent: Receipts to replace lost rental income are taxable as received.

Interest: From banks, savings and loans, credit unions, labor union funds, government agencies, loans to employees or outside parties, money market funds or other investments is taxable income. This is taxed in the year earned.

Keogh Plan proceeds: Withdrawals upon retirement are taxed as withdrawn. Early withdrawal is allowed in the event of permanent disability or death. Otherwise, penalties are applied.

Liquidation proceeds: When a corporation is liquidated, receipts which are higher than the owner's basis in stock are taxed as capital gains.

Lump-sum distributions: From a pension or profit-sharing plan.

Partnership income: Received by individual or corporate partners is taxed in the year acknowledged by the group, whether withdrawn or not.

Professional fees: If you are paid for consulting services, the income is taxed when earned or received.

Refunds: They're income if deducted in a previous period.

Reimbursed casualty losses: If an expense was claimed and deducted in a previous year, proceeds currently received are taxable.

Rent: Received from rental property, the sublease of facilities or office space, or the rental of equipment and machinery.

Sales: Receipts (cash basis) or accruals for earned gross income (accrual basis) from customers.

State tax refunds: Are reported as current income if the gross tax was deducted in a previous year on federal returns.

Strike benefits: Union members who receive benefits under a strike agreement between the union and the employer are receiving taxable income.

Tax refunds: For excess taxes paid and previously deducted (such as excess gasoline or diesel excise taxes).

Unusual receipts: They include gains from changes in foreign currency exchange, rewards, or unexplainable funds.

Damages Recovered Through Legal Action

You're not taxed on damages received for personal injury, libel or slander. These payments are (in theory) compensation for a loss, leaving you no better or worse than before the loss. As a result, you have no actual gain, hence no taxable income. An exception is made for awards that replace income that would have been taxable if rightfully received in the first place. These payments replace lost income. Examples include the following:

Breach of contract: You sue to recover lost profits. The damage award is, in effect, a replacement of your lost income.

Injuries to the reputation of your business: It is assumed that negative influences have resulted in the loss of taxable income. As such, payments compensate you for the lost receipts and are taxable.

Copyright or patent infringement: A copyright or patent is a right which can produce profits. So a damage suit for infringement is brought to replace the lost taxable income.

It's possible for judgments to have taxable and nontaxable portions. For example, a settlement may consist both of slander (nontaxable) and damages for injury to the business reputation (taxable). Personal damages (nontaxable) may be combined in one settlement with breach of contract damages (taxable).

Other Special Situations

There are many examples of income that may or may not be taxable. It depends on the circumstances, definition, and timing. Insurance settlements may be taxable if a deduction was taken for the claimed loss in a previous year. For example, repayment of medical costs, under a group medical policy, may cover itemized deductions. Or, in the case of casualty losses, a reimbursement in one year may be taxed if a deduction was taken in a previous year.

For both accrual and cash-basis builders, recovery on bad debts is taxable. For the accrual-basis builder, a bad debt deduction would have been taken in the past. For the cash-basis builder, neither the original income (receivable) nor a deduction for the bad debt were claimed in the past. A recovery is current income in this case.

However, if you have written off as a bad debt an amount loaned to an employee and then the debt is repaid, the recovery will be taxed in the year it is received.

When reimbursements are received, they are taxed as income (or reduction of expense) when recorded. If the original deduction occurs in the same year, there are two possibilities:

1. Record the reimbursement as miscellaneous income, offset by the original deduction.
2. Use the reimbursement to eliminate the amount of the deduction. The advantage of this is that it eliminates two unusual items on the income statement. They both could be considered extraordinary and might raise questions. Whenever possible, simplify the reporting of income and loss. But do this in a way that does not distort your income and expense statement.

26

Nontaxable Income

Not all income is taxed. This chapter discusses the common types of tax-free income.

Annuities: The amount you receive as repayment of your original cost is a return of capital. A Keogh payment is always taxed, since you received a deduction at the time of contribution.

Appreciated values: The original cost of assets is used for depreciation. None of the appreciation is taxed, even if you pledge the asset to get a loan. No tax is assessed until the asset is sold or exchanged.

Bad debt recoveries: If the original bad debt didn't reduce income, the recovery is not taxed.

Borrowings: Proceeds of a loan are not taxed, just as repayments aren't deductible. Keep accurate records on loans. You might be required to substantiate your bank deposits. If you can't, the difference could be assumed to be taxable income.

Capital: The return to you of your original investment, whether in your own company or another, is not taxed. Any appreciation is a capital gain. Losses are treated as capital losses. But the return of your original investment sum is tax-free.

Casualty insurance: Proceeds from a claim aren't taxed, although they might have to be used to reduce a claimed loss.

Checks held: These are not taxable income. If the funds aren't there to cover a check, you haven't received income.

Checks for partial payment: May be taxable, even if you have refused to cash the check because a larger amount is claimed.

Damages: Some types are nontaxable, as explained at the end of Chapter 25.

Disability benefits: From either a state or a private insurance program are nontaxable.

Disaster relief: Grants paid to victims of natural disasters under provisions of the Disaster Relief Act of 1974 are not taxable.

Dividends: Not taxable if received from a corporation without accumulated earnings. Insurance dividends which are a reduction of your premium cost are not taxable.

Exchanges: Property exchanges can be tax-free if they are properly structured. See the discussion later in this chapter.

Federal tax refunds: Income tax overpayments that are refunded, applied, or carried over are not taxed. Also, operating losses and credits applied against liabilities do not create taxable income.

Foreign income: Is not taxed if it's earned in a country that has a tax treaty with the U.S. This avoids double taxation.

Gifts: Are not taxed to the recipient.

Health insurance payments: They're tax-free, but may reduce itemized deductions if reimbursements are for expenses claimed on your tax return.

Improvements: If your tenant's work increases the value of your property, the improvements may be tax-free. However, if the improvements are performed in lieu of rent payments, they are taxed as ordinary income.

Income earned outside the U.S.: Can be excluded if you live in certain areas. Excess foreign living expenses can also be deducted.

Income in dispute: Is not taxed until the dispute is settled

Income in escrow: Is not taxed until you receive it. Escrow funds being held until job completion are not taxable income until received.

Inherited property: Is not taxed at the time it is inherited. It will be taxed when sold. However, the tax basis is determined by the value of the property back at the time it was inherited. Only the amount above the basis is taxed (as a capital gain).

Interest: Not taxed as income when earned on tax-exempt bonds and tax-free savings accounts.

Mutual fund dividends: Are not taxable if identified as return of capital.

Reductions in the purchase price of property: Do not produce taxable income.

Security deposits: When held for return to tenants, are not taxed as income unless they are not returned.

Stock dividends: Are subject to both individual and corporate exclusions. Only part of dividends received by corporations will be taxed.

Workers' compensation payments: Are not taxable.

Tax-Free Exchanges

The tax status of many types of income depends on the circumstances surrounding the transaction. When you trade one property for another, it can be set up as tax-free exchange. This defers any tax until a subsequent sale.

This rule applies to equipment and machinery, investment real estate, replacement property following condemnation or destruction, and the transfer of property to a corporation in exchange for stock.

For example, suppose you have property that originally cost $80,000 and you exchange it for property worth $120,000. The basis (in a tax-free exchange) of the new property is adjusted to $80,000. The gain won't be recognized until a taxable sale is made of the new property.

Original cost	$80,000
Current value	110,000
Unrecognized gain	$30,000
Tax-free exchange:	
New property's value	$120,000
Basis	80,000
Deferred gain	$40,000

When you transfer property to a corporation in exchange for corporate stock, a tax-free exchange can occur as long as you own 80 percent or more of the stock.

Here's another example. Two builders form a partnership and invest in the following assets:

Equipment and machinery	$82,000
Commercial real estate	392,500
Total	$474,500

Two years later, the partners form a corporation. At that point, the assets have increased in value:

Description	Current Value	Original Cost	Unrealized Gain
Equipment and machinery	$94,300	$82,000	$12,300
Commercial real estate	455,000	392,500	62,500
Total	$549,300	$474,500	$74,800

The two builders, together, must own at least 80 percent of the stock in their new corporation. Then they can engage in a tax-free exchange. The basis of corporate assets will be the original cost to the partnership.

Several years later, all assets are sold. Capital gains (without consideration for depreciation) would be:

Description	Sale Price	Original Cost	Taxable Gain
Equipment and machinery	$135,000	$82,000	$53,000
Commercial real estate	488,950	392,500	96,450
Total	$623,950	$474,500	$149,450

A tax-free exchange isn't necessarily an advantage. If you're holding property that has decreased in value (normal wear and tear on vehicles and machinery, for example), a tax-free exchange causes you to lose write-offs. A capital loss, which you could take individually, is deferred to a corporation which may not use it for years.

In the example above, assume that an asset has a value below the original basis. In this case, the original partners will lose current write-offs in a tax-free exchange when incorporating. If the new corporation won't benefit for several years from such a loss, the partners should structure the deal to take the loss before incorporation. Your tax advisor will help with this.

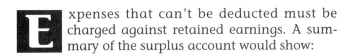

Nondeductible Expenses

xpenses that can't be deducted must be charged against retained earnings. A summary of the surplus account would show:

- Beginning balance
- Plus: net income
- Plus: nontaxable income
- Less: nondeductible expenses
- Less: dividends paid

Here is a list of the more common nondeductible items:

Accident losses: If you use a company automobile for nonbusiness purposes and have an accident, you probably have a nondeductible expense.

Accruals: Not deductible in the year accrued if they're not paid within 75 days after year-end.

Acquisition costs: Must be capitalized as part of the basis in the fixed asset.

Assessments by labor unions: Payments by members for health benefits, when members pay premiums for coverage as part of a labor contract.

Assessments on property: Local assessments (such as sewer or road improvements) that increase the value of your property are added to your basis.

Automobile expenses: Not deductible when used for personal use, such as commuting to and from work.

Bad debts: On receivables, they aren't deductible for cash-basis builders. Only those receivables previously reported as income can be taken in the proper year.

Bank charges: For your personal account.

Bribes: To U.S. Government employees or officials.

Broker commissions: Must be added to the purchase price of investments, and deducted from the selling price of securities.

Capital assets: Must be depreciated over the proper class life. A deduction may be taken under the expensing election rule, subject to annual limits.

Casualty losses: Losses such as termite damage, investment losses not due to natural causes, water erosion, dry rot, rust or corrosion, or losses resulting from your own negligence.

Club memberships: Can be deducted only if used exclusively for business purposes. This is hard to establish in many cases.

Commissions on real estate: They adjust the base price of property and can't be taken as an expense when paid.

179

Commuting expenses: Considered personal and nondeductible. But the additional cost of transporting tools or equipment on that commute is deductible if carrying tools is a requirement of the job.

Compensation: Not deductible if it isn't actually made available to employees. For example, you give an employee a check in the last week of your fiscal year, but tell him he can't cash it for two weeks. The funds aren't available. That employee hasn't received the payment, and you don't have a deductible expense in that year.

Compensation that is unreasonable: Compensation can't be deducted if the IRS rules that it is above a reasonable amount. Unreasonable compensation paid to a stockholder might be construed to be a dividend, thus subject to double taxation (as corporate profits and as income to the recipient).

Construction costs: May be deducted only as related to job progress and income received or accrued. Under the percentage-of-completion method, costs are realized to the extent that the job has progressed. Under the completed-contract method, none of the construction cost can be deducted until the job is completed and accepted.

Contributions: To unqualified groups, including political parties or organizations, lobbying groups, special-interest scholarship funds, professional or fraternal organizations, schools and hospitals that are in business to make a profit, civic groups, labor unions, social clubs, or groups providing you something in return for your contribution. Corporations can accrue contributions in some circumstances. These must be paid in cash or property within 75 days after year-end. Otherwise, only cash-basis contributions can be deducted.

Damages paid: For libel or slander, negligent personal use of a company automobile, breach of promise, or defamation of character.

Debts of others: If you pay voluntarily.

Decreased values: Not deductible until the property is sold, exchanged, abandoned as useless, demolished, or lost through casualty or destruction.

Depreciation: Personal assets may not be depreciated for tax purposes.

Dues and subscriptions: For personal use.

Entertainment: If you can't prove the business nature of the expense, entertainment expenses will be disallowed.

Exempt income expenses: Any expense connected with the production of tax-exempt income. For example, you can't deduct the fees paid to purchase or sell tax-exempt bonds.

Federal income taxes: Payments of liabilities or advance deposits of future taxes.

Fines: Payments for violations of law.

Foreign taxes: Not deductible when a tax credit is also claimed to avoid double taxation.

Gifts: Above $100 per occurrence per year, or of a personal nature.

Hobby losses: The expenses or operating losses of a hobby aren't deductible. Any business can be called a hobby if it doesn't produce profits after a reasonable amount of time. The burden of proof, as always, is on you to show that you are running a business and not a hobby.

Home expenses: Payments to or for a family member for clothing, food, or shelter, or use of part of your home for a business purpose.

Improvements: Must be amortized over the class life of the asset improved. In cases of leased property, this period will normally be the term of the lease. For owned buildings, it will be the remaining class life of depreciation.

Insurance premiums: For personal assets, your residence, the lives of executives, key employees, or yourself.

Insurance prepayments: Even for the cash-basis builder, premiums are deductible only in the period of coverage. Prepayments must be capitalized and amortized over the period of coverage.

Interest: On someone else's liability, on money borrowed to invest, on a debt that is not enforceable, on notes that are really gifts, and on taxes that are past due.

Living expenses: Are not deductible except as part of an allowable travel deduction while away from home on business.

Losses: On illegal transactions or sham sales, or on sales to family members. Distinguish between illegal *transactions* and illegal *activities*. An illegal transaction would be a bribe or kickback to a U.S. Government official. But expenses that are ordinary and necessary are deductible, even if the activity is illegal. The courts have allowed drug dealers, for example, to deduct travel and the cost of merchandise.

Organizational costs: These are costs necessary to prepare to go into business. They're not current operating expenses. Organizational costs must be capitalized as assets and amortized over a period of time (commonly five years).

Penalties assessed by the IRS: For delinquent taxes or returns.

Reference libraries: Must be depreciated over a class life as a capital asset if they have a use beyond one year. Small purchases may be written off within a reasonable minimum as company policy.

Rent advances: Prepayments of your rent can't be deducted until the period in which rent is due.

Repayment of loans: Are not deductible, just as loan proceeds are not taxable.

Sewer taxes: Must be added to your basis in the property.

Social Security: Self-employment taxes and taxes withheld from your employees' paychecks aren't expenses.

Taxes: When paid on sales, they can't be deducted. Payments to the state agency are not deductible. If you include sales taxes in gross receipts, payment of those taxes reduces income.

Travel: To investigate potential business sites or properties for investment can't be deducted.

Uniforms: Are not deductible if they can be worn away from the job. A deduction is allowed only for clothing specifically required during your work.

Withheld taxes: Payroll taxes withheld from your employees' checks are liabilities. They are subsequently paid to the federal, state, or local government. Withholding for insurance or union benefits should not be considered a deduction, but rather a transfer of funds to an outside source.

28

Inventories

Most builders have at least some inventory on hand awaiting installation on a job (or left over from a previous job). Tax law requires that you consider this inventory an asset. But there are many ways to calculate the value of your inventory. And how you calculate the inventory cost can have a major impact on the taxes you pay.

This chapter discusses the tax considerations of inventory, and explains how to minimize taxes without increasing the burden of managing your inventory.

You aren't required to keep an inventory of items that don't go into a salable product, or that aren't held for installation. For example, if you buy a three-year supply of letterhead stationery, you can take the entire cost as an expense in the current year. This isn't considered inventory.

Items that must be kept as inventory can't be treated as an expense until they are installed or sold. These items, in many industries, fall into four classifications:

Finished goods: Inventory items that are ready for installation or sale in their present form

Work in progress: Goods that are partially ready for resale, to be finished at a later date. For example, cabinets that are partially constructed, but not yet sanded and stained, would be work in progress.

Raw materials: Materials purchased for use in a finished product. When the inventory of raw materials is counted, the materials are still in their original form. Nothing has been done to them yet.

Supplies: Directly-related accessory items necessary to prepare products for resale.

At the time an inventory is counted, it should include everything in your possession, and any goods in transit for which you have received title.

It might not be necessary to make a distinction between different types of inventory. If you aren't involved in manufacture for resale, you probably have only one class of inventory — finished goods — and don't need to concern yourself with the other three types.

Recording Inventory

If you keep an inventory of merchandise for resale, you must report on the accrual basis. The level of inventory on hand is taken into account at the beginning and end of your tax year. The net change affects your net income.

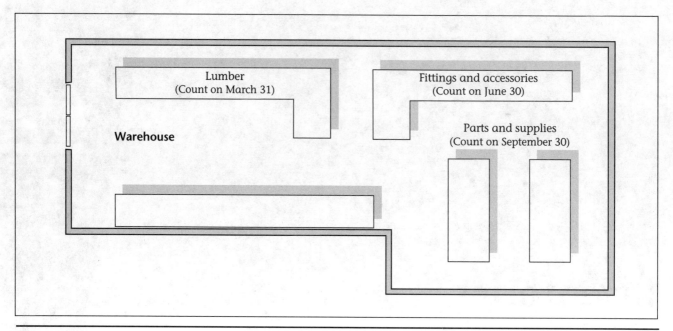

Figure 28–1
Revolving physical count

If your inventory is greater at the end of the year, you have invested in inventory. The money invested isn't totally deductible. Part of it reduces the cost of construction. If your inventory level has decreased by year-end, you will receive a higher deduction for purchases than the amount actually paid or accrued. Part of the inventory must be applied against profits in the current year.

Cost of Goods Sold:	Net Change
Beginning inventory	—
Plus: purchases	—
Plus: other direct costs	—
	—
Less: ending inventory	(—)
Cost of goods sold	—

There is no incentive for overbuying. It only puts a burden on your cash flow and reduces efficiency. High inventory reduces available storage space, increases time needed for counting, and invites risk of loss from obsolescence or damage.

Inventory presents a special problem for tax planning. If your inventory changes seasonally, it's hard to judge your true profit or loss. You must take the change into account, or estimates of your performance will be greatly misleading.

To overcome this problem, track inventory levels. Knowing approximately what you have on hand will improve estimates. To maximize cash flow, minimize inventory. Identify and move dead stock, and arrange remaining items logically and safely.

❏ Make a Revolving Count

If an inventory problem can be narrowed to a specific inventory item, you can increase accuracy by taking physical counts of this item only. Make physical counts on a revolving basis. Count a quarter of your stock every two or three months, breaking out various classifications by location and type. This procedure will highlight problem areas. At the end of the tax year, take a full physical count and save complete documentation for tax record purposes.

The revolving count is illustrated in Figure 28–1. For inventory-counting purposes, builders usually have three types of stock:

- lumber
- fittings and accessories
- parts and supplies

Larger items will probably be closest to the delivery gate. The different types of stock should be segregated and enough space should be allowed for easy passage.

The records you keep must be in line with business standards. Tax regulations don't spell out how or what kind of records you must keep. But your system should support your claim about inventory levels and valuation basis. The final result must accurately reflect your true income or loss.

Inventories are important because of your investment and your income statement. Inventory is an exception to the standard tax rule. An inventory item held for resale can't be deducted even if it is an ordinary and necessary business expense.

Inventory Valuation Methods

There are several ways to set the value of your inventory. The method you choose has a major effect on taxable income. The right system for your business depends on the economic conditions, your volume of purchases, and whether inventory is growing or declining.

❏ The Cost Method

This is the simplest way to value inventory. All items on hand at the end of the year are valued at their original cost, even though the market value may have changed.

The cost method won't be accurate when the market value changes. You may have stock worth considerably more or less than the listed value. The cost method does provide two tax benefits:

1. It's easier to keep records on the cost basis. This is especially true in a market where costs change rapidly.
2. It lets you judge margins on items bought for resale. Changes in your supply cost are viewed as a factor of doing business. In a market where the costs have increased, you make a profit on your investment in inventory. If market values have declined, the loss carries through as a cost factor.

The cost method of inventory valuation gives a misleading impression when market prices go up or down. Failing to recognize the change in value tends to distort income. Current retail prices could have no relation to what you paid. Profit on a specific job may depend more on the market prices for some material than on the accuracy of your construction estimate. This is especially true for materials such as lumber or copper wire that may increase or decrease in value by 10 percent or more in a week.

❏ The Lower of Cost or Market Method

Gains or losses on an investment are taxed only as realized. The lower of cost or market value method provides an exception to this rule. In cases where the market value is lower than your original cost, items still in inventory are marked down to their current market value. A loss is recorded by showing lower gross profits on each job.

Cost is the actual price you paid for goods that are still in inventory at the end of the year. It includes freight and other costs necessary to get the items to you.

If you manufacture goods for resale, cost includes materials that go into the finished product, plus the cost of necessary supplies, direct labor on the product still in stock, and indirect expenses and manufacturing costs assigned to the product. For example, part of management salaries and depreciation on manufacturing equipment may be included as part of inventory cost. The cost of inventory has to reasonably reflect the true cost of manufacture.

Market is the current bid value as of the inventory date. You may pay different prices, depending on quantity. The market is the current bid price in the quantity you normally purchase. Consider this typical pricing scale:

Cost per item
$16.00 each
$15.25 for   50 to 100
$14.75 for   101 to 500
$13.50 for   501 to 800

If you normally buy 200 to 300 units, the current market value is $14.75 per unit, regardless of how many you have in stock.

When there's no way to tell what the current market price is, you must estimate it. Be sure to use a method that can be supported in case it's questioned by the IRS.

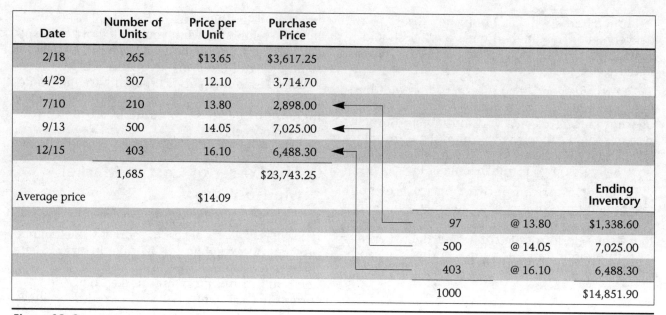

Date	Number of Units	Price per Unit	Purchase Price			Ending Inventory
2/18	265	$13.65	$3,617.25			
4/29	307	12.10	3,714.70			
7/10	210	13.80	2,898.00 ←			
9/13	500	14.05	7,025.00 ←			
12/15	403	16.10	6,488.30 ←			
	1,685		$23,743.25			
Average price		$14.09			97 @ 13.80	$1,338.60
					500 @ 14.05	7,025.00
					403 @ 16.10	6,488.30
					1000	$14,851.90

Figure 28–2
FIFO illustration

For example, if you have items in stock that have been discounted, you can use recent purchases as your basis. If you are offering to install discontinued items at a discount, you can use your price as the current market value. Support for the value would be similar recent sales you have made. Actually, selling the goods is the strongest possible support for a discounted valuation.

The market value of inventory on hand doesn't always mean the prevailing rate. First, there may be no active market. Second, you may need to move unneeded stock quickly. Market value can vary regionally. It may be based on what you can get at a certain time under certain economic conditions.

When using the lower of cost or market method, each item is valued individually. On some items, cost may be higher than market; on others, it may be lower. The lower of the two bases is always the one to use.

❏ The First In, First Out (FIFO) Method

This basis for valuation assumes that the earliest purchases of items are the earliest sales. It also assumes that the latest price paid applies to all items still in inventory.

FIFO, which adjusts to changing markets by reflecting the most recent prices for items still on hand, is illustrated in Figure 28–2. Although the average price of items is $14.09 through the year, the final inventory is valued at the latest price paid. The average price for the ending inventory is $14.85 per unit.

❏ The Last In, First Out (LIFO) Method

This method assumes that the latest purchases of items are the earliest sales. It also assumes that for older items kept in stock, the original prices apply, regardless of current market values.

When prices rise, LIFO gives you a tax advantage. The true value of inventory increases, without being taxed. In the lower of cost or market method, a changing market affects the profitability of specific current jobs using older stock. Under LIFO, the original inventory value is maintained while its true market value has grown.

Figure 28-3 illustrates LIFO. The FIFO method resulted in a closing value of $14.85 per unit, but LIFO holds the valuation down to $13.29.

If you use the LIFO method on your income tax return, you must also use it on financial statements for loan applications, for stockholders or business partners, and for consolidated statements

No. of Units	Price per Unit	LIFO Value
265	$13.65	$3,617.25
307	12.10	3,714.70
210	13.80	2,898.00
218	14.05	3,062.90
1,000		$13,292.85

Figure 28–3

LIFO — Ending inventory

between parent and subsidiary companies. The election to use LIFO is made by filing Form 970 with your tax return. You must include an analysis of your inventory. The election must be approved by the IRS. Once made, this election can't be reversed unless the IRS allows (or requires) a change.

What You Can't Do

There are a few basic rules about inventory. You can't:

1. Ignore some of the inventory actually on hand.
2. Count stock in transit when you don't hold title.
3. Deduct a reserve for depreciation on inventory.
4. Take a deduction for a reserve against the effect of price changes or unexpected losses.
5. Count inventory at less than its current value under the method in use.
6. Change methods from one year to another without IRS consent.

The IRS can compare your gross profit and cost of goods sold to detect unexplained changes in inventory levels. There are cases where stock will be eliminated or written down legitimately. Be sure to document any unusual adjustments to inventory.

Writing Off Inventory

Writing off or writing down inventory occurs in three cases:

1. In the lower of cost or market method when market value is lower.
2. To reflect inventory shortages discovered when you take a physical count or learn of losses.
3. When stock is abandoned due to damage or destruction, or sold for scrap below market value.

When using the lower of cost or market method, you must actually compute both. You can't estimate or base your valuation on percentages of cost.

If you adjust the inventory value down to market value and later sell items at the original cost, you must prove that prices fluctuated enough to support your valuation.

Shortages are deductible. But this is normally done by showing the actual (lower) ending inventory. This has the same effect as a deduction.

When you have goods that can't be sold, their value is zero. A complete write-down eliminates them. This can result from obsolescence, damage, wear and tear while in storage, broken lots, or vandalism. When these goods can be sold for salvage, use a reasonable estimate as the inventory basis.

Inventory becomes unsaleable if your customer backs out of the deal and you can't find another use for the materials. If you have worthless inventory, a write-down is allowed in the year it becomes worthless.

29

Accounting Entry Classifications and Taxes

O ne of the most important tax considerations is the proper coding and classifying of transactions. A good account-classification system followed consistently makes documenting your expenses easy and quick.

Every time you write a check, the amount paid should be charged to some numbered account in your bookkeeping system. All similar expenses should be charged to the same account. Your first job is to establish logical account categories that make tax documentation and cost recording easy. Then you have to follow up by enforcing the classification system you've established.

Benefits

Here are the benefits of following a good account-classification system:

1. Yearly comparisons of each account classification will help you control expenses and spot trends. Comparisons are meaningless if you don't select the classifications carefully and follow them consistently.

2. Distortions are avoided, so anyone evaluating your business (such as a bank loan officer) can get a true picture of your financial condition.

3. Proper coding will avoid IRS audits. If a sensitive account is suddenly increased, the IRS may question your deduction. If some items were coded improperly, it will cast doubt on your entire system.

4. The difference between direct costs and general expenses must be well understood, and each category must be correctly assigned. Otherwise, yearly variances in gross profit might raise questions at your bank or with the IRS. It's impossible to judge the quality of your financial reports without proper classification of transactions.

5. Well-defined accounts help your employees code all expenses. A clear and concise chart of accounts is one of the best control tools any construction contractor can have.

10 - Assets	
1100-1199	Current Assets
1300-1399	Long-Term Assets
1500-1599	Prepaid or Deferred Assets
1700-1799	Other Tangible Assets
1900-1999	Intangible Assets
20 - Liabilities	
2100-2199	Current Liabilities
2300-2399	Long-Term Liabilities
2500-2599	Deferred Liabilities
2700-2799	Other Liabilities
2900-2999	Other Credits
30 - Net Worth	
3100-3199	Capital Stock or Equity Accounts
3300-3399	Paid-In Capital
3500-3599	Retained Earnings
3700-3799	Draw Accounts (Non-corporations)
3900-3999	Nondeductible Expenses
40 - Income	
4000-4999	Income Categories
50 - Direct Costs	
5100-5199	Materials Purchased
5300-5399	Direct Labor
5500-5599	Freight and Shipping
5700-5799	Outside Labor and Subcontracting
5900-5999	Other Direct Costs
60 - Selling Expense	
6000-6999	Expense Categories
70 - General Expenses	
7000-7999	Expense Categories
80 - Other Income	
8000-8999	Income Categories
90 - Other Expenses	
9000-9999	Expense Categories

Figure 29–1
Chart of accounts design

Your employees must understand the classifications that apply to them. Use a chart of accounts that is arranged logically, as shown in Figure 29–1.

Also define what should be included in each account, detailing the account location on your financial statement, in the general ledger, and any special handling required. An account definition is shown in Figure 29–2. The code includes number, name and statement location.

Common Flaws

Virtually every coding system has potential problems. Some are minor. Others will be chronic and can lead to serious tax and accounting problems. All of these can be overcome if you follow a few basic rules. I'll point out some common flaws found in coding systems.

If more than one employee codes transactions, your system probably has inconsistencies. Review one month's coding to see how serious the problem is. Point out the errors for your employees so that they can correct and avoid them.

Even with one employee doing the coding, there will be problems. Many coding decisions involve judgment. Even identical transactions may be coded differently. Your written explanation of each account should resolve as many ambiguities as possible.

Sometimes similar transactions are coded to an expense category one month and a direct cost category the next month. A delivery charge may be lumped with a material cost (direct cost) or with a subcontracting cost (expense). Guard against this by being specific in account definitions, and establishing guidelines for specific costs.

If you find certain accounts are mishandled every month, the problem is probably in the definition. Make sure your employees know the difference between an expense and a cost. And make sure that costs and direct expenses are assigned to the right job.

Several accounts are often misused. These include travel, office supplies, and miscellaneous. When an employee isn't sure of a transaction, the temptation is to dump it into a catch-all account. As a result, this category ends up with a lot of items that belong elsewhere. The more this happens, the harder it is to correct. It requires a detailed analysis of the account, and instructing the employees to avoid repeating the error.

Be especially thorough in defining the problem accounts. Avoid posting costs to the account titled "Miscellaneous." Only a few insignificant transactions should go into this category. If similar trans-

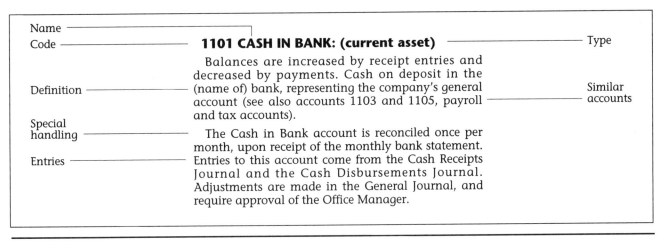

Figure 29–2
Account definition

---

actions end up in the miscellaneous account each month, create a new account.

If you have an account to eliminate offsetting entries, be especially careful. Commonly called the *suspense account*, it's intended for items that will be canceled out by an offsetting entry within a short time. If the two sides of the entry occur in different months, you will have a balance in the suspense account at month-end. You can generally reverse it out the next month. This suspense account is appropriate for handling returned checks and other bank charges (especially if you believe there is a bank error).

The suspense account is often misused and becomes difficult to correct. Be sure that all entries are being reversed out within several months. Make correcting entries when the matter is cleared up. For example, the bank was in error and they correct their records, or they were right and you correct your cash records.

Analyze all asset and liability accounts to make sure that errors aren't being carried from one month to the next. You already analyze some accounts regularly:

- Cash (monthly bank reconciliations)
- Accounts Receivable (subsidiary system)
- Inventory (physical counts)
- Long-term Assets (equipment record)
- Accounts Payable (subsidiary system)
- Taxes Payable (quarterly filing and balancing)

Some accounts don't need to be examined monthly, because there is little activity or trans-

actions are limited to one entry. A *deposits account* for rent, telephone, and utility deposits, will have little activity. But you should know exactly what makes up the balance. Prepaid insurance has one journal entry per month to amortize the total. Again, be sure you know how much is in the account for each amortization, how long it has to go, and when to stop the monthly journal entry.

When you complete a tax return, review your chart of accounts. Eliminate accounts that have little activity. The fewer you keep, the easier it is to control balances, and the less chance for employee coding errors.

Basic Rules for Coding

Here are some fundamentals to follow that don't take much time but can make your system more efficient.

Review disbursements in key areas:

- Prepare a monthly summary of taxes, as shown in Figure 29–3. This helps in preparing your tax returns, and establishes the validity of entries to the expense account. You might discover that current-year federal tax deposits are being coded as expenses. This will distort your estimates of net profit.

- Analyze contributions, advertising, bad debt entries, and all assets and liabilities for which you're likely to need documentation if

Description	Jan	Feb	Mar	Apr	May	Jun	Jul	Aug	Sep	Oct	Nov	Dec
Federal:												
Excise												
Vehicle												
State:												
Vehicle registration												
Use tax												
Local												
Business license												
Permits												
Total												

Figure 29–3

Analysis of taxes

you're audited. Also check subsidiary coding to specific jobs to make sure costs are being assigned to the right job.

■ Each month, before disbursements are entered or posted to your bookkeeping system, have someone review the coding of charges. Look for errors in coding before they become "buried" and hard to find.

Mid-Year Changes

Adding or eliminating accounts during the year can cause some special problems. It's better to eliminate accounts at year-end only. If entries were made to these accounts in previous years, you may have trouble comparing categories from year to year.

Don't eliminate an account with substantial activity. If you're changing the method of classifying transactions, wait until year-end to install new policies.

Add accounts as they're needed. But if you add an account that will be deleted later, you'll have to reclassify every comparative statement. For example, if you lease equipment for the first time and expect to continue to do so for some time, create an "equipment leases" account right away.

Any significant, permanent, new type of transaction needs its own category. But add accounts during the year only when necessary.

Avoid adding accounts that require you to change previous coding. Moving entries around makes them hard to trace. In the event of an audit, you'll want the simplest possible system.

Timing of Corrections

Don't correct the previous years' coding errors unless they were major. Once you've closed the books and completed your tax return, the year is over and done.

You can still make coding adjustments when preparing your tax return. Your accountant will discover some errors and correct them on a trial balance form. Keep these adjustments, documented by journal entries, as part of your permanent records. Include them on comparative financial statements.

The sooner corrections are made, the better. Monthly comparisons are distorted when you continuously move transactions around. It's better to find and correct errors within the month, before financial statements are prepared. Monthly profit comparisons, expense levels, and tax liabilities are more easily tracked in a clean and simple system. Your audit trail is also less confusing.

The best system checks coding before entries are made. Follow these rules for consistency in coding:

1. Have all coding done by one employee.
2. Make one person responsible for checking and approving coding.
3. Follow some logical order in your chart of accounts so that they're easy to remember, and have written descriptions of all categories.
4. Eliminate unneeded accounts at year-end only.
5. Create new categories when needed, rather than miscoding new transactions.
6. Review key tax accounts on a regular basis.
7. Review problem accounts as needed.
8. Avoid using the miscellaneous category except for unusual one-time expenses.
9. Reconcile all asset and liability accounts every month, and understand each balance.
10. Check for the proper use of suspense accounts.
11. Be sure the difference between direct costs and expenses is well understood by whoever does the coding.

Tax Considerations

A good account-coding system will reduce the cost of tax preparation and help avoid trouble during audits. The IRS may review your tax return by comparing year-to-year ratios of gross profit (income minus direct expenses), the level of general expenses, net profits as a percentage of sales, and by analyzing individual accounts. The more you move things around, the higher the chance of an audit.

The most significant comparison is the analysis of the ratio between gross profit and gross sales. Be sure someone in your office clearly understands the difference between direct cost and expense, or this figure will be distorted.

Direct costs are those costs that go into a product and can be assigned to a specific job. Direct costs include materials, direct labor, freight, shipping, and a variety of miscellaneous costs.

Expenses are coded two ways: direct expenses relate to projects and indirect expenses do not.

Direct expenses may include telephone (for calls made specifically for one particular project), entertainment and travel, rental or lease of a particular type of equipment needed for one project, an estimator's consulting fee, and retention of certain employees.

Indirect expenses include rental of your office and warehouse space, office supplies, professional fees, and office expenses such as postage, supplies, rental of general office equipment, and so on.

Most coding errors occur because of confusion over whether a disbursement should be treated as a cost or an expense. Consider the following examples.

Payroll taxes: These can be assigned to a particular project and coded as a direct cost. They represent about 10 percent of labor costs. But payroll taxes can also be treated as an expense. An allowance could be added to all projects if you use the following argument: Payroll taxes are higher in the beginning of a calendar year when you have not yet reached the maximum limits for FICA and state disability. It's unrealistic to burden these early jobs with higher taxes just because of job timing.

No matter what system you follow, be sure to code payroll taxes consistently from one year to the next. Otherwise, a labor-heavy year can distort the relative gross profits of your operation.

Shipping and delivery: These expenses can be assigned to specific projects in some cases and not in others. For example, if you receive delivery of a large amount of inventory, part of it may be for general stock. The balance could be for a number of ongoing projects or projects about to begin. In this case, how should you divide up the cost of shipping? Whatever you decide, don't consider it a cost one year and an expense the next year.

Union welfare: This is generally treated as an expense, but may also be coded as a cost. It varies with payroll costs. If you have a larger payroll this year than last, your union costs will be higher too. It's relatively simple to assign welfare costs to jobs, using the same breakdown as direct labor. But again, be sure to assign it consistently from one year to the next.

Insurance: This is generally considered an expense, except for special types of insurance obtained only for the duration of one project. As is the case with many costs and expenses, it's probably wise to include (in your chart of accounts) two classifications for insurance: one for direct costs and one for expenses. If you do this, be sure to control what is coded to each. Only direct-cost insurance bills, such as those for liability insurance

limited to one job site, should be assigned to the cost account. Expenses should be limited to those coverages that can't be assigned to specific projects.

But this raises another question: How do you code workers' compensation? Part of it is definitely expense, assigned to cover your time and your administrative employees. But the balance will vary with the payroll of your direct labor force. Again, however you do the coding, do it the same way every year.

Budgeting Time for Account Analysis

Coding accounts is important. But don't waste time unnecessarily. Here are some ground rules that should help you avoid excessive analysis in even the largest construction office:

1. Low-volume accounts should be analyzed less frequently.
2. Several errors in a single account don't mean that more analysis is needed. Use better account-definitions to eliminate the problem.
3. Design forms that are easy to use and let you analyze your accounts quickly.
4. Be sure files and document sources are easy to get at.
5. Be sure to follow up on analysis results. When you see something that's out of whack, fix it.

6. Every error found should make it less likely that the same error will happen again.

Identifying and Solving Coding Problems

Once you've found the errors, you should understand the reasons they were made. Usually, errors result from poor definition of accounts, poor training, lax procedures, or a combination of these. In any event, you should be able to identify what's wrong and solve the problem.

Here are some suggestions for solving the more common account-coding problems and preventing their recurrence:

1. Set up subsidiary classifications (within the general ledger) for key problem accounts.
2. Write coding procedures that clearly define the use of each account.
3. Have a responsible employee review or do all coding of checks.
4. Concentrate on eliminating errors in asset and liability accounts.
5. Be sure that suspense accounts are eliminated or cleared every month.
6. Write procedures which let you establish separate accounts when they're needed.
7. Review your chart of accounts for flaws that invite errors.

Appendix: Tax Publications

For detailed information on a specific area of taxation, current forms and publications are available free of charge. Contact the I.R.S. Distribution Center for your area for copies of the publications listed below. The addresses of the three Distribution Centers are given on page 196.

Number	Title
538	Accounting Periods and Methods
909	Alternative Minimum Tax for Individuals
556	Appeal Rights, Examination of Returns, and Claims for Refund
544	Assets, Sales and Other Dispositions of
908	Bankruptcy and Other Debt Cancellation
551	Basis of Assets
535	Business Expenses
587	Business Use of Your Home
917	Business Use of a Car
15	Circular E, Employer's Tax Guide
594	Collection Process, Understanding
526	Contributions, Charitable
542	Corporations, Tax Information on
946	Depreciating Your Property, How to Begin
534	Depreciation
15	Employer's Tax Guide (Circular E)
937	Employment Taxes and Information Returns
463	Entertainment, Travel, and Gift Expenses
505	Estimated Tax and Tax Withholding
510	Excise Taxes (Current Year)
556	Examination of Returns, Appeal Rights, and Claims for Refund
501	Exemptions, Standard Deductions and Filing Information
378	Fuel Tax Credits, Nonhighway Business Equipment
910	Guide to Free Tax Services
553	Highlights of Tax Changes (Current year)
349	Highway Use Tax on Trucks and Truck-Trailers
525	Income, Taxable and Nontaxable
590	Individual Retirement Arrangements (IRAs)
537	Installment and Deferred-Payment Sales
550	Investment Income and Expenses
536	Net Operating Losses
541	Partnerships, Tax Information on
1546	Problem Resolution Program of the IRS, How to Use
552	Recordkeeping for Individuals
527	Rental Property
560	Retirement Plans for the Self-Employed
589	S Corporations, Tax Information on
544	Sales and Other Dispositions of Assets
560	Self-Employed Retirement Plans, Tax Information on
533	Self-Employment Tax
509	Tax Calendars (Current Year)
334	Tax Guide for Small Business
505	Tax Withholding and Estimated Tax
525	Taxable and Nontaxable Income
583	Taxpayers Starting a Business

463   Travel, Entertainment and Gift Expenses

594   Understanding the Collection Process

17   Your Federal Income Tax (for individuals)

1   Your Rights as a Taxpayer

If you are located in:

Alaska, Arizona, California, Colorado, Hawaii, Idaho, Kansas, Montana Nevada, New Mexico, Oklahoma, Oregon, Utah, Washington, Wyoming, Guam, Northern Marianas, America Samoa.

Write to:

I.R.S. Western Area Distribution Center
Rancho Cordova, CA 95743-0001

If you are located in:

Alabama, Arkansas, Illinois, Indiana, Iowa, Kentucky, Louisiana, Michigan, Minnesota, Mississippi, Missouri, Nebraska, North Dakota, Ohio, South Dakota, Tennessee, Texas, Wisconsin.

Write to:

I.R.S. Central Area Distribution Center
P.O. Box 8903
Bloomington, IL 61702-8903

If you are located in:

Connecticut, Delaware, District of Columbia, Florida, Georgia, Maine, Maryland, Massachusetts, New Hampshire, New Jersey, New York, North Carolina, Pennsylvania, Rhode Island, South Carolina, Vermont, Virginia, West Virginia.

Write to:

I.R.S. Eastern Area Distribution Center
P.O. Box 85074
Richmond, VA 23261-5074

Index

Other Practical Resources

Basic Engineering for Builders

If you've ever been stumped by an engineering problem on the job, yet wanted to avoid the expense of hiring a qualified engineer, you should have this book. Here you'll find engineering principles explained in non-technical language and practical methods for applying them on the job. With the help of this book you'll be able to understand engineering functions in the plans and how to meet the requirements, how to get permits issued without the help of an engineer, and anticipate requirements for concrete, steel, wood and masonry. See why you sometimes have to hire an engineer and what you can undertake yourself: surveying, concrete, lumber loads and  stresses, steel, masonry, plumbing, and HVAC systems. This book is designed to help the builder save money by understanding engineering principles that you can incorporate into the jobs you bid. **400 pages, 8½ x 11, $34.00**

Basic Plumbing with Illustrations, Revised

This completely-revised edition brings this comprehensive manual fully up-to-date with all the latest plumbing codes. It is the journeyman's and apprentice's guide to installing plumbing, piping, and fixtures in residential and light commercial buildings: how to select the right materials, lay out the job and do professional-quality plumbing work, use essential tools and materials, make repairs, maintain plumbing systems, install fixtures, and add to existing systems. Includes extensive study questions at the end of each chapter, and a section with all the correct answers.
384 pages, 8½ x 11, $33.00

Blueprint Reading for the Building Trades

How to read and understand construction documents, blueprints, and schedules. Includes layouts of structural, mechanical, HVAC and electrical drawings. Shows how to interpret sectional views, follow diagrams and schematics, and covers common problems with construction specifications.
192 pages, 5½ x 8½, $11.25

Builder's Guide to Accounting Revised

Step-by-step, easy-to-follow guidelines for setting up and maintaining records for your building business. A practical, newly-revised guide to all accounting methods showing how to meet state and federal accounting requirements and the new depreciation rules. Explains what the 1986 Tax Reform Act can mean to your business. Full of charts, diagrams, blank forms, simple directions and examples. **304 pages, 8½ x 11, $22.50**

Contractor's Guide to the Building Code Revised

This completely revised edition explains in plain English exactly what the Uniform Building Code requires. Based on the most recent code, it covers many changes made since then. Also covers the Uniform Mechanical Code and the Uniform Plumbing Code. Shows how to design and construct residential and light commercial buildings that'll pass inspection the first time. Suggests how to work with an inspector to minimize construction costs, what common building shortcuts are likely to be cited, and where exceptions are granted. **544 pages, 5½ x 8½, $28.00**

Builder's Office Manual Revised

Explains how to create routine ways of doing all the things that must be done in every construction office — in the minimum time, at the lowest cost, and with the least supervision possible: organizing the office space, establishing effective procedures and forms, setting priorities and goals, finding and keeping an effective staff, getting the most from your record-keeping system (whether manual or computerized), and more. Loaded with practical tips, charts, and sample forms for your use. **192 pages, 8½ x 11, $15.50**

Building Layout

Shows how to use a transit to locate a building correctly on the lot, plan proper grades with minimum excavation, find utility lines and easements, establish correct elevations, lay out accurate foundations, and set correct floor heights. Explains how to plan sewer connections, level a foundation that's out of level, use a story pole and batterboards, work on steep sites, and minimize excavation costs. **240 pages, 5½ x 8½, $15.00**

Carpentry Estimating

Simple, clear instructions on how to take off quantities and figure costs for all rough and finish carpentry. Shows how to convert piece prices to MBF prices or linear foot prices, use the extensive manhour tables included to quickly estimate labor costs, and how much overhead and profit to add. All carpentry is covered; floor joists, exterior and interior walls and finishes, ceiling joists and rafters, stairs, trim, windows, doors, and much more. Includes *Carpenter's Dream* a material-estimating program, at no extra cost on a 5¼" high-density disk. Double-density 3½" or 5¼" disks are available for $10 extra. **336 pages, 8½ x 11, $35.50**

Rough Framing Carpentry

If you'd like to make good money working outdoors as a framer, this is the book for you. Here you'll find shortcuts to laying out studs; speed cutting blocks, trimmers and plates by eye; quickly building and blocking rake walls; installing ceiling backing, ceiling joists, and truss joists; cutting and assembling hip trusses and California fills; arches and drop ceilings — all with production line procedures that save you time and help you make more money. Over 100 on-the-job photos of how to do it right and what can go wrong. **304 pages, 8½ x 11, $26.50**

Construction Surveying & Layout

A practical guide to simplified construction surveying. How to divide land, use a transit and tape to find a known point, draw an accurate survey map from your field notes, use topographic surveys, and the right way to level and set grade. You'll learn how to make a survey for any residential or commercial lot, driveway, road, or bridge — including how to figure cuts and fills and calculate excavation quantities. Use this guide to make your own surveys, or just read and verify the accuracy of surveys made by others.
256 pages, 5½ x 8½, $19.25

National Electrical Estimator

This year's prices for installation of all common electrical work: conduit, wire, boxes, fixtures, switches, outlets, loadcenters, panelboards, raceway, duct, signal systems, and more. Provides material costs, manhours per unit, and total installed cost. Explains what you should know to estimate each part of an electrical system. Includes an electronic version of the book on computer disk with a stand-alone *Windows* estimating program **FREE** on a 3½" high-density (1.44 Mb) disk. If you need 5¼" high-density or 3½" double-density disks add $10 extra. **512 pages, 8½ x 11, $31.75. Revised annually**

Construction Forms & Contracts

 125 forms you can copy and use — or load into your computer (from the FREE disk enclosed). Then you can customize the forms to fit your company, fill them out, and print. Loads into Word for Windows, Lotus 1-2-3, WordPerfect, or Excel programs. You'll find forms covering accounting, estimating, fieldwork, contracts, and general office. Each form comes with complete instructions on when to use it and how to fill it out. These forms were designed, tested and used by contractors, and will help keep your business organized, profitable and out of legal, accounting and collection troubles. Includes a 3½" high-density disk for your PC. Add $15.00 if you need double-density or Macintosh disks. **432 pages, 8½ x 11, $39.75**

Contractor's Survival Manual

How to survive hard times and succeed during the up cycles. Shows what to do when the bills can't be paid, finding money and buying time, transferring debt, and all the alternatives to bankruptcy. Explains how to build profits, avoid problems in zoning and permits, taxes, time-keeping, and payroll. Unconventional advice on how to invest in inflation, get high appraisals, trade and postpone income, and stay hip-deep in profitable work. **160 pages, 8½ x 11, $16.75**

Commercial Electrical Wiring

Make the transition from residential to commercial electrical work. Here are wiring methods, spec reading tips, load calculations and everything you need for making the transition to commercial work: commercial construction documents, load calculations, electric services, transformers, overcurrent protection, wiring methods, raceway, boxes and fittings, wiring devices, conductors, electric motors, relays and motor controllers, special occupancies, and safety requirements. This book is written to help any electrician break into the lucrative field of commercial electrical work. **320 pages, 8½ x 11, $27.50**

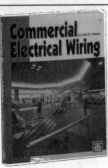

Cost Records for Construction Estimating

How to organize and use cost information from jobs just completed to make more accurate estimates in the future. Explains how to keep the records you need to track costs for sitework, footings, foundations, framing, interior finish, siding and trim, masonry, and subcontract expense. Provides sample forms. **208 pages, 8½ x 11, $15.75**

Drywall Contracting

How to start and keep your drywall business thriving and do professional quality drywall work. Covers the eight essential steps in making any drywall estimate. Shows how to achieve the six most commonly-used surface treatments, how to work with metal studs, and how to solve and prevent most common drywall problems. **288 pages, 5½ x 8½, $18.25**

National Building Cost Manual

Square foot costs for residential, commercial, industrial, and farm buildings. Quickly work up a reliable budget estimate based on actual materials and design features, area, shape, wall height, number of floors, and support requirements. Includes all the important variables that can make any building unique from a cost standpoint. **240 pages, 8½ x 11, $23.00. Revised annually**

Estimating Home Building Costs

Estimate every phase of residential construction from site costs to the profit margin you include in your bid. Shows how to keep track of manhours and make accurate labor cost estimates for footings, foundations, framing and sheathing finishes, electrical, plumbing, and more. Provides and explains sample cost estimate worksheets with complete instructions for each job phase. **320 pages, 5½ x 8½, $17.00**

Roof Framing

Shows how to frame any type of roof in common use today, even if you've never framed a roof before. Includes using a pocket calculator to figure any common, hip, valley, or jack rafter length in seconds. Over 400 illustrations cover every measurement and every cut on each type of roof: gable, hip, Dutch, Tudor, gambrel, shed, gazebo, and more. **480 pages, 5½ x 8½, $22.00**

Roofers Handbook

The journeyman roofer's complete guide to wood and asphalt shingle application on new construction and reroofing jobs: how to make smooth tie-ins on any job, cover valleys and ridges, handle and prevent leaks. Includes how to set up and run your own roofing business and sell your services. Over 250 illustrations and hundreds of trade tips. **192 pages, 8½ x 11, $19.00**

Concrete Construction & Estimating

Explains how to estimate the quantity of labor and materials needed, plan the job, erect fiberglass, steel, or prefabricated forms, install shores and scaffolding, handle the concrete into place, set joints, finish and cure the concrete. Full of practical reference data, cost estimates, and examples. **571 pages, 5½ x 8½, $20.50**

Spec Builder's Guide

Shows how to plan and build a home, control construction costs, and sell to get a decent return on the time and money you've invested. Includes professional tips to ensure success as a spec builder: how government statistics help you judge the housing market, cutting costs at every opportunity without sacrificing quality, and taking advantage of construction cycles. Includes checklists, diagrams, charts, figures, and estimating tables. **448 pages, 8½ x 11, $27.00**

Handbook of Construction Contracting

Volume 1: Everything you need to know to start and run your construction business; the pros and cons of each type of contracting, the records you'll need to keep, and how to read and understand house plans and specs so you find any problems before the actual work begins. All aspects of construction are covered in detail, including all-weather wood foundations, practical math for the job site, and elementary surveying. **416 pages, 8½ x 11, $24.75**

Volume 2: Everything you need to know to keep your construction business profitable; different methods of estimating, keeping and controlling costs, estimating excavation, concrete, masonry, rough carpentry, roof covering, insulation, doors and windows, exterior finishes, specialty finishes, scheduling work flow, managing workers, advertising and sales, spec building and land development, and selecting the best legal structure for your business. **320 pages, 8½ x 11, $26.75**

How to Succeed With Your Own Construction Business

Everything you need to start your own construction business: setting up the paperwork, finding the work, advertising, using contracts, dealing with lenders, estimating, scheduling, finding and keeping good employees, keeping the books, and coping with success. If you're considering starting your own construction business, all the knowledge, tips, and blank forms you need are here. **336 pages, 8½ x 11, $24.25**

HVAC Contracting

Your guide to setting up and running a successful HVAC contracting company. Shows how to plan and design all types of systems for maximum efficiency and lowest cost — and explains how to sell your customers on your designs. Describes the right way to use all the essential instruments, equipment, and reference materials. Includes a full chapter on estimating, bidding, and contract procedure. **256 pages, 8½ x 11, $24.50**

Construction Estimating Reference Data

Provides the 300 most useful manhour tables for practically every item of construction. Labor requirements are listed for sitework, concrete work, masonry, steel, carpentry, thermal and moisture protection, door and windows, finishes, mechanical and electrical. Each section details the work being estimated and gives appropriate crew size and equipment needed. This new edition contains *DataEst*, a computer estimating program on a high-density disk. This fast, powerful program and complete instructions are yours free on a high-density 5¼" disk when you buy the book. Double-density 5¼" or 3½" disks are available for $10 extra. **432 pages, 11 x 8½, $39.50**

Paint Contractor's Manual

How to start and run a profitable paint contracting company: getting set up and organized to handle volume work, avoiding mistakes, squeezing top production from your crews and the most value from your advertising dollar. Shows how to estimate all prep and painting. Loaded with manhour estimates, sample forms, contracts, charts, tables and examples you can use. **224 pages, 8½ x 11, $24.00**

National Construction Estimator

Current building costs for residential, commercial, and industrial construction. Estimated prices for every common building material. Manhours, recommended crew, and labor cost for installation. Includes an electronic version of the book on computer disk with a stand-alone *Windows* estimating program **FREE** on a 3½" high-density (1.44 Mb) disk. If you need 5¼" high-density or 3½" double-density disks add $10 extra.
592 pages, 8½ x 11, $31.50. Revised annually

Residential Electrical Estimating

A fast, accurate pricing system proven on over 1000 residential jobs. Using the manhours provided, combined with material prices from your wholesaler, you quickly work up estimates based on degree of difficulty. These manhours come from a working electrical contractor's records -- not some pricing agency. You'll find prices for every type of electrical job you're likely to estimate -- from service entrances to ceiling fans.
320 pages, 8½ x 11, $29.00

Wood-Frame House Construction

Step-by-step construction details, from the layout of the outer walls, excavation and formwork, to finish carpentry and painting. Contains all new, clear illustrations and explanations updated for construction in the '90s. Everything you need to know about framing, roofing, siding, interior finishings, floor covering and stairs — your complete book of wood-frame home-building.
320 pages, 8½ x 11, $19.75. Revised edition

Remodeler's Handbook

The complete manual of home improvement contracting: evaluating and planning the job, estimating, doing the work, running your company, and making profits. Pages of sample forms, contracts, documents, clear illustrations, and examples. Includes rehabilitation, kitchens, bathrooms, adding living area, reflooring, residing, reroofing, replacing windows and doors, installing new wall and ceiling cover, repainting, upgrading insulation, combating moisture damage, selling your services, and bookkeeping for remodelers. **416 pages, 8½ x 11, $27.00**

Drafting House Plans

Here you'll find step-by-step instructions for drawing a complete set of home plans for a one-story house, an addition to an existing house, or a remodeling project. This book shows how to visualize spatial relationships, use architectural scales and symbols, sketch preliminary drawings, develop detailed floor plans and exterior elevations, and prepare a final plot plan. It even includes code-approved joist and rafter spans and how to make sure that drawings meet code requirements. **192 pages, 8½" x 11, $27.50**

Roofing Construction & Estimating

Installation, repair and estimating for nearly every type of roof covering available today in residential and commercial structures: asphalt shingles, roll roofing, wood shingles and shakes, clay tile, slate, metal, built-up, and elastomeric. Covers sheathing and underlayment techniques, as well as secrets for installing leakproof valleys. Many estimating tips help you minimize waste, as well as insure a profit on every job. Troubleshooting techniques help you identify the true source of most leaks. Over 300 large, clear illustrations help you find the answer to just about all your roofing questions. **432 pages, 8½ x 11 x 11, $35.00**

Painter's Handbook

Loaded with "how-to" information you'll use every day to get professional results on any job: the best way to prepare a surface for painting or repainting; selecting and using the right materials and tools (including airless spray); tips for repainting kitchens, bathrooms, cabinets, eaves and porches; how to match and blend colors; why coatings fail and what to do about it. Lists 30 profitable specialties in the painting business. **320 pages, 8½ x 11, $21.25**

Estimating & Bidding for Builders & Remodelers w/ CD-ROM

If your computer has a CD-ROM drive, the CD Estimator disk enclosed in the book *Estimating & Bidding for Builders & Remodelers* could change forever the way you estimate construction. You get over 2,000 pages from five 1995 cost databases published by Craftsman, plus an estimating program you can master in minutes, plus a 40-minute interactive video on how to use this program, plus an award-winning book. This package is your best bargain for estimating and bidding construction costs. **272 pages, 8½ x 11, $69.50**

Profits in Building Spec Homes

If you've ever wanted to make big profits in building spec homes yet were held back by the risks involved, you should have this book. Here you'll learn how to do a market study and feasibility analysis to make sure your finished home will sell quickly, and for a good profit. You'll find tips that can save you thousands in negotiating for land, learn how to impress bankers and get the financing package you want, how to nail down cost estimating, schedule realistically, work effectively yet harmoniously with subcontractors so they'll come back for your next home, and finally, what to look for in the agent you choose to sell your finished home. Includes forms, checklists, worksheets, and step-by-step instructions. **208 pages, 8½ x 11, $27.25**

Audiotapes: Estimating Remodeling

Listen to the "hands-on" estimating instructions in this popular remodeling seminar. Make your own unit price estimate based on the prints enclosed. Then check your completed estimate with those prepared in the actual seminar. After listening to these tapes you will know how to establish an operating budget for your business, determine indirect costs and profit, and estimate remodeling with the unit cost method. **Includes seminar workbook, project survey and unit price estimating form, and six 20-minute cassettes, $65.00**

Residential Steel Framing Guide

Steel is stronger and lighter than wood — straight walls are guaranteed — steel framing will not wrap, shrink, split, swell, bow, or rot. Here you'll find full page schematics and details that show how steel is connected in just about all residential framing work. You won't find lengthy explanations here on how to run your business, or even how to do the work. What you will find are over 150 easy-to-ready full-page details on how to construct steel-framed floors, roofs, interior and exterior walls, bridging, blocking, and reinforcing for all residential construction. Also includes recommended fasteners and their applications, and fastening schedules for attaching every type of steel framing member to steel as well as wood. **170 pages, 8½ x 11, $38.80**

Video: Drywall Contracting 1

How to measure, cut, and hang: the tools you need and how to use them to do top quality work on any job in the shortest time possible. Explains how to plan the job for top productivity, straighten studs, use nails, screws or adhesive to best advantage, and make the most of labor-saving tools. **33 minutes, VHS, $24.75**

Video: Drywall Contracting 2

How to use mechanical taping tools, mix and apply compound, use corner bead, finish and texture board, and solve the most common drywall problems. Includes tips for making a good living in the drywall business. **38 minutes, VHS, $24.75**

Roof Framing — The Video

Made-to-order for any carpenter, remodeler or builder who wants to become a master roof cutter. Marshall Gross, author of the popular book *Roof Framing*, shows how to cut gable, hip, Dutch, Tudor, gambrel, shed, and even gazebo roofs. After watching these videos and reading the companion book *Roof Framing*, you'll be ready to take on just about any type of roof cutting job, even an irregular roof with a non-centered ridge.

These two videos, and the 480-page book, are a complete training system designed to teach you the art of roof cutting. Running time for each videotape is approximately 90 minutes. Video 1 covers the basics: calculating rise, run and pitch, and laying out and cutting common rafters. Video 2 covers more difficult work: framing a hip or irregular roof and making tie-ins to an existing roof. **$80.00 each**

Profits in Buying & Renovating Homes

Step-by-step instructions for selecting, repairing, improving, and selling highly profitable "fixer-uppers." Shows which price ranges offer the highest profit-to-investment ratios, which neighborhoods offer the best return, practical directions for repairs, and tips on dealing with buyers, sellers, and real estate agents. Shows you how to determine your profit before you buy, what "bargains" to avoid, and how to make simple, profitable, inexpensive upgrades. **304 pages, 8½ x 11, $19.75**

Estimating Electrical Construction

Like taking a class in how to estimate materials and labor for residential and commercial electrical construction. Written by an A.S.P.E. National Estimator of the Year, it teaches you how to use labor units, the plan take-off, and the bid summary to make an accurate estimate, how to deal with suppliers, use pricing sheets, and modify labor units. Provides extensive labor unit tables and blank forms for your next electrical job. **272 pages, 8½ x 11, $19.00**

Residential Electrical Design Revised

If you've ever had to draw up an electrical plan for an addition, or add corrections to an existing plan, you know how complicated it can get. And how many electrical plans — no matter how well designed — fit the reality of what the homeowner wants? Here you'll find everything you need to know about blueprints, what the NEC requires, how to size electric service, calculate and size loads and conductors, install ground-fault circuit interrupt-ers, ground service entrances, and recommended wiring methods. It covers branch circuit layout, how to analyze existing lighting layouts and install outdoor lighting, methods for remote-control switching, residential HVAC systems and controls, and more. **256 pages, 8½ x 11, $22.50**

Audiotapes: Estimating Electrical Work

Listen to Trade Service's two-day seminar and study electrical estimating at your own speed for a fraction of the cost of attending the actual seminar. You'll learn what to expect from specifications, how to adjust labor units from a price book to your job, how to make an accurate take-off from the plans, and how to spot hidden costs that other estimators may miss.

Includes six 30-minute tapes, a workbook that includes price sheets, specification sheet, bid summary, estimate recap sheet, blueprints used in the actual seminar, and blank forms for your own use. **$65.00**

Craftsman's Illustrated Dictionary of Construction Terms

Almost everything you could possibly want to know about any word or technique in construction. Hundreds of up-to-date construction terms, materials, drawings and pictures with detailed, illustrated articles describing equipment and methods. Terms and techniques are explained or illustrated in vivid detail. Use this valuable reference to check spelling, find clear, concise definitions of construction terms used on plans and construction documents, or learn about little-known tools, equipment, tests and methods used in the building industry. It's all here. **416 pages, 8½ x 11, $36.00**

Craftsman Book Company
6058 Corte del Cedro, P.O. Box 6500
Carlsbad, CA 92018

☎ **24 hour order line**
1-800-829-8123
Fax (619) 438-0398

In A Hurry?
We accept phone orders charged to your
Visa, MasterCard, Discover or American Express

Name _____

Company _____

Address _____

City/State/Zip _____

Total enclosed_____(In California add 7.25% tax) *We pay shipping when your check covers your order in full. If you prefer,* use your ☐ Visa ☐ MasterCard ☐ Discover or ☐ American Express

Card#_____

Expiration date_____Initials_____

10-Day Money Back Guarantee

- ☐ 65.00 Audiotape: Estimating Electrical Work
- ☐ 65.00 Audiotape: Estimating Remodeling Work
- ☐ 34.00 Basic Engineering for Builders
- ☐ 33.00 Basic Plumbing with Illustrations
- ☐ 11.25 Blueprint Reading for Building Trades
- ☐ 22.50 Builder's Guide to Accounting Revised
- ☐ 15.50 Builder's Office Manual Revised
- ☐ 15.00 Building Layout
- ☐ 35.50 Carpentry Estimating with **FREE** *Carpenter's Dream* material-estimating program on a 5¼" HD disk.*
- ☐ 27.50 Commercial Electrical Wiring
- ☐ 20.50 Concrete Construction & Estimating
- ☐ 39.50 Construction Estimating Reference Data with **FREE** *DataEst* program on a 5¼" HD disk.*
- ☐ 39.75 Construction Forms & Contracts with a 3½" HD disk. Add $15.00 if you need ☐ DD or ☐ Macintosh disks.
- ☐ 19.25 Construction Surveying & Layout
- ☐ 28.00 Contractor's Guide to Building Code Revised
- ☐ 16.75 Contractor's Survival Manual
- ☐ 15.75 Cost Records for Construction Estimating
- ☐ 36.00 Craftsman's Illustrated Dictionary of Construction Terms
- ☐ 27.50 Drafting House Plans
- ☐ 18.25 Drywall Contracting
- ☐ 69.50 Estimating & Bidding for Builders & Remodelers w/ CD-ROM
- ☐ 19.00 Estimating Electrical Construction
- ☐ 17.00 Estimating Home Building Costs
- ☐ 24.75 Handbook of Construction Contracting Volume 1
- ☐ 26.75 Handbook of Construction Contracting Volume 2
- ☐ 24.25 How to Succeed w/Your Own Construction Business
- ☐ 24.50 HVAC Contracting
- ☐ 23.00 National Building Cost Manual
- ☐ 31.50 National Construction Estimator with **FREE** stand-alone *Windows* estimating program on a 3½" HD disk.**
- ☐ 31.75 National Electrical Estimator with **FREE** stand-alone *Windows* estimating program on a 3½" HD disk.**
- ☐ 24.00 Paint Contractor's Manual
- ☐ 21.25 Painter's Handbook
- ☐ 27.25 Profits in Building Spec Homes
- ☐ 19.75 Profits in Buying & Renovating Homes
- ☐ 27.00 Remodeler's Handbook
- ☐ 22.50 Residential Electrical Design Revised
- ☐ 29.00 Residential Electrical Estimating
- ☐ 38.80 Residential Steel Framing
- ☐ 22.00 Roof Framing
- ☐ 19.00 Roofers Handbook
- ☐ 35.00 Roofing Construction & Estimating
- ☐ 26.50 Rough Framing Carpentry
- ☐ 27.00 Spec Builder's Guide
- ☐ 24.75 Video: Drywall Contracting 1
- ☐ 24.75 Video: Drywall Contracting 2
- ☐ 80.00 Video: Roof Framing, 1
- ☐ 80.00 Video: Roof Framing, 2
- ☐ 19.75 Wood-Frame House Construction
- ☐ 26.50 Contractor's Year-Round Tax Guide
- ☐ **FREE** Full Color Catalog

*If you need ☐ 5¼" DD or ☐ 3½" DD disks add $10 extra.

**If you need ☐ 5¼" HD or ☐ 3½" DD disks add $10 extra.

Craftsman Craftsman Book Company
6058 Corte del Cedro, P.O. Box 6500
Carlsbad, CA 92018

☎ **24 hour order line**
1-800-829-8123
Fax (619) 438-0398

In A Hurry?
We accept phone orders charged to your
Visa, MasterCard, Discover or American Express

Name_____

Company_____

Address_____

City/State/Zip_____
Total enclosed_____(In California add 7.25% tax)
We pay shipping when your check covers your order in full.
If you prefer, use your
☐ Visa ☐ MasterCard ☐ Discover or ☐ American Express
Card#_____
Expiration date_____Initials_____

10-Day Money Back Guarantee

☐ 65.00 Audiotape: Estimating Electrical Work
☐ 65.00 Audiotape: Estimating Remodeling Work
☐ 34.00 Basic Engineering for Builders
☐ 33.00 Basic Plumbing with Illustrations
☐ 11.25 Blueprint Reading for Building Trades
☐ 22.50 Builder's Guide to Accounting Revised
☐ 15.50 Builder's Office Manual Revised
☐ 15.00 Building Layout
☐ 35.50 Carpentry Estimating with **FREE** *Carpenter's Dream* material-est. prog. on a 5¼" HD disk.*
☐ 27.50 Commercial Electrical Wiring
☐ 20.50 Concrete Construction & Estimating
☐ 39.50 Construction Estimating Reference Data with **FREE** *DataEst* program on a 5¼" HD disk.*
☐ 39.75 Construction Forms & Contracts with a 3½" HD disk. Add $15.00 if you need ☐ DD or ☐ Macintosh disks.
☐ 19.25 Construction Surveying & Layout
☐ 28.00 Contractor's Guide to Building Code Revised
☐ 16.75 Contractor's Survival Manual
☐ 15.75 Cost Records for Construction Estimating
☐ 36.00 Craftsman's Illus. Dictionary of Const. Terms
☐ 27.50 Drafting House Plans
☐ 18.25 Drywall Contracting
☐ 69.50 Estimating & Bidding for Builders & Remodelers w/ CD-ROM
☐ 19.00 Estimating Electrical Construction
☐ 17.00 Estimating Home Building Costs
☐ 24.75 Handbook of Construction Contracting Vol. 1

☐ 26.75 Handbook of Construction Contracting Vol. 2
☐ 24.25 How to Succeed w/Your Own Construction Bus.
☐ 24.50 HVAC Contracting
☐ 18.00 National Building Cost Manual
☐ 31.50 National Const. Estimator with **FREE** stand-alone *Windows* est. prog. on a 3½" HD disk.**
☐ 31.75 National Electrical Estimator with **FREE** stand-alone *Windows* est. prog. on a 3½" HD disk.**
☐ 24.00 Paint Contractor's Manual
☐ 21.25 Painter's Handbook
☐ 27.25 Profits in Building Spec Homes
☐ 19.75 Profits in Buying & Renovating Homes
☐ 27.00 Remodeler's Handbook
☐ 22.50 Residential Electrical Design Revised
☐ 29.00 Residential Electrical Estimating
☐ 38.80 Residential Steel Framing
☐ 22.00 Roof Framing
☐ 19.00 Roofers Handbook
☐ 35.00 Roofing Construction & Estimating
☐ 26.50 Rough Framing Carpentry
☐ 27.00 Spec Builder's Guide
☐ 24.75 Video: Drywall Contracting 1
☐ 24.75 Video: Drywall Contracting 2
☐ 80.00 Video: Roof Framing, 1
☐ 80.00 Video: Roof Framing, 2
☐ 19.75 Wood-Frame House Construction
☐ 26.50 Contractor's Year-Round Tax Guide
☐ **FREE** Full Color Catalog
*If you need DD ☐ 5¼" or ☐ 3½" disks add $10 extra.
**For HD ☐ 5¼" or DD ☐ 3½" disks add $10 extra.

Mail This Card Today For a Free Full Color Catalog

Over 100 books, videos, and audios at your fingertips with information that can save you time and money. Here you'll find information on carpentry, contracting, estimating, remodeling, electrical work, and plumbing.

All items come with an unconditional 10-day money-back guarantee. If they don't save you money, mail them back for a full refund.

Name_____

Company_____

Address_____

City/State/Zip_____

Craftsman Book Company / 6058 Corte del Cedro / P.O. Box 6500 / Carlsbad, CA 92018